I0146091

Texas Slave Narratives & Photographs—Part 3

A Traditional History of Slavery in the United States
From Interviews with Former Slaves
Illustrated with Photographs

Part 3

COMPILED
BY
J. MITCHELL, MA

PREPARED FOR PUBLICATION
BY
HISTORIC PUBLISHING

INTERVIEWS ORIGINAL TYPEWRITTEN RECORDS PREPARED BY
WORK PROJECTS ADMINISTRATION
FEDERAL WRITERS' PROJECT

1936-1938

ASSEMBLED BY

THE LIBRARY OF CONGRESS PROJECT

WORK PROJECTS ADMINISTRATION

FOR THE DISTRICT OF COLUMBIA

SPONSORED BY THE LIBRARY OF CONGRESS

WASHINGTON 1941

PREPARED FOR PUBLICATION
BY
HISTORIC PUBLISHING

All Rights Reserved
San Antonio, Texas
©2017

ISBN:978-1-64227-012-9

HISTORIC PUBLISHING
©2017 All Rights Reserved

Historic Publishing Slave Narrative Series™

Florida Slave Narratives
ISBN: 978-1-64227-001-3

Texas Slave Narratives & Photographs—Part 3
ISBN:978-1-64227-012-9

Kentucky Slave Narratives: A Folk History of Slavery in the United States From Interviews
with Former Slaves
ISBN:978-1946640758

TEXAS NARRATIVES—PART 3

Table of Contents
Slave Narratives
INFORMANTS (Lewis – Ryles)

Van Moore

William Moore

Mandy Morrow

Patsy Moses

Andy Nelson

Virginia Newman

Margrett Nillin

John Ogee

Annie Osborne

Horace Overstreet

Mary Overton

George Owens

Mary Anne Patterson

Martha Patton

Ellen Payne

Henderson Perkins

Daniel Phillips

Lee Pierce

Ellen Polk

Betty Powers

Tillie R. Powers

Allen Price

John Price and wife Mirandy

Reverend Lafayette Price

Henry Probasco

Jenny Proctor

A.C. Pruitt

Harre Quarls

Eda Rains

Millie Randall

Laura Redmoun

Elsie Reece

Mary Reynolds

Walter Rimm

Mariah Robinson

Susan Ross

VOLUME XVI
TEXAS NARRATIVES—PART 3

Prepared by the Federal Writers' Project of

the Works Progress Administration

for the State of Texas

[HW:] Handwritten note

[TR:] Transcriber's note

INFORMANTS

[HW:] Handwritten note
[TR:] Transcriber's note

Cinto Lewis
Hagar Lewis
Henry Lewis
Lucy Lewis
Amos Lincoln
Annie Little
Abe Livingston
John Love
Louis Love
John McCoy
Hap McQueen
Bill McRay
C.B. McRay
Julia Malone
Adeline Marshall
Isaac Martin
James Martin
Louise Mathews
William Mathews
Hiram Mayes
Susan Merritt
Josh Miles
Anna Miller
Mintie Maria Miller
Tom Mills
La San Mire
Charley Mitchell
Peter Mitchell
Andrew Moody and wife Tildy

A.M. Moore

Jerry Moore

John Moore

Van Moore

William Moore

Mandy Morrow

Patsy Moses

Andy Nelson

Virginia Newman

Margrett Nillin

John Ogee

Annie Osborne

Horace Overstreet

Mary Overton

George Owens

Mary Anne Patterson

Martha Patton

Ellen Payne

Henderson Perkins

Daniel Phillips

Lee Pierce

Ellen Polk

Betty Powers

Tillie R. Powers

Allen Price

John Price and wife Mirandy

Reverend Lafayette Price

Henry Probasco

Jenny Proctor

A.C. Pruitt

Harre Quarls

Eda Rains

Millie Randall

Laura Redmoun

Elsie Reece

Mary Reynolds

Walter Rimm

Mariah Robinson

Susan Ross

Annie Row

Gill Ruffin

Martin Ruffin

Florence Ruffins

Aaron Russel

Peter Ryas

Josephine Ryles

ILLUSTRATIONS

Mary Reynolds
Walter Rimm
Gill Ruffin
Martin Ruffin
Aaron Russel

[HW:] Handwritten note
[TR:] Transcriber's note

Cinto Lewis

Uncle Cinto Lewis, ex-slave, claims to be 111 years old. He lived in a brick cabin with his wife, Aunt Lucy, on the Huntington Plantation, in Brazoria Co., Texas. Miss Kate Huntington says the cabin occupied by the old couple is part of the old slave quarters built by J. Greenville McNeel, who owned the plantation before Marion Huntington. Miss Kate's father bought it. Although Uncle Cinto claims to be 111, he says he was named San Jacinto because he was born during the "San Jacinto War", which would make his age 101.

"Yes, suh, I's Cinto. That's Lucy over there, she my wife and I calls her Red Heifer, 'cause her papa's name was Juan and he was a Mexican. She and me marry right after 'mancipation. We come long way and we goin' to die together.

"They named me San Jacinto 'cause I's born durin' de San Jacinto war, but they calls me Cinto. I's born in Fort Bend County, up near Richmond, and my old marster was Marse Dave Randon, and his wife, Miss Nancy, was my missus. She was sister to Marse John McNeel, what with his brothers owned all de land hereabouts.

"I 'members once I slips away come dark from de plantation, with some others. We is slippin' 'long quiet like and a paddle roller jump out from behin' a bush and say, 'Let's see your pass.' We didn't have none but I has a piece of paper and I gives it to him and he walks to where it am more light, and then we run, right through old burdock bushes with briars stickin' us and everything. Iffen he cotched us we sho' gits a hidin'.

"I fust went to de field when I 'bout 15 year old, but they larned us to work when we was chaps, we would he'p our mammas in de rows. My mamma's name Maria Simmons and my papa, Lewis. They rared me up right.

"Marse Dave wasn't mean like some. Sometimes de slaves run away to de woods and iffen they don't cotch 'em fust they finally gits hongry and comes home, and then they gits a hidin'. Some niggers jus' come from Africa and old Marse has to watch 'em close, 'cause they is de ones what mostly runs away to de woods.

"We had better houses then, good plank houses, and de big house was sho' big and nice. 'Course they didn't larn us read and write, and didn't 'low no church, but us steal off and have it sometimes, and iffen old Marse cotch us he give us a whalin'. We didn't have no funerals like now, they jus' dig a hole and make you a box, and throw you in and cover you up. But de white folks fed us good and give us good clothes. We wore red russet shoes and good homespun clothes, and we done better'n now.

"Come Christmas time old marse sometimes give us two-bits and lots of extra eats. Iffen it come Monday, we has de week off. But we has to watch the eats, 'cause niggers what they marsters don't give 'em no Christmas sneak over and eat it all up. Sometimes we have dances, and I'd play de fiddle for white folks and cullud folks both. I'd play, 'Young Girl, Old Girl', 'High Heel Shoes,' and 'Calico Stockings.'

"When we was freed we was all glad, but I stayed 'round and worked for Marse Dave and he pays me a little. Finally Lucy and me gits married out of de Book and comes down here to Marse McNeel's. They puts us in debt and makes us work so many years to pay for it. They gives us our own ground and sometimes we makes two bales of cotton on it. 'Course, we works for them, too, and they pays us a little and when Christmas comes we can buy our own things. I used to haul sugar and 'lasses for Papa John up to Brazoria and sometimes to Columbia.

"Yes, suh, I been here a long time, long time. All my own stuff is dead now, I guess. I got grandchillen in Galveston, I think, but all my own stuff is dead."

Hagar Lewis

Hagar Lewis, tall and erect at 82 years of age, lives at 4313 Rosa St., El Paso, Texas. She was born a slave of the Martin family and was given with her mother and family to Mary Martin, when she married John M. McFarland. They lived near Tyler, Smith Co., Texas. When freed she remained with the McFarlands until she married A. Lewis and moved to San Antonio, Texas. Widowed early, she raised two sons. One, chief electrical engineer with the U.S. government, lives in New York City. He provides for his aged mother.

[HW: Illegible]

"I was born Jan. 12th, 1855. My first owners was the Martins, and when their daughter, Mary, married, I was give to her. My mama lived to 112 years old. She had sixteen children. I was the baby.

"Missus Mary McFarland, my mother's missus and mine, taught us children with her own; learned us how to read and write. She treated us just like we were her children. We had very strict leaders, my mother and Missus Mary. She'd say, 'Mammy Lize (my mother), 'you'll have to come and whop Oscar and Hagar, they's fightin!' Mammy Lize would say, 'No, I won't whop 'em, I'll just punish 'em.' And we'd have to stand with our backs to each other. My missus never did much whoppin'.

"We lived in cabins made of logs and chinked with mud mortar. We had beds that had only one leg; they fit in each corner of the walls. They was strong, stout. We could jump on 'em and have lots of fun. We didn' stay in quarters much. The cabins was near a creek where willows grew and we'd make stick horses out of 'em. We called it our horse lot. On the farm was a spring that threw water high, and we'd go fishing in a big lake on one corner of the farm. Marster owned half a league, maybe more.

"I was 12 years old when freed. I can remember the way my marster come home from the war. The oldest son, Oscar, and I was out in the yard, and I saw marster first, comin' down the road, and I hollered and screamed, 'O, Oscar, Marse John's a-comin! Marse John's a-comin' home!' We stayed on with them 'till they all died off but Oscar.

"We never changed our name 'till after the Civil War. Then Marse John said, 'Mammy Lize, you gotta choose a name.' He carried us into Tyler to a bureau or something. Mammy Lize say, 'I'm going to keep the name McFarland. I ain't got no other name.'

"My father was a slave from another farm. My mother was the cook. She cooked it all in the same place for white folks and us. We ate the same, when the white folks was finished. They's a big light bread oven in the yard of the big house and in front of the quarters, under a big tree. That one baked the pies. The cabins had a big fireplace wider than that piano there. They'd hang meat and sausage and dry them in the fireplace. Cut holes in ham and hang them there. Had big hogsheads filled up with flour, corn and wheat.

"Some pore niggers were half starved. They belonged to other people. Missus Mary would call them in to feed 'em, see 'em outside the fence pickin' up scraps. They'd call out at night, 'Marse John, Marse John.' They's afraid to come in daytime. Marse John'd say, 'What's the matter now?' They'd say, 'I'se hongry.' He'd say, 'Come in and git it.' He'd cure lots of meat, for we'd hear 'em hollerin' at night when they'd beat the pore niggers for beggin' or stealin', or some crime.

"Marse John would saddle up Old Charlie and go see. He had a big shot gun across his lap. We'd hear that ole bull whip just a poppin'. They'd turn 'em loose when Marse John got after 'em. He prosecuted some marsters for beatin' the slaves. He knew they was half feedin' 'em. One time he let us go see where they'd drug two niggers to death with oxen. For stealin' or somethin'. I can't say we were treated bad, 'cause I'd tell a story. I've always been treated good by whites, but many of the niggers was killed. They'd say bad words to the bosses and they'd shoot 'em. We'd ask Miss Mary why did they kill old Uncle so and so, and Miss Mary would say, 'I don't know. It's not right to say when you don't know.' I'm glad to see slavery over.

"When I was turned loose Miss Mary was training me and sister to do handwork, knittin' and such. Mama wouldn't let us dance, didn't want any rough children. Miss Mary'd say, when I'd get sleepy, 'Owl eyes, ain't you sleepy?' I'd say, 'No, ma'am, anything you want us to do?' I cried to sleep in the big house with Miss Mary and the children, 'cause my sister Belle did. Said she's goin' to turn white 'cause she stayed with the white folks, and I wanted to turn white, too.

"Miss Mary'd make our Sunday dresses. My mother put colored thread in woven material and they was pretty. We had plenty of clothes. Miss Mary saw to that. They paid my mother for every child she had that was big enough to work, and Marse John saw that others did the same.

"Some whites had a dark hole in the ground, a 'dungeon,' they called it, to put their slaves in. They'd carry 'em bread and water once a day. I'se afraid of the hole, they'd tell me the devil was in that hole.

Hagar Lewis

"We set traps for 'possum, coons and squirrels. We used to have big sport ridin' goats. One near busted me wide open. Miss Mary's brother put me on it, and they punished him good for it. He didn't get to play for a long time. And we had an old buck sheep. He'd keep Oscar and I up on the oak patch fence all the time.

"We'd watch the doodle bugs build their houses. We'd sing, 'Doodle, Doodle, your house burned down.' Those things would come up out of their holes just a-shakin'.

"One game I remember was, 'Skip frog, Skip frog, Answer your Mother, she's callin' you, you, you.' We'd stand in a circle and one would be skip frog. We'd slap our hands and skip frog would be hoppin' just like frogs do. Oh, I wish I could call them times back again. I'd go back tomorrow. But I'm tryin' to live so I can meet 'em once again."

Henry Lewis

Henry Lewis was born in 1835, at Pine Island, in Jefferson Co., Texas. He was owned by Bob Cade. Henry's voice is low and somewhat indistinct and it was evidently a strain on his vocal chords and also on his memory, to tell the story of his life. He lives with one of his daughters, in Beaumont, who supports him, with the aid of his pension.

"Old Bob Cade, he my massa, and Annie Cade, she my missus. Dey had a big plantation over in Louisiana and 'nother in Jefferson County, out at Pine Island. I's born a hunnerd and one year ago, on Christmas Day, out at Pine Island. If I lives to see next Christmas day 'gain, I'll be a hunerd two year old.

"My mammy she come from Mis'sippi and she name' Judy Lewis. Washington Lewis, one de slaves on Massa Bob's Louisiana plantation, he my daddy. I can't 'member nobody else 'cept my greatgramma, Patsy. She's 130 when she die. She look awful, but den she my folks. My own dear mammy was 112 year old when she die. She have ten chillen and de bigges' portion dem born in slavery time. Dey two sister older'n me, Mandy and Louise. I name' after my daddy brudder, Henry Lewis.

"My white folks have a plantation in Louisiana, at Caginly, and stay over dere mos' de time. I 'member when old Massa Bob used to come to Pine Island to stay a month or two, all us li'l chillen gather round him and he used to throw out two bitses and big one cent pieces 'mongst us, jis' to see us scrammel for dem. When Christmas time come round dey give us Christmas gift and a whole week for holiday.

"I never been no nearer east dan Lake Charles and dat been lately, so I ain't never see de old plantation. At Pine Island us have de big woods place with a hunerd workin' hands, without de underlin's (children). All he niggers say Cade de good man. He hire he overseers and say, 'You can correct dem for dey own good and make dem work right, but you ain't better cut dey hide or draw no blood.' He git a-holt some mean overseers but dey don't tarry long. He find out dey beatin' he niggers and den he beat dem and say, 'How dat suit you?'

"Old massa he a big, stocky Irishman with sandy hair and he ain't had no beard or mustache. When he grow old he have de gout and he put de long mattress out on de gallery and lay down on it. He say, 'Come here, my li'l niggers,' and den he make us rub he foots so he kin git to sleep.

"Dey used to have old slavery-day jedge and jury of white folks and dey hear de case and 'cide how many lashes to give de darky. Dey put de lash on dem, but dey never put no jail on dem. I seed some slaves in chains and I heared of one massa what had de place in de fence with de hole cut out for de nigger's neck. Dey hist up de board and de nigger put he head through de hole and den dey beat him with a lash with holes bored in it and every hole raise de blister. Den he bus' dem blisters with de handsaw and dey put salt and pepper in de bucket water and 'noint dem blisters with de mop dip in de water. Dey do dat when dey in 'ticular bad humor, iffen de nigger ain't chop 'nough cotton or corn. Sometime a overseer kilt a nigger, and dey don't do nothin' to him 'cept make him pay for de nigger. But our massa good.

"Old massa 'low us praise Gawd but lots of massas didn't 'low dem to git on de knees. Us have church-house and de white folks go in de mornin' and us go after dinner. Us used to sing:

"'My knee bones achin',
My body's rackin' with pain,
I calls myself de chile of Gawd,
Heaven am my aim.
If you don't 'lieve I's a chile of Gawd,
Jis' meet me on dat other shore,
Heaven is my home.
I calls myself a chile of Gawd,
I's a long time on my way,
But Heaven am my home.'

"Old massa have de house make out hand-sawed planks in slavery time. It put together with home-made nails, dem spike, square nails dey make deyselfs. It have de long gallery on it. De slaves have li'l log cabin house with mud-cat chimney on de side and de furn'ture mostly Georgia hosses for beds and mattress make out tow sacks. Dey no floor in dem house, 'cept what Gawd put in dem.

"When I six or seven year old dey 'cides I's big 'nough to start ridin' hosses. Dey have de big cattle ranch and I ride all over dis territory. I's too li'l to git on de hoss and dey lift me up, and dey have de real saddle for me, too. I couldn't git up, but I sho' could stay up when I git dere, I's jis' like a hoss-fly.

"Beaumont was jis' a briarpatch in dem time. Jis' one li'l store and one blacksmith shop, and Massa John Herring he own dat. Dat de way I first see my wife, ridin' de range. De

Cade brand was a lazy RC [TR: letters R and C turned 90 degrees] dat done register 'fore I's born. Us brand from de first of March to de 15th of December.

"Old massa have de big field 'vided in trac's and each slave could have a part and raise what he want, and old massa buy de crop from de slave. He's purty good to he slaves, and us have good clothes, too, wool for winter and cotton for summer. Us have six suit de year, unnerwear and all. Dey a trunk like in de cabin for Sunday clothes and de res' hang on a peg.

"Us have plenty good food to eat, too. Beef and hawgs and bacon and syrup and sugar and flour was plenty. All de possums and rabbits and fish and sich was jis' dat much more. He give us de barrel whiskey every year, too.

"Dey 'low de li'l chillen lots of playtime and no hard task. Us play stick hoss and seven-up marble game with marbles us make and de 'well game.' De gal or boy sot in de chair and lean way back and 'tend like dey in de well. Dey say dey so many feet down and say, 'Who you want pull you out?' And de one you want pull you out, dey sposed to kiss you.

"Dey used to be nigger traders what come through de country with de herd of niggers, jis' like cattlemen with de herd of cattle. Dey fix camp and de pen on de ridge of town and people what want to buy more slaves go dere. Dey have a block and make de slaves git up on dat. Maybe one man say, 'I give you, $200.00,' and when dey's through de slave sold to de highes' bidder. Old massa warn us look out and not let de trader cotch us, 'cause a trader jis' soon steal a nigger and sell him.

"De patterrollers come round befo' de war to see iffen de massas treat dere slaves good. My wife's gramma say dey come round to her massa's place, but befo' dey git dere he take a meat skin and make dem rub it round dey mouth and git dey face all greasy so it look like dey have plenty to eat and he tell dem dey better tell de patterrollers dey gittin' plenty to eat. But dere one big nigger and he say, 'Hell, no, he ain't give us 'nough to eat.' Den dat nigger say, 'Please take me with you, 'cause if you don't massa gwineter kill me when you git gone.'

"Old massa he die befo' de war and den he son, John Cade, take over de place, and he brudders help. Dey name' Overton and Taylor and Bob, Junior. Us all want to git free and talk 'bout it in de quarters 'mongst ourselfs, but we ain't say nothin' where de white folks heared us.

"When war come on I seed sojers every day. Dey have de camp in Liberty and I watches dem. I heared de guns, too, maybe at Sabine Pass, but I didn't see no actual fightin'. Dat a long year to wait, de las' year de war. Dey sont de papers down on March 5th, I done heared, but dey didn't turn us loose den. Dis de last state to turn de slaves free. When dey didn't let dem go in March, de Yankee sojers come in June and make dem let us go. Next mornin' after de sojers come, de overseer reads de papers out and say we's free as he is and we can go. Some stay on de old place a long time and some go off. You know dey jis' slaves and wasn't civilize'. Some ain't never git civilize' jet. Old massa never give us nothin', but he told us we would stay on iffen we want, but I left.

"I goes down close to Anahuac and builds a li'l log cabin at Monroe City, and dat's where dey puttin' in oil wells now. Washington Lewis, dat my daddy, he have 129 acres dere. De white folks say to sign de paper to let dem put de well on it and dey give us $50.00 and us sign dat paper and dey have de land.

"I marries in slavery time, when I's 'bout 22 year old. My first wife name' Rachel an she live on Double Bayou. She belong to de Mayes place. I see her when I ridin' de range for Massa Bob. I tells massa I wants to git marry and he make ma ask Massa Mayes and us have de big weddin'. She dress all in white. I have de nice hat and suit of black clothes and daddy a shoemaker and make me de good pair of shoes to git marry in. Us stand front Massa Mayes and he read out de Bible. Us had a real big supper and some de white folks give us money.

"De first money I makes am workin' for de gov'ment in Galveston. After de war de gov'ment hire folks to clean up de trash what de fightin' make and I am hired. Dey lots of wood and stones and brick and trees and sich dem big guns knock down.

"I goes back to ridin' de prairie and rides till I's 94 year old. I stops de same year Mr. Joe Hebert dies. When I quits I's out workin', tendin' Mr. Langham's chickens and I forgits it Christmas and my birthday till Mr. Langham comes ridin' out with my money. Dat's de last work I done and dat in 1931 and I's 94 year old, like I say. I bet dese nineteen hunerd niggers ain't gwine live dat long.

"I didn't had no chillen by my first wife and she been dead 'bout 70 year now. My last wife name' Charlotte and she been dead 22 year and us have 16 chillen. Dey six gals and ten boys and ten am livin' now. Mos' of dem am too old to work now. I stays with Ada, here, and she got a gif'. She know what kind of herb am good for medicine for diff'rent ailments. She born with a veil over de face and am wise to dem things. Dey's de fever weed and de debil's shoestring, and fleaweed cures neuralgy and toothache. Spanish mulberry root, dat good for kidneys. When anybody git swolled feets give dem wild grapevine. Prickly ash bark good for dat, too. Red oak bark good for women's troubles and pumpkin head for de heart. Camphor and asafoetida in de bag round de neck good for de heart. When de chile git convulsion make dem drink li'l bluin'. Dat good for growed-up folks, too. It good for burns, too."

Lucy Lewis

Lucy Lewis, wife of Cinto Lewis, does not know her age, but is very aged in appearance, about four feet tall and weighs around 65 or 70 pounds. She was born on the McNeel plantation at Pleasant Grove, land now occupied by No. 2 Camp of the Clemens Prison Farm. Her master was Johnny McNeel, brother of J. Greenville McNeel. His sister married Dave Randon, Cinto's master. Cinto and Lucy's cabin is furnished with an enormous four-poster bed and some chairs. Pots, pans, kettles and jugs hang on the walls. The fireplace has a skillet and beanpot in the ashes. The old people are almost blind.

"You all white folks jus' set a bit while I eats me a little breakfast. I got me a little flap jack and some clabber here. Dem old flies gobble it up for me, don't I git to it fust. Me and Cinto 'bout starve, old hard time 'bout git us. I sure wishes I could find some of Marse John Dickinson's folks, I sho' go to them.

"Me and Cinto got nine head grandchillen down in Galveston, but dey don't write or nothin'. All our own children are dead. Dey was Lottie and Louisa and Alice. Dey was John, too, but he was so little and scrawny he die when he a month old. We call him after Marse John, which we all love so much.

"My mama's name was Lottie Hamilton and she was born at de Cranby Camp for Johnny McNeel. My papa was a Mexican and went by name of Juan.

"I don't hardly recollec' when we git married. I hardly turn fifteen and dey was fat on dese here old bones den, and I had me a purty white calico dress to git married in. It was low in de neck with ruffles and de sleeves come to my elbow purty like. We sho' had de finest kind of a time when Cinto and me gits married, we-all fishes down on de bayou all day long. Marse John marry us right out of de Bible.

"I were bred and born in No. 2 Camp over thar, but it called McNeel Plantation at Pleasant Grove in them days. It was Greenville McNeel's brother and his sister, Nancy, marry Dave Randon. When my marster and wife separate, de wife took part de slaves and de marster took some others and us and we come down here.

"I had five brothers and one sister and I jus' 'member, Cinto' s step-pappy try cross de ribber on a log in high water and a old alligator swaller him right up.

"My marster and his missy were mighty good to us, mighty good. We used to wear good clothes--real purty clothes--most as good as dat Houston cloth you-all wearin'. And, sho' 'nough, I had some purty red russet shoes. When we-all real good, Marse John used to give us small money to buy with. I spent mos' of mine to buy clothes. We used to go barefoot and only when I go to church and dances I wore my shoes.

"We sho' had some good dances in my young days, when I was spry. We used to cut all kind of steps, de cotillion and de waltz and de shotty (schottische) and all de rest de dances of dat time. My preacher used to whup me did he hear I go to dances, but I was a right smart dancin' gal. I was little and sprite and all dem young bucks want to dance with me.

"Cinto didn't know how to do no step, but he could fiddle. Dere was a old song which come back to me, 'High heels and Calico Stockin's.'

"'Fare you well, Miss Nancy Hawkins,
High heel shoes and calico stockin's.'

"I can't sing now from de time I lost my teeth with de Black John fever. When I git dat fever, my missy told me not to drink a mite of water 'cepting she told me to. I git so hot I jus' can't stand it and done drink a two-pint bucket of water, and my teeth drop right out.

"Missy sho' good to me. Dey 'bout 20 slaves but I stay in de house all de time. Our house have two big rooms and a kitchen and de boys and men have rooms apart like little bitty houses on de outside. When we don't have to green up, I gits up 'bout sun-up to make coffee, but when we has to green up de house for company I gits up earlier.

"Missy Nancy used to whup me if I done told a lie, but I didn't git whupped often. She used to whup me with a cattle whup made out of cowhide.

"Some of de slaves wore charms round dey necks, little bags of asfeddity. Me, I got me three vaccinations--dat all I need.

"We used to git lots to eat, greens and suet, fish from de ribber, cornmeal and plenty of sugar, even in de war time. Soldiers was around here as thick as weeds. We had to give 'em a tithe of corn and we makes clothes for 'em, and bandages and light jackets. We made de heavy leaded jackets, with lead in de skirts of de coat to hold it down. De lead looked like a marble and we cut it in long strips and hammer it down.

"One of dem Yank gunboats come up de river and shell around here. Right here. Dem shells come whistlin' through de trees and lop de limbs right off. Dem were sho' scare times.

"I didn't want to be free, I was too happy with missy. But I had to be free, jus' like de others."

Amos Lincoln

Amos Lincoln, 85, was born a slave of Elshay Guidry, whose plantation was in the lower delta country of Louisiana, about fifty miles south of New Orleans. His memories of slave days are somewhat vague. He has lived in Beaumont fifty-two years.

"My tongue's right smart I think. I's ten year old when they blew up that fort. I mean Fort Jackson. Grandpa was cookin'. They wouldn't let him fight. The fort was in New Orleans. They kilt lots of people. They bore holes in the ground and blow it up. A square hole, you know, a machine went in there. A man could crawl in the hole, yes, yes, sho'. The fort was long side the river. They bore holes from the river bank. They had a white paper, a order for 'em not to come to New Orleans. They drag cannon in the hole and shoot up the fort.

"Soon's freedom come my pa and ma was squatters on gov'ment land. It was good land and high land. My pa had 'bout 100 acres. One night somebody come shoot him. Shoot him in the back. Ma took the chillen to Shady Bayou to grandpa.

"My grandpa come from Africy. I never see my other people 'cause dey 'longs to other masters. My grandpa die when he 115 year old.

"Elisha Guidry he my master in slavery. He had lots of slaves. He whip my pa lots of times. He was unwillin' to work. He whip my ma, too. One time he cut her with the whip and cut one her big toes right off. Ma come up on the gallery and wrap it up in a piece of rag.

"Us have a dirt house. The chimney made with mud. It's a good house. It hot in summer. The beds made with moss and shucks and the big old ticks made at the big house. Us didn't have no chairs. Jes' benches. In the room's a big trough. Us sit 'round the trough and eat clabber and bread with big, wood spoon. I eat many a meal that way myself.

"Dem's moral times. A gal's 21 'fore she marry. They didn't go wanderin' 'round all hours. They mammies knowed where they was. Folks nowadays is wild and weak. The gals dress up come Sunday. All week they wear they hair all roll up with cotton they unfold from the cotton boll. Sunday come they comb the hair out fine. No grease on it. They want it natural curly.

"Us have good food most time. Steel and log traps fo' big game. Pit traps in the woods 'bout so long and so deep, and kivered with bresh and leaves. That cotch possum and coon and other things what come 'long in the night. Us lace willow twigs and strings and put a cross piece on top and bottom, and little piece of wood on top edge. The trap 'bout two feet off the ground to cotch the birds. Doves, blackbirds, any kind birds you can eat. Us clean them li'l birds good and rub 'em down in lard. After they set awhile us broil 'em with plenty black pepper and salt. Us shoot plenty ducks with musket, too.

"Greens was good, too. Us eat parsley greens and shuglar weed. That big, two foot plant what have red flower on it. Us git lots of 'em in Wade's Bayou. Us put li'l bit flour in ashes and make ashcake. Us cook pumpkin in ashes, too.

"After slavery I hoe cotton. No money at first, jes' work on halves. The trouble that there no equal halves. The white folks pay jes' like they wants. A man couldn't work that way no time. I had to come over to Texas 'cause a man what want my land say I stoled a barrel from he house. He try arres' my old woman 'cause she say she find the barrel. Now, I never have the case in lawsuit and I 'spect to die that way. But I has to stay 'way from Mauriceville for three year 'cause that man say I thiefed he barrel.

"Things was bad after us come to Texas for a time. That Lizal Scizche, he sho' rough man. Us cropped on the share and he take the crop and the money and lef' fast. Us didn't have a mess of nothin' left.

"I manages to live by croppin'. I been here 52 year now. My first wife name Massanne Florshann, that the French. My wife what I got now name Annie. Massanne she give me six chillen and Annie four."

Annie Little

Annie Little, 81, was born a slave of Bill Gooden, in Springfield, Missouri. Her master owned a plantation in Mississippi, and sent Annie's family there while she was a baby. Annie now lives in Mart, Texas.

"I's first a baby in Springfield. Dat in Missouri and dere am where I's birthed in January, 1856. My daddy and mammy was Howard and Annie and dey 'longed to Massa Bill Gooden. He have de plantation in Missipp' and send us dere while I's still de li'l baby. Dat am what dey call de Delta now, and de cotton so high I clumb up in de trees to reach de top of de stalks, and de corn so high a man on he mule only have de top he hat showin'.

"If us mind massa and missus, dey good to us, but if de hands lazy and not work den de overseer whop dem. When dey run 'way he sot de bloodhounds on dem and dey clumb de tree. I's heared dem hounds bayin' de nigger up a tree jes' lots of times. Massa never sold none my family and we stays with him till he wife die and he die, too.

"In de cold days de women spin and weave de cloth on looms. I stands by and pick up de shuttle when dey fall. Us niggers all wore de clothes make on de spinnin' wheel, but de white folks wore dresses from de store. Dey have to pay fifty and seventy-five cents de yard for calico den.

Annie Little

"Den de war come. I 'member how massa come home on de furlough and when word come he on de way, us all git ready for de big cel'bration. Dey kill the yearlin' or hawg and all us niggers cook for de big feast. Sometimes iffen he stay a week, we jes' do nothin' but eat and cook.

"Dem de good old days, but dey didn't last, for de war am over to sot de slaves free and old massa ask if we'll stay or go. My folks jes' stays till I's a growed gal and gits married and has a home of my own. Den my old man tell me how de Yankees stoled him from de fields. Dey some cavalry sojers and dey make him take care of de hosses. He's 'bout twict as old as me, and he say he was in de Bull Run Battle. He's capture in one battle and run 'way and 'scape by de holp of a Southern regiment and fin'ly come back to Mississip'. He like de war songs like 'Marchin' Through Georgia,' but bes' of all he like dis song:

"'I ain't gwine study war no more,
i gwine lay down my burden,
down by de river side,
down by de river side.

"'Gwine lay down my sword and shield
Down by de riverside,
Down by de riverside.

"'I ain't gwine study war no more,
Gwine try on my starry crown,
Down by de river side,
Down by de river side.'
"Well, he done lay he burden down and quit dis world in 1916.

"Do I 'member any hant stories? Well, we'd sit round de fire in de wintertime and tell ghos' stories till us chillen 'fraid to go to bed at night. Iffen I can 'lect, I'll tell you one. Dis story am 'bout a old, haunted house, a big, old house with two front rooms down and two front rooms up and a hall runnin' from back to front. In back am de li'l house where Alex, massa's boy kep' he hoss, stay.

"Dis big house face de river. Old Massa go to war and never come back no more. Old missy jes' wait and wait, till fin'ly dey all say she am weak in de head. Every day she tell de niggers to kill de pig, dat massa be home today. Every day she fix up in de Sunday best and wait for him. It go on like dat for years and years, till old miss am gone to be with old massa, and de niggers all left and dere am jes' de old house left.

"One day long time after freedom Alex come back, and he hair turned white. He go up de river to de old plantation to tell Old Miss dat Old Massa gone to he Heavenly Home, and won't be back to de old place. He come up to de old house and de front gate am offen de hinges and de grass high as he head, and de blinds all hangin' sideways and rattle with de wind. Dey ain't no lightnin' bug and no crickets on de fireplace, jes' de old house and de wind a-blowin' through de window blinds and moanin' through de trees.

"Old Alex so broke up he jes' sot down on de steps and 'fore he knowed it he's asleep. He saw Old Massa and hisself gwine to war and Old Massa am on he white hoss and he new gray uniform what de women make for him, and de band am playin' Dixie. Old Alex seed hisself ridin' he li'l roan pony by Old Massa's side. Den he dream o' after de battle when he look for Old Massa and finds him and he hoss lyin' side by side, done gone to where dere ain't no more war. He buries him, and--den de thunder and lightnin' make Alex wake up and he look in Old Miss' room and dere she am, jes' sittin' in her chair, waitin' for Old Massa. Old Alex go to talk with her and she fade 'way. Alex stay in he li'l old cabin waitin' to tell Old Miss, and every time it come rain and lightnin' she allus sot in her chair and go 'way 'fore he git in her room. So Old Alex fin'ly goes to sleep forever, but he never left he place of watchin' for Old Miss.

"De white folks and niggers what live in dem days wouldn't live in dat big, old house, so it am call de 'hanted house by de river.' It stands all 'lone for years and years, till de new folks from up North come and tore it down." (See pictures of house at end of story.)

"I well 'lect my old man sayin' how de steamboat come whistlin' up de river and all de darkies go to singin', 'Steamboat Comin' Round da Bend.' Dis am in de cotton patch jes' 'yond da hanted house and de steamboat whistle mean time to go to dinner. Dat am de Little Red River up in Arkansas, where my old man, Dolphus Little, am birthed, right near de hanted house.

"Dolphus and me marries in Missipp' but come to Texas and lives at Hillsboro on Massa John Willoughby's farm. We has ten chillen and I'm livin' with my baby boy right now. I'll tell you de song I gits all dem chillen to sleep with:
"Mammy went 'way--she tell me to stay,
And take good care of de baby.
She tell me to stay and sing disaway,
O, go to sleepy, li'l baby,

"O, shut you eye and don't you cry,
Go to sleepy, li'l baby.
'Cause mammy's boun' to come bime-by,
O, go to sleepy, li'l baby.

"We'll stop up de cracks and sew up de seams,
De booger man never shall cotch you.
O, go to sleep and dream sweet dreams,
De booger man never shall cotch you.

"De river run wide, de river run deep,
O, bye-o, sweet li'l baby.
Dat boat rock slow, she'll rock you to sleep,

O, bye-o, sweet li'l baby.

Chorus

"O, go to sleepy, sleepy, li'l baby,
'Cause when you wake, you'll git some cake,
And ride a li'l white hossy.
O, de li'l butterfly, he stole some pie,
Go to sleepy, li'l baby.
And flew so high till he put out his eye,
O, go to sleepy, li'l baby."

Abe Livingston

Abe Livingston, 83 years old, was born a slave to Mr. Luke Hadnot, Jasper Co., Texas, the owner of about 70 slaves. He now lives in Beaumont, Texas.

"I done well in slavery, 'cause I belonged to Massa Luke Hadnot and he had some boys and they and me grew up together. When my daddy beat me I'd go up to the big house and stay there with the boys and we'd git something to eat from the kitchen. When de white folks has et, we gits what lef'. Massa Luke done well by his niggers, he done better'n mos' of 'em.

"Us boys, white boys and me, had lots of fun when us growin' up. I 'member the games us play and we'd sing this:

"'Marly Bright, Marly Bright,
Three score and ten;
Kin you git up by candlelight?
Yes, iffen your legs
Are long and limber and light.'

"Sometimes us boys, not the white ones 'cause they couldn', would go in the woods and stay all night. We builds campfires and watches for witches and hants. I seen some but what they was I don' know. By the waterhole, one tall white hant used to come nearly every night. I couldn' say much how it looked, 'cause I was too scart to git close.

Abe Livingston

"I was jus' about big enough to handle the mule when the war bust out. My daddy was a servant in the army and he helped dig the breastwork round Mansfield for the battle.

"News of the freedom come 'bout 9 or 10 o'clock on a Tuesday morning. Mos' us goes home and stays there till nex' Monday. Then Yankees come and told us we's free. About 80 of 'em come and they sho' laughed a lot, like they's glad war is through. Seem like they's more for eatin' than anything else and dey steal the good hosses. They take everything to eat, and 40 big gobblers and they eat the hawgs and beeves, too. How them Yankees could eat! I never seen nothin' like it.

"I come to Jefferson County after freedom and got me a job. It was spikin' on the railroad. Freedom didn' mean much to me, 'cause I didn' know the difference. I done well anyhow."

John Love

John Love, 76, was born near Crockett, Texas, a slave of John Smelley. John tells of the days of Reconstruction, and life in the river bottoms. He now lives in Marlin, Texas.

"I's born on de Neches River and spends all my earlies' life right down in de river bottoms, 'cause I done live in de Brazos bottom, too. Mammy and pappy 'longed to John Smelley and was Rose and John.

"It was wild down in de Neches bottom den, plenty bears and panthers and deers and wolves and catamounts, and all kind birds and wild turkeys. Jes' a li'l huntin' most allus fill de pot dem days. De Indians traps de wild animals and trade de hides for supplies. We was right near to de Cherokee and Creek res'vation. I knowed lots of Indians, and some what was Alabama Indians and done come over here. Dey said de white people was wrong when dey thinks Alabama mean 'here we rest.' It don't mean dat a-tall. It mean "people what gathers mulberries.' You see, dem Alabama Indians right crazy 'bout mulberries and has a day for a feast when de mulberries gits ripe. Dat where de tribe git its name and de town named after de tribe.

"Massa Smelley fit in de Mexico War and in de Freedom War, but I don't know nothin' 'bout de battles. De bigges' thing I 'members am when de soldiers come back, 'cause dey finds all dey cattle stoled or dead. De soldiers, both kinds, de 'Federates and Yankees, done took what dey want. De plantations all growed up in weeds and all de young slaves gone, and de ones what stayed was de oldes' and faithfulles'.

"Times was hard and no money, and if dere wasn't plenty wild animals everybody done starve. But after 'while, new folks come in, and has some money and things picks up a li'l more'n more.

"We has de sugar cane and makes sorghum, and has our own mill. Us all, mammy and pappy and us chillun, done stay with Massa Smelley long time after freedom, 'cause we ain't got nowhere to go or nothin'. I'd help in de 'lasses mill, and when we grinds dat cane to cook into syrup, dis am de song:

"'Ain't no more cane on de Neches,
Ain't no more cane on de land;
Oh---- ooooo---- ooooo---- oO!
Done grind it all in 'lasses,

Oh---- ooooo---- ooooo---- oO!

"After I's 'bout growed, I moves to de Brazos bottom and works for a stockman, den I works for de man what driv de first post on de Houston & Texas Central right-of-way. I helped build dat railroad from Houston to Waco, and build de fences and lay de cross-tires. Den I broke wild hosses for Mr. Curry. He give me my groceries and twenty-five cents a day. I was sho' proud of de job.

"After dis, I carries de mail from Marlin to Eddy, on hossback. De roads went through de Brazos bottom. Dey was jes' cowtrails, 'stead of roads. Dere was a road through dat bottom so bad de white man wouldn't carry dat mail, so dey gives it to me and I ain't got no better sense dan to try it. Dat six miles through de bottom was all mudholes and when de river git out de banks dat was bad. But I helt out for eight years, till de mail sent by train.

"I knows why dat boll-weevil done come. Dey say he come from Mexico, but I think he allus been here. Away back yonder a spider live in de country, 'specially in de bottoms. He live on de cotton leaves and stalks, but he don't hurt it. Dese spiders kep' de insects eat up. Dey don't plow deep den, and plants cotton in February, so it made 'fore de insects git bad.

"Den dey gits to plowin' deep, and it am colder 'cause de trees all cut, and dey plows up all de spiders and de cold kill dem. Dey plants later, and dere ain't no spiders left to eat up de boll-weevil.

"I knows an old boll-weevil song, what us sing in de fields:
"De bollweevil is a li'l bug, from Mexico, dey say,
He come try dis Texas soil, and think he better stay,
A-lookin' for a home--jes' lookin' for a home.

"De farmer took de bollweevil and put him in de sand.
Boll weevil said to farmer, 'I'll stand it like a man,
For it's jes' my home--it's jes' my home.'

"First time I seed de weevil, he on de eastern train,
Nex' time I seed dat weevil, he on de Memphis train,
A-lookin' for a home--jes' lookin' for a home.

"If anybody axes you who writ dis li'l song,
It's jes' a dark-skin nigger, with old blue duckin's on."

Louis Love

Louis Love, 91, was born in Franklin, Louisiana, a slave of Donaltron Cafrey, whom Louis describes as a "leadin' lawyer and once United States Senator." At the start of the Civil War, Louis was sent to Texas with about 300 other slaves to escape the "Yankee invaders." Louis now lives in Orange, Texas, and says he spends most of his time sitting on the gallery. One handshakes constantly and his reedy voice is tremulous.

"Well, I guess I's 'bout 91 year old. I 'member when freedom come. I goes up to reg'stration de year I gits free. I walks up to old Doc Young and say, 'I come reg'ster for de vote.' He say, 'You too young to vote. You ask your missus.' Missus git de big book 'bout six inch thick where she got all de births and deaths on dat place since she been missus and she give me a letter sayin' I nineteen year old. I kep' dat letter till not so long ago and burns it by mistake, 'cause I can't read.

"Dave Love he was my daddy and Tildy Love was my mama. My grandmama raise me, though. My massa's name Donaltron Cafrey and he statue stand in de court house square now. He was a leadin' lawyer and a United States senator. When Senator Gibson die massa he serve out he term. Young massa name Donaltron Cafrey, junior, and he keep de big bank in New Orleans now.

"I never was sold to nobody. I heared folks say my folks come from Kentucky, but my mama born on Massa Cafrey's place. He have de big house, fine old house with galleries all 'round and big lawns. It's far back from de road, pushin' clost to a mile, I guess. He have seven sugar plantation and after freedom come dey rents it out at $3.00 a acre to raise 'taters in.

"Us live in shacks 'bout like dese 'round here. Dese times am better'n slavery times, 'cause den you couldn't go nowheres 'thout de pass or de patterrollers git you. Dat mean 25 lashes and more when you gits home.

"My missus took us chillen to de Baptis' church and de white preacher he preach. De cullud folks could have church demselves iffen dey have de manager of 'ligion to kinder preach. Course he couldn't read, he jus' talk what he done heared de white preachers say.

"I git ship one time. Dat time de overseer give me de breakin'. Dey have stocks dey put a man in. Dey put de man leg through de holes and shut it down. De man jus' lay dere and bawl.

"De clothes us wore was shirts and us didn't git no britches till us big. I's wearin' britches a good many year 'fore freedom, though. Dey give us two suit de year and us have beefhide shoes what us call moc'sins.

"Dey wasn't no better people dan my white folks. Dey didn't 'low us to be brutalize', but dey didn't 'low us to be sassy, neither. I holp my grandma milk de cows.

"When de Yankees come to New Orleans dey go on to Port Hudson and have de big fight dere. Massa order everybody be ready to travel nex' mornin'. Dey 'bout 300 peoples in dat travel wagon and dey camps dat night at Camp Fusilier, where de 'federates have de camp. Dey make only five mile dat day. Dey stops one night at Pin Hook, in Vermilionville. My brudder die dere. Dey kep' on dat way till dey come to Trinity River. I stay dere five year.

"De overseer on de new plantation name Smoot. I wait on de table and grandma she cook for Smoot. Dey raise sugar cane and corn and peas and sich like. Dey have lots of pork meat. Dey have stock and one time a calf git eat by a panther. Massa hunt dat panther and shoot him in a tree.

"One day Smoot tell me to bring all de hands to de house when dey blows de horn at noon. When dey gits dere old massa say dey's free as he was. If dey stays he say he give 'em half de crop, but didn't one stay. Six or seven what wants go back to de old home massa done give teams to and it take dem 'bout six week comin' home. I's glad to git dere. I couldn't see free meant no better. Missus plantation seem mighty pleasant.

"I been marry twict. Fust time a gal name Celeste, but she 'fuse to come to Texas with me and dat 'solve de marriage. I marry dis wife, Sarah, 'bout a few year ago. Us been marry 'bout 22 year."

John McCoy

John McCoy, ex-slave, who lives in a small shack in the rear of 2310 State St., Houston, Texas, claims to have been born Jan. 1, 1838. Although his memory is hazy, John is certain that "folks had a heap more sense in slave times den dey has now."

"Well, suh, my white folks done larn me to start de cotton row right and point for de stake at de far end of de field, and dat way a nigger don't git off de line and go dis-a-way and dat-a-way. He start right and end right, yes, suh! Dat de way to live--you start right and go de straight way to de end and you comes out all right.

"I's been here a mighty long time, I sho has, and done forgit a heap, 'cause my head ain't so good no more, but when I first knowed myself I 'longs to old Marse John McCoy. Old Miss Mary was he wife and dey de only white folks what I ever 'longs to. Dat how come I's a McCoy, 'cause all de niggers what old marse have goes by his name.

"My pappy's name was Hector and mammy's name Ann, and dey dies when I's jes' a young buck and dat been a long time 'fore freedom. Ain't got no brudders and sisters what I knows 'bout. All a slave have to go by am what de white folks tells him 'bout his kinfolks.

"Old Marse John have a big place round Houston and raises cotton and corn and hawgs and cows. Dere was lots of wilderness den, full of varmints and wildcats and bears. Old Marse done larn me 'bedience and not to lie or steal, and he larn me with de whip. Dat all de larnin' we gits. Does he cotch you with de book or paper, he whip you hand down. He don't whip de old folks none, jes' de young bucks, 'cause dey wild and mean and dat de onlies' way dey larns right from wrong.

"I tells you jes' like I tells everyone--folks had heap more sense in slave times dan dey has now. Long as a nigger do right, old marse pertect him. Old Marse feed he niggers good, too, and we has plenty clothes. Course, dey home-made on de spinnin' wheel, but dey good. De shoes jes' like pen'tentiary shoes, only not fix up so good. Old Marse kill a cow for meat and take de hide to de tanner and Uncle Jim make dat hide into shoes. Dey hard and heavy and hurt de feets, but dey wear like you has iron shoes.

"Old Marse don't work de niggers Sunday like some white folks do. Dat de day we has church meetin' under trees. De spirit jes' come down out de sky and you forgits all you troubles.

"Slave times was de best, 'cause cullud folks am ig'rant and ain't got no sense and in slave times white folks show dem de right way. Now dey is free, dey gits uppity and sassy. Some dese young bucks ought to git dere heads whipped down. Dat larn dem manners.

"Freedom wasn't no diff'rence I knows of. I works for Marse John jes' de same for a long time. He say one mornin, 'John, you can go out in de field iffen you wants to, or you can git out iffen you wants to, 'cause de gov'ment say you is free. If you wants to work I'll feed you and give you clothes but can't pay you no money. I ain't got none.' Humph, I didn't know nothin' what money was, nohow, but I knows I'll git plenty victuals to eat so I stays till old marse die and old miss git shet of de place. Den I gits me a job farmin' and when I gits too old for dat I does dis and dat for white folks, like fixin' yards.

"I's black and jes' a poor, old nigger, but I rev'rence my white folks 'cause dey rared me up in de right way. If cullud folk pay 'tention and listen to what de white folks tell dem, de world be a heap better off. Us old niggers knows dat's de truth, too, 'cause we larns respec' and manners from our white folks and on de great day of jedgment my white folks is gwineter meet me and shake hands with me and be glad to see me. Yes, suh, dat's de truth!"

Hap McQueen

Hap McQueen, 80, was born in Tennessee, a slave of the McQueen family, who later brought Hap to Texas. He now lives in Beaumont.

"I's born in Tennessee but dey brings me 'way from dere when I's a little chile, what my mammy say is eight year gwine on nine. My daddy name' Bill McQueen and my mammy name Neelie.

"We come from Tennessee in de fall in de wagons and it takes us a long time, 'cause we camps on de way. But we gits dere and starts to work on de new place.

"Massa have three cook women and two was my grandma and my mammy. De dinin' room was right by de kitchen and we has plenty to eat. He was a good massa and I wouldn't knowed it been slavery iffen dey hadn't told me so, I was treat so good.

"Dey have a big house to take care de chillen when dey mammies workin' in de fields, and old missus sho good to dose chillen. She comes in herse'f every day to see dem and sometime play with dem.

"Massa son John was de overseer but de old massa wouldn't 'low him to whip de slaves. Iffen it got to be done, old massa do it, but he never draw blood like on de plantations 'round us. Some of dem on dose plantations say dey ain't want Massa McQueen's niggers 'round de place, 'cause dey's free, dey fed too good and all, and dey afraid it make dere slaves unsatisfy.

"Dey allus stop workin' Saturday afternoons and Sunday and gits pass to go fishin' or huntin'. Sometime dey has preachin' under de arbor. Den at dinner time dey blow de horn and de cullud folks eats at de same time as de white folks, right where massa kin watch 'em, and if dey not enough to eat, he say, 'How come? What de matter with de cooks?'

"He live in a two-story house builded out of lumber and all 'round in de yard was de quarters. Dey make out of logs and most has a little patch de massa 'lows 'em, and what dey raise dey own. My daddy raise cotton each year and he raise sweet 'taters and bank 'em.

"Dey has Georgia hosses in de quarters. Dey was dem bed places what de niggers slep' on. Dey bores holes in de wall of de house and makes de frame of de bed and puts cotton mattress and quilt on dem. De white folks have house make bedsteads, too. De first bought bed I see was a plumb 'stonishment to me. It have big posties to hang 'skeeter bar over. De chairs was homemake too, with de white oak splits for de bottoms.

"Massa he didn't go to de war, but he sent he oldest boy, call John. He takes my daddy 'long to feed de stock and like dat. I goes to de camp once to see my daddy and stays a good while. Dey fixin' to fight de Yankee and dey rest and eat and talk. Dey shoot at de rifle ring and dey make dem practise all dey got to know to be good soldier.

"When freedom come 'long, massa line us all up by de gallery and say, 'You is you own women and men. You is free. Iffen you wants to stay, I gives you land and a team and groceries.' My daddy stays.

Hap McQueen

"I marry long time after freedom and raise' two batch of chillen. My first wife have eight and my second wife have nine.

"I 'members de story 'bout de man what owned de monkey. Dat monkey, he watch and try do everything a man do. One time a nigger make up he mind scare 'nother nigger and when night time come, he put a white sheet over him and sot out for de place dat nigger pass. De monkey he seed dat nigger with de sheet and he grab de nice, white tablecloth and throw it over him and he follow de nigger. Dat nigger, he hear something behin' him and look 'round and see somethin' white followin' him and he think it a real ghostie. Den he took out and run fitten to kill hissel'f. De monkey he took out after dat nigger and when he fall 'zausted in he doorway he find out dat a monkey chasin' him, and he want to kill dat monkey, but he can't do dat, 'cause de monkey de massa's pet.

"So one day dat nigger shavin' and de monkey watchin' him. He know right den de monkey try de same thing, so when he gits through shavin' he turn de razor quick in he hand, so de monkey ain't seein' him and draw de back of de razor quick 'cross he throat. Sho' 'nough, when he gone, de monkey git de bresh and rub de lather all over he face and de nigger he watchin' through de crack. When dat monkey through shavin' he drew de razor quick 'cross he throat, but he ain't know for to turn it, and he cut he own throat and kill hissel'f. Dat what de nigger want him to do and he feel satisfy dat de monkey done dead and he have he revengence."

Bill McRay

Bill McRay was born in Milam, fifteen miles north of San Augustine, Texas, in 1851. He is a brother of C.B. McRay. Col. McRay was his owner (the name may have been spelled McCray, Bill says). Bill now lives in Jasper, Texas. He is said to be an expert cook, having cooked for hotels, boats and military camps 40 years.

"I was born in Milam in 1851 and dat makes me 86 year ole. My mother and father was slaves and dey brung me to Jasper in 1854. Colonel McRay, he was our marster and dis' our boss. He have 40 head of niggers, but he never hit one of 'em a lick in his life. He own a big farm and have a foreman named Bill Cummins. I stay with de Colonel till after I's free.

"Us have good marster, but some of de neighbors treat dere slaves rough. Ole Dr. Neyland of Jasper, he have 75 or 80 slaves and he was rich and hard on de slaves. One day two run away, Tom and Ike, and Dr. Neyland takes de bloodhoun's and ketch dose two niggers and brung 'em in. One of de niggers takes a club and knock one of de houn's in de head and kilt him. Dey cook dat dog and make dem niggers eat part of him. Den dey give both of 'em a beatin'.

"De ole log jail in Jasper, it useter stan' whar de Fish Store is now. Dey have a place t'other side de jail whar dey whip niggers. De whippin' pos' was a big log. Dey make de niggers lie down on it and strap 'em to it. I was a lil' boy den and me and two white boys, Coley McRay and Henry Munn, we useter slip 'round and watch 'em. Coley and Henry both grow up and go to war but neither one come back.

Bill McRay

"Sam Swan, he was sheriff, and he ketch two run-away niggers one day. Dey was brudders and dey was name Rufe and John Grant. Well, he takes 'em and puts dem in jail and some of de men gits 'em out and takes 'em down to de whippin' pos' and den strap 'em down and give 'em one terrible lashin' and den throw salt in dere wounds and you could hear dem niggers holler for a mile. Den dey took 'em back to de farm to wo'k.

"Dey hanged good many niggers 'round Jasper. In slavery times dey hangs a nigger name Jim Henderson, at Mayhew Pond. Us boys wen' dere and mark de tree. Two cullud men, Tom Jefferson and Sam Powell, dey kill anudder nigger and dey hang dem to de ole white oak tree what is south of Jasper Court House.

"After I's free I cooks for Cap'n Kelly in his mil'tary camps for 21 year. Den I cook for boats what run up and down de Neches and Angelina rivers. I wants to say, too, dat I wo'ks for every sheriff in Jasper County 'ceptin' de las' one. Guess I's too young to wo'k for him!"

C.B. McRay

C.B. McRay was born in Jasper, Texas, in 1861, a slave to John H. McRay, a slave trader. C.B. is rather unapproachable, and has a secretive manner, as though he believes the human race will bear a little watching. He told of only one wife, but his present wife explained, confidentially, that he has had six. He lives in Jasper.

"My name is C.B. McRay, better knowed as 'Co'nstalk', 'cause I's long and thin. Also knowed as 'Racer', 'cause I useter be fleet on the feet. When I's ten year ole I often caught a rabbit what jump 'fore me, jus' by runnin' him down. Don' see why my boys can't do the same.

"I's bo'n in Jasper, on Main street, right where Lanier's Store stan's, on the 12th of April, in 1861. My father's name was Calvin Bell McRay, de same as mine, and mother's name was Harriet McRay. Father was bo'n in Virginny and mother in Sabine County, in Texas. My brudders' names was Bill McRay and Robert and Duckin Dacus. Father and mother was slaves right here in Jasper, and so was my gran'parents, who was bo'n in Africy.

"John McRay was us marster. He was call a 'nigger trader', and was sich a easy marster dat other people call he slaves, 'McRay's free niggers'. He make trips to New Orleans to buy slaves and brung 'em back and sol' 'em to de farmers. Missus was de bestes' white woman to cullud folks dat ever live.

"I's too lil' to wo'k much but I 'member lotsa things. Us have a big dinin'-room with a big, long table for de cullud folks and us git jus' the same kin' of food dat the white folks have on dere table. Iffen a nigger sass marster and he couldn' control him, he was de fus' one to be sol' and git rid of. He sol' my uncle dat way. But marster was good to us when we done right.

"The nigger women spinned and weaved cloth. I 'spec' dat's the onlies' place in Jasper whar you could go any time of day and see a parlor full of nigger women, sittin' up dere fat as dey could be and with lil' to do. Marster have no plantation for de men to wo'k but he rented lan' for them to cult'vate.

"Marster's niggers all got Sunday clothes and shoes. Every one of dem have to dress and come to the parlor so he could look dem over 'fore dey goes to church.

"Us have a foreman, name Charlie. It was his duty to keep de place stock' with wood. He take slaves and wo'k de wood patches when it needed, but onct marster come home from New Orleans and foun' dem all sufferin' for want of fire. He call ole Charlie and ask him why he not git up plenty wood. 'Well,' old Charlie say, 'wood was short and 'fore I could git more dis col' spell come and it too awful col' to git wood.' Marster say, 'You keep plenty wood or I gwinter sell you to a mean marster.' Charlie git better for a while, then he let wood git low again. So he was sol' to Ballard Adams, who had the name of bein' hard on his slaves. Charlie couldn' do enough wo'k to suit Marster Adams, so he put him in what's knowed as the 'Louisiana shirt.' Dat was a barrel with a hole cut in the bottom jus' big enough for Charlie to slip he head through. Dey pull dis on to him every mornin' and then he couldn' sit down or use he arms, coul' jus' walk 'roun' all day, de brunt of other slaves' jokes. At night dey took it off and chain him to he bed. After he have wo'n dis Louisiana shirt a month de marster task he again. He fail and run off to the woods. So Marster Adams, he come to Marster McRay and want to sell Charlie back again, but he couldn', 'cause freedom jus' come and they couldn' sell slaves no more, but Marster McRay say Charlie coul' come back and stay on he place if he wanted to.

C.B. McRay

"Dey didn' try to teach us readin' and writin', but Miss Mary read de Bible to us every Sunday. Iffen us git sick dey git ol Dr. Haynes or Dr. Perkins.

"When us chillun, we plays 'Town Ball' and marbles. Mother's fav'rite lullaby was Bye-o Baby Buntin'.

"I never seed any sojers till after de War close, den I seed dem camp on Court House Square right here in Jasper. When freedom was 'clared, Miss Mary call us niggers into the parlor and den Marster McRay come and tol' us we's free. He 'vise 'em to wo'k 'round Jasper, whar they knows people, and says iffen any wan's to stay with him to please rise up. Every person riz up. So dey all stay with him for a time. After 'while he 'gin to rent and cult'vate differen' plantation, and dere treatment not so good, so dey 'gin to be dissatisy and pull loose."

Julia Malone

Julia Malone, 79, was born a slave of Judge Ellison, who owned a thousand acre plantation near Lockhart, Texas. Julia's mother was killed by another slave. Julia stayed with the Ellison family several years after she was freed. She lives at 305 Percy St., Fort Worth, Texas.

"Jedge Ellison owned 'bout a tousand acres land near Lockhart, a few miles up de Clear Fork river. Right dere I is borned, and it were a big place and so many goin' and comin' it look like de beehive. De buildin's and sheds look like de li'l town.

"I 'member bein' left in de nursery whilst my mammy work in de fields. One night she go to de river for to wash clothes. She has to wash after dark and so she am washin' and a nigger slave sneak up on her and hit her on de neck, and it am de death of her. So de woman what mammy allus live with takes care of me den and when freedom came she moves to town, but massa won't let her took me. I stays on with him and runs errands, while I is not fannin' de new baby. Dey has six while I'm dere. I fans dem till I drops asleep, and dat call for de whippin'.

"My foster mammy comes out and asks massa to let her have me, but he won't do dat. But she puts one over on him fin'ly and gits me anyway. He am gone and missus am gone and I has to stay home alone with de last baby, and a man and woman what was slaves on de place 'fore surrender, comes by in a wagon and tells me to jump in. Dey takes me to my foster mammy and she moves and won't 'low me outside, so massa can't ever find me.

"She 'splains lots of things to me. I done see de women stick dere heads in de washpot and talk out loud, while us in slavery. She tells me day prayin' for de Lawd to take dem out from bondage. Dey think it right to pray out loud so de Lawd can hear but dey mustn't let de massa hear dem.

"I asks her 'bout my father and she says him on de place but die 'fore I's borned. He was make de husband to lots of women on de place, 'cause he de big man.

"She am good to me and care for me till I meets de boy I likes. Us lives together for fifteen years and den him dies. My chillen is all dead. He name am William Emerson and I waits nine years 'fore I marries 'gain. Den I marries Albert Malone and I's lucky 'gain. He's de good man. One day he am fixin' de sills under de house and de whole house moves over and falls on him. I feels so grievous over dat I never marries 'gain. Dat thirty-four year ago, and I lives alone all de time. It ain't 'cause I doesn't have de chance, 'cause lots of bucks wants me, 'cause I's de hard worker.

"I washes for de livin' and washes old massa's daughter's clothes. Massa am de powerful man durin' slavery and have de money and fine clothes and drives de fine teams and acts like de cock of de walk. All dat changes after freedom. I seed him layin' in de sun like de dog. I offers to wash he clothes and he jus' grunt. He done turned stone deaf, and de white folks say it 'cause he done treat he slaves so bad.

"I done live here in Fort Worth 'bout fifteen years with my daughter, Beulah Watkins. I's mighty happy here, and has de $10.00 pension and thanks de Lawd fer dat."

Adeline Marshall

Adeline Marshall, 3514 Bastrop St., Houston, Texas, was born a slave somewhere in South Carolina. She was bought by Capt. Brevard and brought to Texas while still a baby, so she remembers nothing about her family and has no record of her age. Adeline is evidently very old.

"Yes, suh, Adeline Marshall am my name, all right, but folks 'round here jes' calls me 'Grandma.'

"Lawd have mercy, I's been in dis here land too long, too long, and jes' ain't no 'count no more for nothin'. I got mis'ries in my bones and jes' look at what I's got on my feet! Dem's jes' rags, dat's all, rags. Can't wear nothin' else on 'em, dey hurts so. Dat's what de red russet shoes what we wears in slave times done--jes' pizen de feets.

"Lawd, Lawd, dat sho' bad times--black folks jes' raise up like cattle in de stable, only Cap'n Brevard, he what own me, treats he hosses and cattle better'n he do he niggers.

"Don't know nothin' 'bout myself, 'cept on Cap'n Brevard's place down on Oyster Creek. He has de plantation dere, what de only place I knows till I's freedomed. He says I's a South Carolina nigger what he bought back dere and brung to Texas when I jes' a baby. I reckon it de truth, 'cause I ain't never knowed no mama or papa, neither one.

"Cap'n he a bad man, and he drivers hard, too, all de time whippin' and stroppin' de niggers to make dem work harder. Didn't make no difference to Cap'n how little you is, you goes out to de field mos' soon's you can walk. De drivers don't use de bullwhip on de little niggers, but dey plays de switch on us what sting de hide plenty. Sometimes dey puts a nigger in de stocks and leaves dem two or three days, don't give dem nothin' to eat or a drink of water, jes' leaves dem till dey mos' dead. Does dey die, jes' put dem in a box and dig a hole out back of de hoss lot and dump dem in and cover up. Ain't no preachin' service or nothin', but de poor nigger out he mis'ry, dat's all.

"Old Cap'n jes' hard on he niggers and I 'member one time dey strops old Beans what's so old he can't work good no more, and in de mornin' dey finds him hangin' from a tree back of de quarters. He done hang himself to 'scape he mis'ry!

"We works every day 'cept Sunday and has to do our washin' den. Does anybody git sick week days, he has to work Sunday to make it up. When we comes in at night we has to go right to bed. Dey don't 'low no light in de quarters and you better be in bed if you don't want a whippin'.

"We gits a plain cotton slip with a string 'round de neck, de stuff dey makes pickin' sacks of. Summer or winter, dat all we gits to wear.

"Old Cap'n have a big house but I jes' see it from de quarters, 'cause we wasn't 'lowed to go up in de yard. I hear say he don't have no wife, but a black woman what stays at de house. Dat de reason so many 'No Nation' niggers 'round. Some calls dem 'Bright' niggers, but I calls dem 'No Nation' 'cause dat what dey is, ain't all black or all white, but mix. Dat come from slave times.

"I knows I's good size when Old Cap'n calls us in and say we's free, but nobody tell me how old I is and I never found out. I knows some of us stays and works for somethin' to eat, 'cause we didn't know no one and didn't hab nowheres to go.

"Den one day, Cap'n come out in de field with 'nother man and pick me and four more what's workin' and say we's good workers. Dat was Mr. Jack Adams, what have a place clost to Stafford's Run. He say if we wants to work on his place he feed us and give quarters and pay us for workin', and dat how come I leaves old Cap'n, and I ain't never see him or dat place where I's raise sence, but I reckon he so mean de debbil done got him in torment long time ago.

"I works in de field for Mr. Jack and dat where Wes Marshall, what I marries, works, too. After we gits married we gits a piece of ground and stays on de same place till Mr. Jack die and we come to Houston. Dat 'fore de 1900 storm.

"I tells folks when dat storm comin'. I ain't 'lieve in no witch doin's, but some way I knows when dat storm comin'. Dey laughs at dis old nigger, but it come and dey loses hosses and cattle and chickens and houses.

"I tells de truth jes' like it am, and I's had a hard time in de land. Why, in dis sinful town, dey don't do like de Good Book say. No, suh, dey don't. It say, 'Love thy neighbor,' and folks don't love nobody but theyselves!

"Jes' look at me! I's old with mis'ry and 'lone in de world. My husband and chillen done die long ago and leave me here, and I jes' go from house to house, tryin' to find a place to stay. Dat why I prays Gawd to take me to his bosom, 'cause He de onlies' one I got to call on."

Isaac Martin

Quite black, with close-cut hair and stubby gray whiskers, Isaac Martin is contentedly spending the evening of his life. But two or three darkened teeth show between his thick lips as he talks. He was enjoying the friendly shade of the old tree in his backyard from his comfortable seat in an old rocker. His feet were bare and his once striped trousers were rolled up above his knees to keep him cool in the hot midsummer weather. Beside the chair was a pair of brogan shoes with gaping splits across the toes to avoid cramping his feet. He told the story of by-gone days with evident enjoyment.

"Dis ol' man jes' layin' 'roun'. Ain't nuttin' to him no mo'. I done wo' out. I jes' waitin' for de Good Marster to call po' ol' Isaac home to Glory.

"When dey read de proclamation to my mammy and daddy dey mek 'em give eb'rybody' age in de fam'ly. I was twelve year' ol' den.

"I was bo'n up here in Montgomery county 'bout t'ree mile from Willis upon de I&GN Railroad. I holp to buil' dat I&GN Railroad.

"Ol' Major Wood he my daddy' marster, and 'course he mine too. He was well fixed. He had 'bout seb'nty or eighty wukkin' slaves and I dunno how many li'l niggers. I didn' know nuttin' 'bout ol' Missus, Mrs. Wood. I jis' 'member she a big fat woman. Dey didn' 'low no li'l nigger chillun up in de yard 'roun' de big house 'cep'n' to clean up de yard, and dem what done dat, dey hatter be jis' like dat yard, clean as peckerwoods.

"Ol' marster he warn't mean. He nebber whip' 'em jis' so iffen anybody say de slave orter be whip. Dey hafter see him and tell him what dey done befo' he give de order to de overseer to whip. Iffen he don' t'ink dey orter be whip, he say don' whip 'em and dey don' git whip.

"I had to mind de cows and de sheep. I had a mule to ride 'roun' on. It was dis way, I hafter mind de cows. Ol' marster he plant dif'rent fiel's in co'n, fifty or sixty or a hundred acres. When dey harvestin' de co'n, when dey git one fiel' done dey tu'n de cows in so dey kin eat on de stalks and nubbins what lef' in dat fiel'. I got to ride 'roun' and see de cows don' bus' over from one fiel' what dey done harves' into de other fiel' where dey wukkin', or what ain't been harves' yet. I jis' like dat, ridin' dat mule 'roun' de fiel' and keepin' de cows in.

"Den dere was five or six of us boys to keep de dogs out de sheep. You know iffen de dogs git in de sheep dey ap' to kill 'em.

"Us go huntin' wid de dogs lots of time, and lots of time us ketch rabbits. Dey was six dogs, and de rabbits we kotch was so much vittles for us. I 'member one night us went out huntin' and ketch fo' or five rabbits. Us tek 'em home and clean and dress 'em, and put 'em in de pot to have big rabbit supper. I was puttin' some red pepper in de pot to season 'em, and den I rub my eyes wid my han' and git dat pepper in my eyes and it sho' burn. You know how red pepper burn when it git in your eyes, I nebber will forget 'bout dat red pepper. De ol' folks uster show us how to fix de t'ings we ketch huntin', and cook 'em.

"Ol' marster sho' t'ought mo' of his li'l nigger chillen. He uster ride in de quarters 'cause he like to see 'em come runnin'. De cook, she was a ol' woman name' Forney, and she had to see atter feedin' de chillen. She had a way of callin' 'em up. She holler, 'Tee, tee, t-e-e;' and all us li'l niggers jis' come runnin'. Ol' marster he ride up and say, 'Forney, call up dem li'l pickaninnies,' and ol' Forney she lif' up her voice and holler, 'Tee, t-e-e, t-e-e,' and ol' marster jis' set up on de hoss and laugh and laugh a lot to see us come runnin' up. He like to count how many li'l niggers he did have. Dat was fun for us too. I 'member dat jes' like yestiddy.

"Nuttin' went hard wid me. Fur's I know 'bout slav'ry dem was good times.

"Dey had 'bout t'ree or fo' hundred of sheep. My father hafter kill a mutton eb'ry Friday for de house. Dey bring up de sheep and somebody hol' de head 'cross a block and my father cut de head off wid a hatchet. Sheeps is de pitifullest t'ings to kill. Day jis' give up. And dey cries, too. But a goat, he don' give up, naw suh, he talk' back to you to de las'.

"I 'member one time dey gwine to give a school feas', and dey gwine kill a goat. Dey hang dat goat up to a tree by he hind legs so de blood dreen good. Dey cut he t'roat, dat's de way dey gwine kill 'im. Dat goat seem like he kep' on talkin' and sayin' 'Please, God, don' kill me' to de las', but dat ain't done no good. Dat goat jis' beg to de las'.

"My ol' marster he live in a big house. Oh, it was a palace. It had eight or nine rooms. It was buil' outer logs, and moss and clay was stuff' twixt de logs. Dere was boards on de outside and it was all coil' nice on de inside. He lived in a mansion.

"Dey was plenty rich. Ol' marster he had a ol' waitin' man all dress up nice and clean. Now if you wanter talk to ol' marster you hafter call for dat ol' waitin' man. He come and you tell him what you want and den he go and tell ol' marster and den he say, 'Bring him in,' and den you go in and see de ol' marster and talk your business, but you had to be nice and hol' your hat under your arm.

"Dey's big rich people. Sometime' dey have parties what las' a week. Dey was havin' dere fun in dere way. Dey come in kerridges and hacks.

"My father was de hostler and he hafter keep de hosses and see 'bout feedin' 'em. Dey had a sep'rate li'l house for de saddles. Ol' marster he kep' good hosses. He warn't mean.

"He had a great big pasture and lots of times people go camp in it. You see it was dis-away, de Yankees dey got rushin' de American people, dat de Confed'rates, dey kep' comin' furder and furder wes', 'till dey come to Texas and den dey can't go much furder. De Yankees kep' crowdin' 'em and dey kep' on comin'. When dey camp in ol' marster' pasture, he give 'em co'n. I see 'em dribe a whole wagon load of co'n and dump it on de groun' for dey hosses. De Yankees nebber come 'till de war close. Den dey come all through dat country. Dat was destruction, it seem to me like. Dey take what dey want.

"When freedom come and de proclamation was read and de ol' marster tol' 'em dey was free and didn' have no ol' marster no mo' some of de slaves cried. He tell 'em, 'I don't want none of you to leave. I'll give you $8.00 a mont'.' All de ol' folks stay and help gadder dat crop. It sho' griebe ol' marster and he didn' live long atter dey tek his slaves 'way from him. Well, it jis' kill' him, dat's all. I 'members de Yankees on dat day dey sot to read de proclamation. Dey was gwine 'roun' in dey blue uniform' and a big long sword hangin' at dey side. Dat was cur'osity to dem niggers.

"When ol' marster want to go out, he call he li'l nigger serbent to go tell my father what was de hostler, to saddle up de hoss and bring him 'roun'. Den ol marster git on him. He had t'ree steps, so he could jis' go up dem steps and den his foot be right at de stirrup. My daddy hol' de stirrup for him to put he other foot in it.

"I was big 'nuff to run after him and ax him to gimme a dime. He laugh and sometime he gimme de dime. Sometime he pitch it to me and I run and grab it up and say, 'T'ankee, marster,' and he laugh and laugh.

"Ol' mistus she had a reg'lar cook. Dat was my mudder's mudder. Eb'ryt'ing had to be jis' so, and eb'ryt'ing nice and clean.

"Dey didn' do no reg'lar wuk on Sunday. Eb'ry Sunday one of de other wimmins hafter tek de place of de cook so she could git off. All of 'em what could would git off and go to de chu'ch for de preachin'. Dem what turn didn' come one Sunday, would go anudder 'till dey all got 'roun' to go.

"Marster had two or t'ree hundred head of cattle. My gran'father, Guilford, had a mule and hoss of he own. Uncle Hank was his brudder, and he had de sheep department to look attar. Sometime de niggers git a hoss or a sheep over, den de marster buy 'im. Some of de niggers had a li'l patch 'roun' dey cabin' and dey raise veg'table. Ol' marster he buy de veg'table sometime. I didn' know what freedom was. I didn' know wedder I needed it or not. Seem to me like it was better den dan now, 'cause I gotter look out for myself now.

"Us uster be on de watch-out for ol' marster. De fus' one see him comin' lit out and open de gate for him to ride froo and ol' marster toss him a nickle.

"When it was time to eat, de ol' cook she holler out, 'T-e-e, t-e-e, t-e-e-e' and all us li'l niggers come runnin'. She have a big tray and each of us have a wessel and a spoon. She fill' us wessel and us go eat and den us go back for mo'. Us git all us want. Dey give us supper befo' de han's come in from de fiel' and what wid playin' 'roun' all day and eatin' all us could hol' in de afternoon, twarn't long befo' us li'l niggers ready to go to sleep.

"One t'ing, ol' marster didn' want his niggers to run about. Sometime dey want to go over to anudder plantation on Sunday. Den he give 'em a pass iffen he willin' for 'em to go. Dey had patterrollers to ride from plantation to see iffen dey was any strange niggers dere.

"When dey wanter marry, de man he repo't to ol' marster. He want his niggers to marry on his own plantation. He give 'em a nice li'l supper and a big dance. Dey had some sort of license but ol' marster tek care of dat. He had two sons what had farms and slaves of dere own. Ol' marster didn' care if his slaves marry on his sons' farms. If any of de slaves do mean, he mak 'em work on Sunday. He didn' b'leeb in beatin' 'em.

"So many of 'em as could, usually go to de white folks chu'ch on Sunday and hear de white preacher. Dey sit off to deyse'fs in de back of de chu'ch. Dem what stay at home have a cullud preacher. Dey try to raise 'em up social.

"Dey had a ol' woman to look after de babies when dey mammies was out in de fiel'. Dey have a time sot for de mammies te come in and nuss de babies. De ol' woman she had helpers. Dey had a big house and cradle' for dem babies where de nuss tek care of 'em.

"When anybody die dey have a fun'rel. All de han's knock off work to 'tend de fun'rel. Dey bury de dead in a ho'made coffin.

"I nebber pay no 'tenshun to talk 'bout ghos'es. I nebber b'leeb in 'em. But one time comin' from chu'ch my uncle' wife say, 'Ike, you eber see a ghos'? Want to see one?' and I tell her 'I don't give a cent, yes I want to see one.' She say, 'I show you a man dress' all in white what ain't got no head, and you gwine feel a warm breeze.' After a while down de hill by de graveyard she say, 'Dere he go.' I look' but I neber see nuttin', but I feel de warm breeze.

"I uster go to see a gal and I uster hafter pass right by a ol' graveyard. It was all wall' up wid brick but one place dey had steps up over de wall so when dey hafter bury a body two men kin walk up dem steps side by side, and dat de way dey tek de corpse over. Well, when I git to dem steps I hear sump'n'. Den I stop and I ain't hear nuttin'. When I start walkin' ag'in I hear de noise ag'in. I look 'roun' and den I see sump'n' white come up right dere where de steps go over de wall. I had a stick in my han' and nex' time it come up I mek a rush at it and hit it. It was jis' a great big ol' billy goat what got inside de wall and was tryin' to git out. He get out jis' when I hit him and he lit out froo de woods. Dat's de only ghos' I eber see and I's glad dat warn't no ghos'.

"Ol' marster he had twenty head of cows. Dey give plenty milk. Dey uster git a cedar tub big as dat dere one full of milk. De milkers dey pack it en dey head to de house. Us cow-pen boys had to go drive up de caffs. Cow-pen boys? Cow-pen boys, dem de boys what keep away de caffs when dey do de milkin'. Co'se, lots of times when dey froo milkin' us jump on 'em and ride 'em. Wheneber dey ketch us doin' dat dey sho' wear us out. Dat warn't yestiddy.

"Fur as I's concern we had a plum good time in slav'ry. Many a year my grampa raise a bale of cotton and marster buy it. Dat was encouragin' us to be smart.

"My daddy name' Edmond Wood and my ma name' Maria. I had a brudder and a sister; dey name' Cass and Ann. I been a farmer all my life. I kep' on farmin' 'till de boll weevil hit dese parts and den I quit de farm and went to public work. I work in de woods and cut logs. I buy dis house. I been here 'roun' Voth 'bout twenty-five year'.

"I been marry twict. De fus' time I marry--I git so stinkin' ol' I can't 'member when it were, but it been a long ways back. My fus' wife, Mary Johnson. She die' and den I marry dis yere woman I got yere now. Her name been Rhoda McGowan when I marry her but she been marry befo'. Befo' of us ol', ain't fit fer nuttin'. Us git pension' and dat what us live on now, 'cause I too ol' to do any work no mo'.

"Me and my fus' wife we had ten chillun. Dey's all dead but fo' and I ain't sho' dey's all livin'. Las' I heerd of 'em one was in Houston, and one in Chicago, and one in Kansas City, and one live here. I see him dis mawnin'.

"I heerd tell of de Klu Klux but I ain't neber seed 'em. I neber did go to school needer.

"I's a member of de C.M.E. Meth'dis' Chu'ch. When I uster could git about I uster be a steward in de chu'ch. Den I was de treasurer of de chu'ch here at Voth for some seben year'. I uster b'long to de U.B.F. Lodge, too.

"Back in slav'ry dey allus had a ol' darky to train de young ones and teach 'em right from wrong. And dey'd whip you for doin' wrong. Dey'd repo't to de overseer. Some of 'em was mean and repo't somebody dey ain't like jis' to git 'em in trouble. De overseer he had to 'vestigate 'bout it and if it was so, somebody git a whippin'. Sometimes some folks repo't sump'n' when it warn't true.

"Ol' marster he was plum ind'pendant. His plantation was off from de town. He uster had his mail brung to him. Fur's I kin 'member I didn' had to look out for nuttin'. Dey had a time to call all de slaves up and give 'em hats, and anudder time dey give 'em shoes, and anudder time dey give 'em clo's. Dey see dat eb'rybody was fit. Ol' marster allus give 'em all some kinder present at Crismus. I dunno what all he give de ol' folks but he give de chillun candy and de like.

"I was allus tickle' to see ol' marster come 'roun'--Oh, good gracious, yes. And it allus tickle' him to come 'roun' and see all his li'l niggers.

"One time Cap'n Fisher was 'sociated wid ol' marster, and him and anudder man come 'long wid ol' marster up de road what run froo de quarters. Dey wanter see de li'l niggers. Ol' marster call 'em up and frow out a han'ful of dimes. It sho' tickle' 'em te see de li'l niggers scramble for dem dimes, and us look' for dimes 'roun' dat place for a week. Dat was enjoyment to de white folks dem days.

"Marster was good to his niggers and none of 'em eber run away. My mudder she raise ol' mistus' baby chile. She uster suckle him jis' like he her own baby and he allus t'ink lots of her. After he a growed up man he uster bring her presents lots of times. He call her 'mammy' all de time.

"He went off to de war. He los' he hearin' and got deef. Muster been de noise from dem big cannons what done it. He got his big toe shot off in de war, too. After de war was over he come home and git married.

"Dat 'bout all dat I kin 'member 'cep'n' dat I vote' in de state and other 'lections when I's twenty-one year' ol'."

James Martin

James Martin, 311 Dawson St., San Antonio, Texas, is 90 years old. His parents were Preston and Lizzie Martin and he was born in Alexandria, Va. Uses little dialect.

"I was born in Virginia in 1847. My mother was a slave and my grandfather was one of the early settlers in Virginia. He was born in Jamaica and his master took him to England. When the English came to Virginia, they brought us along as servants, but when they got here, everybody had slaves, so we was slaves, too. My mother was born in the West Indies.

"A man named Martin brought my grandfather here and we took his name. And when marster was ready to die, he made a will and it said the youngest child in the slaves must be made free, so that was my father and he was made free when he was 16. That left me and my brothers and sisters all free, but all the rest of the family was slaves.

"My mother was born a slave near Alexandria. The marster's daughter, Miss Liza, read to my mother, so she got some learning. When my mother's owner died he left her to Miss Liza, and then my father met my mother and told her they should get married. My mother said to Miss Liza: 'I'd like fine to marry Preston Martin.' Miss Liza says, 'You can't do that, 'cause he's a free nigger and your children would be free. You gotta marry one of the slaves.' Then Miss Liza lines up 10 or 15 of the slave men for my mother to pick from, but mother says she don' like any of 'em, she wants to marry Preston Martin. Miss Liza argues but my mother is just stubborn, so Miss Liza says, 'I'll talk to the marster.' He says, 'I can't lose property like that, and if you can raise $1,200 you can buy yourse'f free.' So my mother and my father saves money and it takes a long time, but one day they goes to the marster and lays down the money, and they gits married. Marster don' like it, but he's promised and he can't back out.

"So me and my brothers and sisters is free. And we sees others sol' on the auction block. They're put in stalls like pens for cattle and there's a curtain, sometimes just a sheet in front of them, so the bidders can't see the stock too soon. The overseer's standin' just outside with a big black snake whip and a pepper box pistol in his hand. Then they pulls the curtain up and the bidders crowds 'round. The overseer tells the age of the slaves and what they can do. One bidder takes a pair of white gloves they have and rubs his fingers over a man's teeth, and he says, 'You say this buck's 20 years old, but there's cups worn to his teeth. He's 40 years if he's a day. So they knock that buck down for $1,000, 'cause they calls the men 'bucks' and the women 'wenches.' Then the overseer makes 'em walk across the platform, he makes 'em hop, he makes 'em trot, he makes 'em jump.

"When I'm old enough, I'm taught to be a saddler and when I'm 17 or 18 I enlist in the Confed'rate Army.

"Did they whip the slaves? Well, they jus' about half killed 'em. When it was too rough, they slipped into Canada.

"A marriage was a event. The bride and groom had to jump over a broom handle. The boss man had a white preacher, sometimes, and there was plenty good beef cornbread. But if the boss didn't care much, he jus' lined 'em up and said, 'Mandy, that's your husband and, Rufus, that's your wife.'

James Martin

"After the war we were sent to Texas, the 9th U.S. Cavalry, under Capt. Francis F. Dodge. I was at Fort Sill, Fort Davis, Fort Stockton and Fort Clark. I was in two battles with Indians in the Guadalupe Mountains. I served under Col. Shafter in 1871 and I got my discharge under Gen. Merritt in 1872. Then I come to San Antonio.

"I helped bring the first railroad here. The S.P. in them days only ran near Seguin and I was a spiker and worked the whole distance. Then I helped build the old railroad from Indianola to Cuero and then from Cuero to Corpus, and Schleister, I think, and Cunningham were the contractors. That was in 1873 and 1874.

"I drove cattle for big outfits, and drove 2,000 or 3,000 head from South Texas sometimes clean up to Dakota. I drove for John Lytle, Brockhaus, Kieran and Bill Sutton. There wasn't no trails and no fences. The Indians would come ask for meat and we knew if we didn't give it to 'em they'd stampede the cattle.

"If I wasn't so old, I'd travel 'round again. I don't believe any man can be educated who ain't traveled some."

Louise Mathews

Louise Mathews, 83, is a sister of Scott Hooper. Her owner was the Rev. Robert Turner. Louise married Henry Daggett when she was twenty, Jim Byers when she was thirty-one and Bill Mathews when she was thirty-three. She lives alone at 2718 Ennis Ave., Fort Worth, about a block from Scott.

"Sho', I 'members dem slavery times, 'cause I's eleven when de break-up come. Everybody call my massa Jedge Turner, but him am a Baptist preacher and have de small farm and gen'ral store. My pappy and mammy don't live together, 'cause pappy am own by Massa Jack Hooper. Massa Turner done marry dem. Mostest de cullud folks jus' lives together by 'greement den, but massa have de cer'mony.

"Us live in log cabins with de dirt floor and no windows, and sleep on straw ticks. All de cookin' done in de eatin' shed but when pappy come over twict de week, mammy cooks him de meal den.

"Let me tell yous how de young'uns cared for. Massa give dem special care, with de food and lots of clabber and milk and pot-liquor, and dey all fat and healthy.

"Massa am a preacher and a farmer and a saloonkeeper. He makes de medicine with whiskey and cherry bark and rust offen nails. It mus' be good, 'cause us all fat and sassy. Gosh for 'mighty. How I hates to take dat medicine! He say to me, 'Take good care de young'uns, 'cause de old ones gwine play out sometime, and I wants de young'uns to grow strong.'

"Massa Turner wants de good day's work and us all give it to him. Every Saturday night us git de pass if us wants to go to de party. Us have parties and dancin' de quadrille and fiddles and banjoes.

"On Sunday massa preach to us, 'cause he de preacher heself. He preach to de white folks, too.

"I 'member dat surrender day. He call us round him. I can see him now, like I watches him come to de yard, with he hands clasp 'hind him and he head bowed. I know what he says, 'I likes every one of you. You been faithful but I has to give you up. I hates to do it, not 'cause I don't want to free you, but 'cause I don't want to lose you all.' Us see de tears in he eyes.

Louise Mathews

"Mos' everybody leaves, and us go to pappy's place, den comes here in 1872, right here where us live now. My sister, Scott, she lives up de street. It warn't no houses here den.

"I gits married in 1874 to Henry Daggett and he dies in 1884. Den I marries Jim Byers in 1885 and he am lazy and no 'count. He leaves on Christmas Day in de mornin', and don't come back. Dat de only present he ever give me! He am what you calls de buck passer. I does de washin' and ironin' and he passes de bucks I makes. I marries Bill Mathews and he my las' husband. He dies on May 15th, dis year. I has seven chillen and four of dem am right in dis town.

"I never votes but once, 'bout four years ago. I jus' don't care 'bout it. Too much fustin' round for me. My husband allus voted de Lincoln ticket.

"I gits 'round and it won't be long 'fore I goes to de Lawd's restin' place. My sister am 81 and I's 83, and she lives in de next block yonder way. Us am de cons'lation to each other."

William Mathews

William Mathews, 89, was born a slave on the Adams plantation, in Franklin Parish, Louisiana. He was driver of the family carriage. After William was freed he supported himself by hiring out as a field hand and by making and selling baskets. Since 1931 he has lived with his daughter, Sarah Colburn, at 812-½ 41st St., Galveston, Texas.

"Course I can 'lect 'bout slavery. I is old and my eyesight am gone, but I can still 'lect. I ain't never forgit it.

"My massa, old Buck Adams, could out-mean de debbil heself. He sho' hard--hard and sneaky as slippery ellum. Old Mary Adams, he wife, was 'most as hard as he was. Sometimes I used to wonder how dere chillen ever stood 'em. Old Buck Adams brung my mammy and daddy from South Car'lina to work in de fields and my daddy's name was Economy Mathews and my mammy's name Phoebe. Simmons was her name 'fore she marry. I is born on old Buck's place, on December 25th, in 1848. Dat plantation was in Franklin Parish, somewhere round Monroe, in Louisiana.

"Me and Bill Adams raised together. When he shoot a deer I run home like greased lightnin' and git de hoss. Sometimes he'd shoot a big hawg and I'd skin him.

"When I got big 'nough I'd drive dere carriage. I was what dey calls de 'waitin' boy.' I sot in dat buggy and wait till dey come out of where dey was, and den driv 'em off. I wasn't 'lowed to git out and visit round with de other slaves. No, suh, I had to set dere and wait.

"De slaves git out in de fields 'fore sun-up and work till black dark. Den dey come home and have to feel dere way in de house, with no light. My mammy and daddy field hands. My grandma was cook, and have to git in de cook pot 'bout four o'clock to git breakfas' by daylight. Dey et by candles or pine torches. One de black boys stand behin' 'em and hold it while dey et.

"De clothes we wore was made out of dyed 'lows.' Dat de stuff dey makes sackin' out of. Summer time us go barefoot but winter time come, dey give you shoes with heels on 'em big as biscuits.

"De quarters is back of de big house and didn't have no floors. Dey sot plumb on de ground and build like a hawg pen. Dey cut down timber and stake it up at de corners and fill it in with timber with de bark on it. Dere was split log houses and round log houses and all sech like dat. Dey have only fifty slaves on dat place, and it a big place, big 'nough for a hundred. But what dey do? Dey take de good slaves and sell 'em. Dat what dey do. Den dey make de ones what am left do all de work. Sell, sell, all de time, and never buy nobody. Dat was dem.

"Every Sat'day evenin' us go to de pitcher poke. Dat what dey calls it when dey issues de rations. You go to de smokehouse and dey weigh out some big, thick rounds of white pork meat and give it to you. De syrup weighed out. De meal weighed out. Dey never give us no sugar or coffee. You want coffee, you put de skillet on de fire and put de meal in it and parch it till it most black, and put water on it. Mammy make salt water bread out of a li'l flour and salt and water.

"Sometimes, dey make de slaves go to church. De white folks sot up fine in dere carriage and drive up to de door and git de slaves out of one cabin, den git de slaves out of de nex' cabin, and keep it up till dey gits dem all. Den all de slaves walks front de carriage till dey gits to church. De slaves sit outside under de shade trees. If de preacher talk real loud, you can hear him out de window.

"If a cullud man take de notion to preach, he couldn't preach 'bout de Gospel. Dey didn't 'low him do dat. All he could preach 'bout was obey de massa, obey de overseer, obey dis, obey dat. Dey didn't make no passel of fuss 'bout prayin' den. Sometimes dey have prayin' meetin' in a cabin at night. Each one bring de pot and put dere head in it to keep de echoes from gittin' back. Den dey pray in de pot. Dat de Gawd's truth!

"Like I done said, massa sol' de good slaves in Monroe. Nobody marry in dem days. A gal go out and take de notion for some buck and dey make de 'greement to live together. Course, if a unhealthy buck take up with a portly gal, de white folks sep'rate 'em. If a man a big, stout man, good breed, dey gives him four, five women.

"Sometimes dey run 'way. It ain't done dem no good, for de dawgs am put on dey trail. If you climb de tree, dem dogs hold you dere till de white folks comes, and den dey let de dogs git you. Sometimes de dogs tore all dey clothes off, and dey ain't got nary a rag on 'em when dey git home. If dey run in de stream of water, de dogs gits after 'em and drowns 'em. Den Nick, de overseer, he whop 'em. He drive down four stakes for de feets and hands and tie 'em up. Den he whop 'em from head to feets. De whip make out a hide, cut in strips, with holes punch in 'em. When dey hits de skin it make blisters.

"All kind of war talk floatin' round 'fore de Yankees come. Some say de Yankees fight for freedom and some say dey'll kill all de slaves. Seems like it must have been in de middle of de war dat de Yankees come by. We hears somebody holler for us to come out one night and seed de place on fire. Time we git out dere, de Yankees gone. We fit de fire but we had to tote water in buckets, and de fire burn up de gin house full of cotton and de cotton house, too, and de corn crib.

"De Yankees allus come through at night and done what dey gwine to do, and den wait for more night 'fore dey go 'bout dere business. Only one time dey come in daylight, and some de slaves jine dem and go to war.

"All de talk 'bout freedom git so bad on de plantation de massa make me put de men in a big wagon and drive 'em to Winfield. He say in Texas dere never be no freedom. I driv 'em fast till night and it take 'bout two days. But dey come back home, but massa say if he cotch any of 'em he gwine shoot 'em. Dey hang round de woods and dodge round and round till de freedom man come by.

"We went right on workin' after freedom. Old Buck Adams wouldn't let us go. It was way after freedom dat de freedom man come and read de paper, and tell us not to work no more 'less us git pay for it. When he gone, old Mary Adams, she come out. I 'lect what she say as if I jes' hear her say it. She say, 'Ten years from today I'll have you all back 'gain.' Dat ten years been over a mighty long time and she ain't git us back yit and she dead and gone.

"Dey makes us git right off de place, jes' like you take a old hoss and turn it loose. Dat how us was. No money, no nothin'. I git a job workin' for a white man on he farm, but he couldn't pay much. He didn't have nothin'. He give me jes' 'nough to git a peck or two of meal and a li'l syrup.

"I allus works in de fields and makes baskets, big old cotton baskets and bow baskets make out of white oak. I work down de oak to make de splits and make de bow basket to tote de lunch. Den I make trays and mix bowls. I go out and cut down de big poplar and bust off de big block and sit down 'straddle, and holler it out big as I wants it, and make de bread tray. I make collars for hosses and ox whops and quirts out of beef hide. But I looses my eyesight a couple years back and I can't do nothin' no more. My gal takes care of me.

"I come here in 1931. Dat de first time I'm out of Franklin Parish. I allus git along some way till I'm blind. My gal am good to me, but de days am passin' and soon I'll be gone, too."

Hiram Mayes

Hiram Mayes thinks he was born in 1862, a slave of Tom Edgar, who owned a plantation in Double Bayou, Texas. Hiram lives with two daughters in a rambling farmhouse near Beaumont, less than three miles from his birthplace on the old Edgar homestead near the Iron Bridge. For thirty years Hiram has served as Worshipful Master of the Masonic Lodge (Negro) in the vicinity. Native intelligence gleams in his deep-set eyes, but his speech shows that he received little schooling.

"De fust thing I 'members back in slavery time was gittin' in de master's strawberry patch. He's right proud of dat patch and git after us plenty. Dey was li'l Tim Edgar, dat de white boy, and me. Tim, he still livin' down in Wallisville. Old master he cut us both a couple times for thiefin' he strawberries, jes' give us a bresh or two to skeer us. Dat de onlies' time he ever did whip me and you couldn' hardly call that a whippin'.

"Old man Tom Edgar was my master and de old Edgar place was down below where Jackson's store is and 'bout two mile from where I lives now. Some de brick from dat house still standin' dere in de woods.

"My mama name Mary and Dolf Mayes my papa, and I's borned 'bout 1862, I guess, 'cause I wasn't very big when freedom come. I did most my playin' with young master, Tim, him and me 'bout de same age.

"Old master was sho' good to he slaves and dey ain't never have no cruel overseer nor no lot of whippin' like some masters did. Mama work in de white folks' house and done de cookin' in de big kitchen. De big house was a big, low place with galleries 'round it. Mama tie me to a chair leg on de gallery to keep me from runnin' off to de bayou. Dey 'fraid of alligators. Dem 'gators never did eat no cullud chillen 'round us place, but dey allus 'fraid day would. Dey sich big snakes in de woods, too, dey skeered of dem.

"De cullud folks all have li'l brick cabin quarters and dey have a brickyard right near de place what a white man own and he make de bricks what dey calls Cedar Bayou brick 'count of de mud being diff'rent. I's born in one dem li'l brick houses. I don't 'member none my grandfolks 'cept my papa's mama, call Martha Godfry. She come from Virginny, and 'long to de Mayes where my papa born.

"I never did bother with Sunday School much, me. Dey one on de bayou and a white lady, Miss Joseph, am de teacher. Dey wasn't no school but after I git free I go to school on de edge of de woods. Dey have teacher name Runnells and a old blue-back speller to larn out of.

"After us freed my papa move up de prairie a ways and hire out to ride de range. Dey done larn me to ride when I 'bout five, six year old and I rid with de old man. Dat ridin' business was jes' my job. My daddy never did like to settle down and farm, but druther ride de range for four bits or six bits de day. De old master done give us nothin', jes' turn us adrift, but he didn't have much and everybody jes' have to shift for demselves dem days. Us git 'long all right makin' money with de cattlemen.

"De prairie lands a good place to git things to eat and us see plenty deers, sometime eight or ten in de bunch. Dey lots of wolves roamin' 'round lookin' for stray cows. Dat when de whip come in handy, to knock dem on de head. Never hear tell of but one bear, and us cotch him on Gum Island and kill him. You know dem funny lookin', horny things dey calls armadillos? Dey been immigrate here 'bout ten year ago. Dey come from somewhere but us ain't knowed why. Dey never was none here in slavery time but plenty horny frogs and 'gators.

"I marry 51 year ago to Wilina Day and I's still marry to her. Us marry in her brudder's house with jes' homefolks. Dey's nine chillen and eight still livin' and most dem farmers, 'cept two boys in de reg'lar army. Dey am Dolf and Robert. Oscar runs de fillin' station at Double Bayou. Oscar was in France in de World War. I has two my gals with me here and two grandchillen.

"I rode de range till 'bout 20 year ago and den I start gittin' purty old, so I settles down to farmin'. Dey charter a Masonic lodge here in 1906, I 'lieve it were number naught six, and dey put me up for Worshipful Master of de bunch. After dey vouch for me I git de chair and I been sittin' in de east for 30 year."

Susan Merritt

Susan Merritt, 87, was born in Rusk Co., Texas, a slave of Andrew Watt. A year after she was freed, Susan moved with her parents to Harrison Co., and stayed on their farm until she married Will Merritt. They reared fifteen children. Susan has little to say of her life from 1865 to the present, stating that they got along on the farm they worked on shares. Since her husband's death Susan lives with a son, Willie, west of Marshall, Texas, on the Hynson Springs Road.

"I couldn't tell how old I is, but does you think I'd ever forgit them slave days? I 'lieve I's 'bout 87 or more, 'cause I's a good size gal spinnin all the thread for the white folks when they lets us loose after surrender.

"I's born right down in Rusk County, not a long way from Henderson, and Massa Andrew Watt am my owner. My pappy, Bob Rollins, he come from North Carolina and belonged to Dave Blakely and mammy come from Mississippi. Mammy have eleven of us chillen but four dies when they babies, but Albert, Hob, John, Emma, Anna, Lula and me lives to be growed and married.

"Massa Watt lived in a big log house what sot on a hill so you could see it 'round for miles, and us lived over in the field in little log huts, all huddled along together. They have home-made beds nailed to the wall and baling sack mattresses, and us call them bunks. Us never had no money but plenty clothes and grub and wear the same clothes all the year 'round. Massa Watt made our shoes for winter hisself and he made furniture and saddles and harness and run a grist mill and a whiskey still there on the place. That man had ev'ything.

"The hands was woke with the big bell and when massa pulls that bell rope the niggers falls out them bunks like rain fallin'. They was in that field 'fore day and stay till dusk dark. They work slap up till Saturday night and then washes their clothes, and sometimes they gits through and has time for the party and plays ring plays. I 'member part the words to one play and that, 'Rolling river, roll on, the old cow die in cold water ... now we's got to drink bad water 'cause old cow die in cold water,' but I can't 'member more'n that. It's too long ago.

"When the hands come in from the field at dusk dark, they has to tote water from the spring and cook and eat and be in bed when that old bell rings at nine o'clock. 'Bout dusk they calls the chillen and gives 'em a piece of corn pone 'bout size my hand and a tin cup milk and puts them to bed, but the growed folks et fat pork and greens and beans and sich like and have plenty milk. Ev'ry Sunday massa give 'em some flour and butter and a chicken. Lots of niggers caught a good cowhiding for slippin' 'round and stealin' a chicken 'fore Sunday.

"Massa Watt didn't have no overseer, but he have a nigger driver what am jus' as bad. He carry a long whip 'round the neck and I's seed him tie niggers to a tree and cowhide 'em till the blood run down onto the ground. Sometimes the women gits slothful and not able to do their part but they makes 'em do it anyway. They digs a hole, 'bout body deep, and makes them women lie face down in it and beats 'em nearly to death. That nigger driver beat the chillen for not keepin' their cotton row up with the lead man. Sometimes he made niggers drag long chains while they works in the field and some of 'em run off, but they oughtn't to have done it, 'cause they chase 'em with hounds and nearly kilt 'em.

"Lots of times Massa Watt give us a pass to go over to George Petro's place or Dick Gregg's place. Massa Petro run a slave market and he have big, high scaffold with steps where he sells slaves. They was stripped off to the waist to show their strengt'.

"Our white folks have a church and a place for us in the back. Sometimes at night us gather 'round the fireplace and pray and sing and cry, but us daren't 'low our white folks know it. Thank the Lawd us can worship where us wants nowadays. I 'member one song we allus sing:
"'I heard the voice of Jesus callin'
Come unto me and live
Lie, lie down, weepin' one
Res' they head on my breast.

"'I come to Jesus as I was
Weary and lone and tired and sad,
I finds in him a restin' place,
And he has made me glad.'
"Us have two white doctors call Dr. Dan and Dr. Gill Shaw, what wait on us when we real sick. Us wore asafoetida bags 'round the neck and it kep' off sickness.

"I stay mos' the time in the big house and massa good but missy am the devil. I couldn't tell you how I treated. Lots of times she tie me to a stob in the yard and cowhide me till she give out, then she go and rest and come back and beat me some more. You see, I's massa nigger and she have her own niggers what come on her side and she never did like me. She stomp and beat me nearly to death and they have to grease my back where she cowhide me and I's sick with fever for a week. If I have a dollar for ev'ry cowhidin' I git, I'd never have to work no more.

Susan Merritt

"Young missy Betty like me and try larn me readin' and writin' and she slip to my room and have me doin' right good. I larn the alphabet. But one day Missy Jane cotch her schoolin' me and she say, 'Niggers don't need to know anything,' and she lams me over the head with the butt of a cowhide whip. That white woman so rough, one day us makin' soap and some little chickens gits in the fire 'round the pot and she say I let 'em do it and make me walk barefoot through that bed of coals sev'ral times.

"I hears 'bout freedom in September and they's pickin' cotton and a white man rides up to massa's house on a big, white hoss and the houseboy tell massa a man want see him and he hollers, 'Light, stranger.' It a gov'ment man and he have the big book and a bunch papers and say why ain't massa turn the niggers loose. Massa say he tryin' git the crop out and he tell massa have the slaves in. Uncle Steven blows the cow horn what they use to call to eat and all the niggers come runnin', 'cause that horn mean, 'Come to the big house, quick.' That man reads the paper tellin' us we's free, but massa make us work sev'ral months after that. He say we git 20 acres land and a mule but we didn't git it.

"Lots of niggers was kilt after freedom, 'cause the slaves in Harrison County turn loose right at freedom and them in Rusk County wasn't. But they hears 'bout it and runs away to freedom in Harrison County and they owners have 'em bushwhacked, that shot down. You could see lots of niggers hangin' to trees in Sabine bottom right after freedom, 'cause they catch 'em swimmin' 'cross Sabine River and shoot 'em. They sho' am goin' be lots of soul cry 'gainst 'em in Judgment!"

Josh Miles

Josh Miles, 78, was born in Richmond, Virginia, a slave of the Miles family. In 1862 Mr. Miles brought his family and slaves to Franklin, Texas. After he was freed, Josh worked for the railroad until he was laid off because of old age. He lives in Mart, Texas.

"I was born in Richmond, in Virginny, back in 1859, and my mammy and pappy was slaves to a man named Miles, what lived in Richmond but owned three plantations out a few miles, and 'bout fifteen hundred niggers. Pappy was de fam'ly coachman and druv de li'l surrey when Massa gwine see he plantations. On Sunday he druv de big coach to church. De Old Massa wear de big stove-pipe hat and de long-skirt coat and he big boots. Pappy, he wear de tall hat with de blue uniform with brass buttons, and black, shiny boots. He have de long horsewhip to crack at dem hosses--he drive four or six hosses, 'cause dat coach am big and heavy and de roads am often muddy.

"Massa allus went to de big fairs in Louisville and Richmond, where de big hoss races am. Dey name de hosses for Abe Lincoln and Steve Douglas, in 1860. De bettin' song what dey sings am like dis:

"'Dere's a old plow hoss, whose name am Doug, doo, dah, doo-dah--
He's short and thick, a reg'lar plug, oh, doo, dah, doo-dah, doo--
We're born to work all night, we're born to work all day,
I'll bet my money on de Lincoln hoss, who bets on Steven A?'

"Well, dat de way us lives jes' befo' de war. When de presidents calls for volunteers, Virginny goes for de Rebels, and dey moves de capitol to Richmond. So Old Massa sees he'll be right in de thick of de war and he 'cides to come to Texas. He gits he slaves and he folks and hosses and cattle and he household things in de covered wagon and starts. Course, de hosses and cattle walks, and so does us niggers. But massa take he time and stops wherever he wants. It takes two years to make de trip. He stay de whole winter one place, and stops in Nashville and Memphis and Vicksburg. All dese places he trade de hosses and mules and oxen and niggers and everything else he have. But he wouldn't trade he pers'nal slaves. Dey have de big warehouse in places like Memphis, and take de nigger de day befo' de sale and give him plenty to eat to make him look in good humor. Dey chain him up de night befo' de sale, and iffen he am de fightin' nigger, dey handcuffs him. De auctioneer say, 'Dis nigger am eighteen year old, sound as de dollar, can pick 300 pounds of cotton a day, good disposition, easy to manage, come up 'xamine him.' Dey strips him to de waist and everybody look him over and de good ones brung $1,500 sometimes. I seed de old mammy and her two boys and gals sold. One man buys de boys and old mammy cry, but it don't do no good. 'Nother man bids de two gals and mammy throw such a fit her old massa throws her in, 'cause she too old to be much 'count.

"De siege of Vicksburg 'gins jus' after old massa done left there, on he way to Texas. He friends tell him all 'bout it. Coffee was $4.00 de pound, tea $18.00, butter to $2.00 de pound, corn $15.00 de bar'l, calico $1.75 de yard and muslin 'bout $7.00 de yard. De Rebels holds de city long as they could. De bluff over de city have de caves in it and dey's rented for high rent. Flour am $10.00 de pound and bacon $5.00. Dey eats mule meat, and dey give it de French name, 'Mule tongue cold, a la bray.'

"We keep's up with what happen and after de war dey tells us 'bout Richmond. De lab'tory am blowed up Friday, and de Stuart home burnt. Befo' Richmond am taken, dey sings dis song:

"Would you like to hear my song?

I'm 'fraid its rather long--

Of de 'On to Richmond,' double trouble,

Of de half a dozen trips

And de half a dozen slips,

And de latest bustin' of de bubble.

"'Pull off you coat and roll up you sleeve,

For Richmond am a hard road to travel--

Then pull off you coat and roll up you sleeve.

For Richmond am a hard road to travel.'

"Dey sung dat song to de old tune call 'Old Rosin de Beau.'

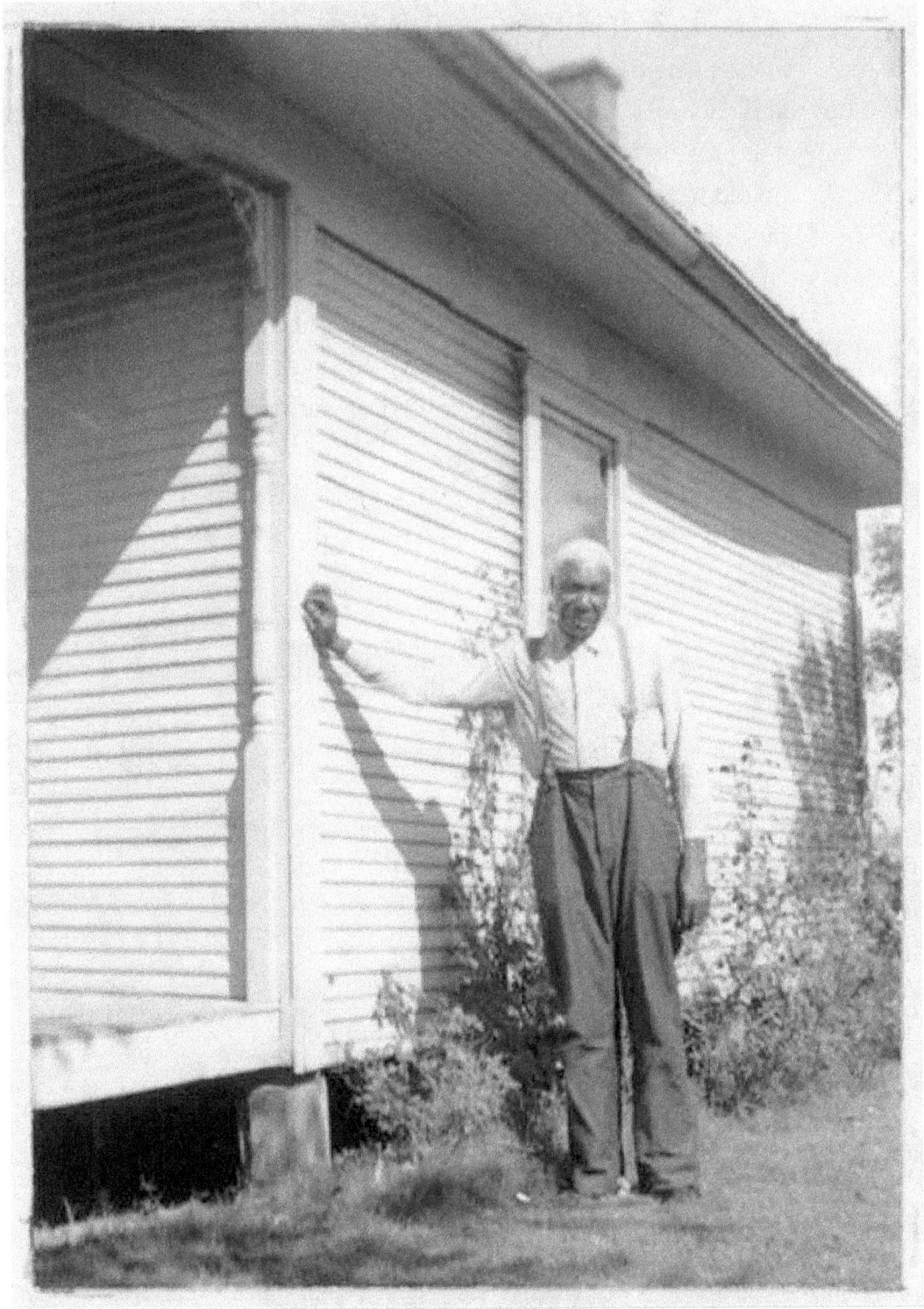

Josh Miles

"De war ends and in de few months old massa sot he slaves free. He give my pappy some money and he starts out for heself. He goes to Milligan and rents land and raises he fam'ly. Old Massa never goes back to Richmond. De Yanks gits what he left so dey no use gwine back dere. He lives in Franklin till 1914. It ain't like Old Virginny, but dey's plenty wild game and hawgs and he raises a bale of cotton to de acre, so he have money once more.

"Dey's folks comin' to Texas all de time from de old states. It am de new world and dey likes it. Dey has de Juneteenth cel'brations after 'while, and de white folks gives us beeves and hawgs to barbecue, so Texas am de good place to stay.

"When I's 'bout growed, I starts workin' on de I. & G.N. railroad and helps build it from Houston into Waco. I works for it for years and years, and allus lives near de Brazos River. I's lived here in Mart forty years.

"I doesn't have de bitter mem'ries like some de niggers. 'Cause Old Massa allus good to us. I's had de good life and am 'bout ready to go to Hebben, and hopes I can see Old Massa dere."

Anna Miller

Anna Miller, 85, lives with her daughter, Lucy Watkins, at 407 W. Bluff St., Ft. Worth, Texas. She was born a slave in Kentucky, and was sold, with her parents, to Mark Loyed, a farmer in Missouri. He later sold Anna's mother, before Anna was old enough to remember her. When Anna was 8, her owner moved to Palo Pinto, Texas.

"I'se now 'bout 85 years ole, dat's what de white folks tells me. I'se bo'n in Kentuck'. My mammy, pappy and I'se sold by our fust marster to Marster Mark Loyed, who lived in Missouri. He takes us to him's farm. When I'se 'bout eight years ole, Marster Loyed sold him's farm and comes to Texas in covered wagons and oxen. He's brung all de slaves wid him. I'se don' 'member much 'bout de trip, cause I'se sick wid de fever. I'se so bad, de marster thinks I'se goin' to die. One mornin' he comes and looks at me and says, 'Dis nigger am too val'able to die. We'd better doctor her.' We camps for six days.

"We comes to Palo Pinto and dat's wild country den. Plenty of Indians, but dey never trouble we'uns. My work, 'twas helpin' wid de chores and pick up de brush whar my pappy was a-clearin' de land. When I gits bigger, I'se plowed, hoed, and done all de goin' to de mill. I'se helps card, spins and cuts de thread. We'uns makes all de cloth for to makes de clothes, but we don' git 'em. In de winter we mos' freeze to death. De weavin' was de night work, after workin' all de day in de fiel'.

"Dey sho whups us. I'se gits whupped lots a times. Marster whups de men and missus whups de women. Sometimes she whups wid de nettleweed. When she uses dat, de licks ain't so bad, but de stingin' and de burnin' after am sho' misery. Dat jus' plum runs me crazy. De mens use de rope when dey whups.

"'Bout eatin', we keeps full on what we gits, such as beans, co'nmeal and 'lasses. We seldom gits meat. White flour, we don' know what dat taste like. Jus' know what it looks like. We gits 'bout all de milk we wants, 'cause dey puts it in de trough and we helps ourselves. Dere was a trough for de niggers and one for de hawgs.

"Jus' 'bout a month befo' freedom, my sis and nigger Horace runs off. Dey don' go far, and stays in de dugout. Ev'ry night dey'd sneak in and git 'lasses and milk and what food dey could. My sis had a baby and she nuss it ev'ry night when she comes. Dey runs off to keep from gittin' a whuppin'. De marster was mad 'cause dey lets a mule cut hisself wid de plow. Sis says de bee stung de mule and he gits unruly and tangle in de plow. Marster says, 'Dey can' go far and will come back when dey gits hongry.'

"I'se don' know much 'bout de war. De white folks don' talk to us 'bout de war and we'uns don' go to preachin' or nothin', so we can't larn much. When freedom comes, marster says to us niggers, 'All dat wants to go, git now. You has nothin'.' And he turns dem away, nothin' on 'cept ole rags. 'Twarn't enough to cover dere body. No hat, no shoes, no unnerwear.

"My pappy and mos' de niggers goes, but I'se have to stay till my pappy finds a place for me. He tells me dat he'll come for me. I'se have to wait over two years. De marster gets worser in de disposition and goes 'roun' sort of talkin' to hisse'f and den he gits to cussin' ev'rybody.

"In 'bout a year after freedom, Marster Loyed moves from Palo Pinto to Fort Worth. He says he don' want to live in a country whar de niggers am free. He kills hisse'f 'bout a year after dey moves. After dat, I'se sho' glad when pappy comes for me. He had settled at Azle on a rented farm and I'se lives wid him for 'bout ten years. Den I'se goes and stays wid my brudder on Ash Creek. De three of us rents land and us runs dat farm.

"I'se git married 'bout four years after I'se goes to Ash Creek, to Bell Johnson. We had four chillen. He works for white folks. 'Bout nine years after we married my husban' gits drowned and den I works for white folks and cares for my chillen for fo'teen years. Then I'se gits married again. I'se married Fred Miller, a cook, and we lived in Fort Worth. In 1915 he goes 'way to cook for de road 'struction camp and dats de las' I'se hears of dat no 'count nigger!

"Lots of difference when freedom comes. Mos' de time after, I'se have what I wants to eat. Sometime 'twas a little hard to git, but we gits on. I'se goes to preachin' and has music and visit wid de folks I'se like. But Marster Loyed makes us work from daylight to dark in de fiel's and make cloth at night."

Mintie Maria Miller

Mintie Maria Miller, 1404 39th St., Galveston, Texas, was born in Tuscaloosa, Alabama, in 1852. She has forgotten her first master's name, but was sold while very young to Dr. Massie, of Lynchburg, Texas. The journey to Texas took three months by ox-cart. After the Civil War Mintie went to Houston and stayed with an old colored woman whose former master had given her a house. Later she went to Galveston, where she has worked for one family 24 years.

"I was born in Alabama in 1852, in Tuscaloosa and my mammy's name was Hannah, but I don't know my pappy's name. When I was still pretty little my brother and uncle and aunt and mother was sold and me with 'em.

"Dr. Massie brung us to Texas in an ox-cart but my sister had to stay with the old mistress and that the last I ever seen my sister. She was four year old then.

"After we reaches Texas we lives on a great big place, somewhere 'round Lynchburg and Dr. Massie have two girls and I sleeps on the foot of they bed. They nice to me, they spoil me, in fac'. I plays with the white gals and they feeds me from they tables and in the evenin' my mammy takes me down to de bayou and wash my face and put me on a clean dress.

"My mammy cook for the white folks and they treats us both fine, but one gal I knowed was 'bout 8 or 9 and she run away from her master and swim de Trinity River and it was winter and her feets freezes. He cotches dis gal and puts her feets in the fire to thaw 'em, and burnt 'em. The law say you could take slaves 'way from sich a man, so Dr. Frost takes her away from that man and gives her to Miss Nancy what was de mistress at Dr. Massie's place.

"Then they says they gwine sell me, 'cause Miss Nancy's father-in-law dies and they got rid of some of us. She didn't want to sell me so she tell me to be sassy and no one would buy me. They takes me to Houston and to the market and a man call George Fraser sells the slaves. The market was a open house, more like a shed. We all stands to one side till our turn comes. They wasn't nothin' else you could do.

"They stands me up on a block of wood and a man bid me in. I felt mad. You see I was young then, too young to know better. I don't know what they sold me for, but the man what bought me made me open my mouth while he looks at my teeth. They done all us that-a-way, sells us like you sell a hoss. Then my old master bids me goodby and tries to give me a dog, but I 'members what Miss Nancy done say and I sassed him and slapped the dog out of his hand. So the man what bought me say, 'When one o'clock come you got to sell her 'gain, she's sassy. If she done me that way I'd kill her.' So they sells me twice the same day. They was two sellin's that day.

"My new master, Tom Johnson, lives in Lynchburg and owns the river boat there, and has a little place, 'bout one acre, on the bayou. Then the war comes and jes' 'fore war come to Galveston they took all the steamships in the Buffalo Bayou and took the cabins off and made ships. They put cotton bales 'round them and builded 'em up high with the cotton, to cotch the cannonballs. Two of 'em was the Island City, and the Neptune.

"Then freedom cries and the master say we all free and I goes to Houston with my mammy. We stays with a old colored woman what has a house her old master done give her and I finishes growin' there and works some. But then I comes to Galveston and hired out here and I been workin' for these white folks 24 year now."

Tom Mills

Tom Mills was born in Fayette Co., Alabama, in 1858, a slave of George Patterson, who owned Tom's father and mother. In 1862 George Patterson moved to Texas, bringing Tom and his mother, but not his father. After they were freed, it was difficult for Tom's mother to earn a living and they had a hard time for several years, until Tom was old enough to go to work on a ranch, as a cow-hand. In 1892 Tom undertook stock farming, finally settling in Uvalde in 1919. He now lives in a four-room house he built himself. A peach orchard and a grape arbor shade the west side of the house and well-fed cows are in the little pasture. Tom is contented and optimistic and says he can "do a lot of work yet."

"I was born in Alabama, in Fayette Co., in 1858. My mother was named Emaline Riley and my father was named Thad Mills. My sisters were named Ella and Ann and Lou and Maggie and Matildy, and the youngest one was Easter. I had two brothers, Richard and Ben. Bob Lebruc was my great-uncle and for a long while he ran a freight wagon from Salt Lakes to this country. That was the only way of getting salt to Texas, this part of Texas, I mean, because Salt Lakes is down east of Corpus, close to the bay. My uncle was finally killed by the Indians in Frio County.

"In Alabama we lived on Patterson's place. The grandmother of all these Pattersons was Betsy Patterson and we lived on her estate. My mother wove the cloth. It kep' her pretty busy, but she was stout and active. My uncle was blacksmith and made all the plows, too.

"We had a picket house, one room, and two beds built in corners.

"My mother done the cookin' up at the house because she was workin' up there all the time, weavin' cloth, and of course we ate up there. The rest of 'em didn't like it much because we ate up there, but her work was there. I guess you never did see a loom? It used to keep me pretty busy fillin' quills. She made this cloth--this four-dollar-a-yard, four-leaf jean cloth, all wool, of course.

"I was too little to work durin' the war; of course we packed a little water and got a little wood. I was goin' to tell you about this scar on my finger. I was holdin' a stick for another little fellow to cut wood and he nearly cut my finger off. That sure woke me up.

"They had field work on the place, but a family by the name of Knowles did the farm work. I worked stock nearly all my life. It used to be all the work there was. I think my mother was allowed to make a little money on this cloth business. That is, cloth she made on the outside. And she was the only one of the slaves that could read. I don't know that they cared anything about her readin', but they didn't want her to read it to the rest of 'em. I never earned no money; I was too little.

"We called Old Man Patterson 'master' and we called Mrs. Patterson 'mistuss'.

"I don't know what the other slaves had to eat--they cooked for themselves, but we had jes' what the Pattersons had to eat. On Sunday mornin' we had flour bread. Always glad to see Sunday mornin' come. We made the co'n meal right on the place on these old hand mills that you turn with both hands like this. When the co'n jes' fust began to get ha'd, they would grate that; but when it got ha'd, they would grind it. We always had meat the year 'round. We called hogshead cheese 'souse'. But we never did make sausage then. It was a long time before we had a sausage mill. Oh, sho' we made 'chittlin's' (chitterlings). We make them even now. Why mama always takes the paunch and fixes it up ever' time we kill hogs. We dried beef, strung it out, and put it on the line. When we got ready to cook it, we'd take it and beat it and make hash and fry it or boil it. We had lots of deer and turkeys, quail and 'possums, but they never did do much eatin' rabbits. I didn't eat no 'possums and I didn't eat no honey; there was sever'l things I didn't like. I like straight beef, turkeys, quail and squirrel is mighty fine eatin'. I set traps and would ketch quail. Armadillos are pretty good meat, but we didn't eat 'em then. Why, I was grown before I ever saw an armadillo. I don't know where they immigrated from. Yes'm, I think they come from Mexico; they must surely have because they wasn't any here when I was a young boy. We used to see 'em in shows before they ever got to be around here.

"I wore a shirt that hit me down about my knees. When my mother made my pants, she made 'em all in one piece, sleeves 'n all. The fust shoes I ever had, my uncle tanned the leather and made 'em. I guess I was about six years old. He made the pegs, tanned the leather, and made the shoes. It taken 18 months to tan the leather. Bark tanned. Huh, I c'n smell that old tannin' vat now. People nowadays, they're livin' too easy. 'Fraid to let a drop of water fall on 'em.

"Ever' day was Sunday with me then. After we got up any size, they put us to work, but we didn't work on Sunday. After I got to be a cowboy, of course, they didn't have no Sunday then.

"I was twenty-two when I fust married. It was in Medina County. Her name was Ada Coston. She had on a white dress, draggin' the groun' in the back, what you used to call these trains. I remember when they wore these hoops, too. We married about 7 o'clock in the evenin'. I had on one of these frock-tail coats, black broadcloth suit. I had on good shop-made shoes. We had better shoes then than we ever have now. We had a supper and then danced. Had a big weddin' cake--great big white one, had a hole in the center, all iced all over. I think my auntie made that cake, or my cousin. We had coffee, but I never did drink whiskey in my life. I think they had chickens--if I remember right, chicken and dressin'. Had a whole lot better to eat then than I can get now. We danced all night. I was at a weddin' where they danced three days and nights, and I tell you where it was. Have you been down to Old Bill Thomas'? You have? Well, that was where it took place. Bill and Ellen married when I was about twelve years old, and I think they danced three days and nights, and maybe longer. Now, if they didn't tell you that, I could'a told you if I had been there. We danced these old square dances, what you call the Virginia Reel, and the round dances like the Schottische, Polka, waltzes, and all them. I was a dancin' fool, wanted to dance all the time. I inherited that from my mother. She was a terrible dancer.

"Old Man George Patterson was a very tall and a dark complected man. He was a kind old man. He was good to my mother and all those that come from Alabama. The old mistuss would whip me, but he didn't. The grandchillun and I could fight all over the house; he would jes' get out of the way. But she would get on us once in awhile. The worst whippin' she ever give me was about some sheep. They had a cane patch down close to the sheep pen and I went down there and got me some cane and stripped it off and I was runnin' 'round down there whippin' the sheep with that stalk of cane and she found me down there and took me to the house and learned me better. They never did whip my mother. I know they whipped two others. Two was all I ever knew of 'em whippin'. Dillard, he married the oldest Patterson girl, and my uncle, he borrowed an auger from Mr. Dillard to make a frame. When dinner time came, he laid it down and went to his dinner. When he got back, this bit was broken and he went and tells him (Dillard) and they came down to make a search about who had used it. They found that another colored man got it and used it to bore some holes with and broke it, so he took it back and laid it down and never said nothin'. Them days, a thing like that steel bit was awful high. They laid 'im over a log and whipped 'im and whipped his wife for not tellin' it when they asked her. They had a boy countin' the licks, but I don't know how many he got. They had me down there too, and I was ready to get away from there. I think they had us down there to show what we would get if we didn't do right.

"The old lady, the mistuss, she was pretty high-tempered--her head kind of bounced, like that--when she got mad. She was slender and tall. I think they lived in a log house; I don't remember much what kind of house it was. I know my mother weaved cloth in one part of it.

"I don't think the field was very large on that place. I often wanted to go back and see it. It was right on the Sabinal, right opposite Knowlton Creek.

"I have heard my mother tell about slaves bein' sold. It was kinda like a fair they have now. They would go there, and some of 'em sold for a thousand dollars. They said somethin' about puttin' 'em on a block; the highest bidder, you know, would buy 'em. I don't know how they got 'em there, for they wasn't much of a way for 'em to go 'cept by oxen, you know. It was back in Alabama where she saw all that. Of course, there was more of that down in Mississippi than Alabama, but she didn't know nothin' about that.

"I remember the cotton they raised on the Patterson place. They picked the seeds out with their fingers and made cloth out of it. They would take coarse wool--not merino wool, for that was too fine--and use the coarse wool for a filler. That was what they would make me do, pick the seed out of that cotton to keep me out of mischief. I remember that pretty well. Kep' me tied down, and I would beg the old man to let me go, and when he did, if I got into anything, I was back there pickin' seeds pretty quick.

"We would get up about daybreak. They might have got up before I knew anything about it, but sometimes I got up with my mother.

"What little school I went to was German, at D'Hanis and Castroville. I went to the priest at D'Hanis and to the sisters at Castroville. No education to amount to anything. That was after we were freed. I went to school at the same time that Johnny Ney and his sister, Mary, went to school. I would like to see Johnny and talk to him now. Your grandmother and her sisters and brothers went to that school and I remember all of 'em well. One of them boys, George, was killed and scalped by the Indians, and that was caused by them boys playin' and scarin' each other all the time. He was with them Rothe boys, and they always had an Indian scare up someway to have fun with each other, especially to scare George. So when they did discover the Indians and hollered to George, he wouldn't run, because they had fooled 'im so much. So the Indians slipped up on him and killed 'im.

"Yes, I knew all the Millers better than I did nearly any of the rest of the old settlers up there. Aunt Dorcas, that was George's mother, she nursed me through the measles. I was awful sick, and when my mother heard it and come up after me, she told my mother to leave me there, she would take care of me. I tell you she took good care of me too.

"But that was after freedom. You see, my mother didn't want to come to Texas. She laid out nearly two years before they got hold of her and got her to come to Texas. Alabama wasn't thickly settled then. There was bottoms of trees and wild fruit she could eat. She stayed out by herself, and would come and get something to eat and leave again. But Patterson told her if she would come to Texas she would be treated right and not be whipped or nothin' like that. And so far as I know, she never was whipped. He kep' his word with her. She was useful and they needed her. She wove the cloth and was such a good worker.

"The first cow we ever owned, we cut cockleburrs out of a field of about seven or eight acres. Mr. John Ware gave her a cow to cut the burrs out.

"After the war, my uncle carried my mother and his wife and chillen away, and when they started with Margaret--she was his niece and my cousin--they overtook 'em and took Margaret back. She was house girl, she didn't do nothin' but work in the house. I don't know whether they ever paid her anything or not. They needed her to wait on the old lady.

"I don't know how that come about when they told 'em they was free. I don't know whether mother read it in the paper or he come and told 'em. We went on, and came right on up the same creek to a place where a man had a ranch by the name of Roney. It was an old abonded (abandoned) place, and we didn't have anything to eat. My uncle got out and rustled around to get some bread stuff and got some co'n, but while he was gone was when we suffered for something to eat. We didn't have anything to kill wild game with. We would fish a little. When he left he went up in the Davenport settlement, up there about where your grandfather lived. We got milk and careless weeds, but that was all we had, and we were awful glad to see the co'n come. And that was my first taste of javelin (javelina). It evidently was an old male javelin, for I couldn't eat it. I don't think my uncle ever stole anything in his life. I was with him all the time and I know he didn't. My mother, she went over to Davenports' and my uncle got out and rustled to see where he could get something to do. So they moved up in the Sabinal Canyon and he got on Old Man Joel Fenley's place.

"Old Man 'Parson' Monk, I think, was the first person I ever heard preach. That was down here in the Patterson settlement (formerly a settlement six miles south of the present town of Sabinal). The preachin' was right there on the place. I joined the church after I was grown, but that was the cullud church, then. My mother she joined the white church. She joined the Hardshell Baptist. She never did live in any colony and the cullud church was too far. They had lots of camp meetin's. I never was at but one camp meetin' that I know of. They would preach and shout and have a good time and have plenty to eat. That was what most of 'em went for. But the churches then seemed to be more serious than they are now. They preached the 'altar.' You know, like anyone wanted to join the church, they was a mourner, you see, seekin' for religion. And they would sing and pray with 'em till they professed the religion. I had a sister that never went to a meetin' that she didn't get to shoutin' and shout to the end of the sermon. I always tried to get out of the way before I joined because if she got to me, she would beat on me and talk to me. We always tried to get to her, if she had her baby in her arms, because she would jes' throw that baby away when the Spirit moved her.

"Did you ever know of Monroe Brackins over at Hondo City? Well, I and him was both jes' boys and was with Jess Campbell, Joe Dean and a man named McLemore. They was white men. We went down on the Frio River, and there was some pens down there on the Johnson place. They was three brothers of them Johnsons. We had a little bunch of cattle, goin' down there. This Jess Campbell and Joe Dean was full of devilment and they knew Monroe was awful scarey. When we penned the cattle that evenin' it was late and Monroe noticed a pile of brush at the side of the gate. He asked 'em what you reckin that was there, and they told him they was a man killed and buried there. That night after dark they was fixin' to get supper ready and told Monroe to go get some water down at the river, but he wouldn't do it. Well, I never was afraid of the dark in my life, so I had to go get the water. Well, we made a fire and fixed supper and then these men put a rope on Monroe and took him off a little piece and wrapped the rope around a tree and never even tied the rope fast. The other man, McLemore, he went around the camp and came up on the other side. He had an old dried cow hide with the tail still on it. The old tail was all bent, crimped up. Here he come from down the creek, from where they told Monroe that fellow was buried, and right toward Monroe with that hide on. Tail first and in the dark it looked pretty bad, and, I tell you, Monroe got to screamin'. I believe he would have died if they hadn't let him loose. I never laughed so much in my life. When he would get scared, he would squeal like a hog. He sure was scarey.

"Sometimes, I know, we would be woke up in the night and they would be cookin' chicken and dumplin's, or havin' somethin' like that. I'd like for 'em to come ever' night and wake me up. I don't know where it come from, but they would always wake the chillen up and let 'em have some of it. (This is an early recollection of his childhood during slavery.)

"My mother's daddy, if he was here, he could tell plenty of things. He could remember all about them days, and sing them songs too. I've heard him tell some mighty bad things, and he told somethin' pretty bad on hisself. He said they captured some Indian chillen and he was carryin one and it got to cryin' and he jes' took his saber and held it up by its feet and cut its head off. Couldn't stan' to hear it cry. He got punished for it, but he said he was a soldier and not supposed to carry Indian babies. Usually when Indians captured little fellows like that, they carried 'em off. Like when they carried off Frank Buckilew, a white boy. And a cullud boy that got away up close to Utopia. They kep' the Buckilew boy a long time, long enough that he got to where he understood the language. It was a long time that the Indians didn't kill a darky, though. But after the war, when they brought these cullud soldiers in here to drive 'em back, that started the war with the cullud people then.

"After freedom, I remember one weddin' the white folks had. That was when John Kanedy (Kennedy) married Melinda Johnson. He was a man that lived there on the river and was there up to the time he died. I wasn't at the weddin', but I was at the infair. They were married east of Hondo City. They had the infair then and it was a kind of celebration after the weddin'. Ever'body met there and had a big dance and supper and had a big time. They danced all night after the supper and then had a big breakfast the next mornin'. I was little, but I remember the supper and breakfast, for I was enjoyin' that myself. They was lots to eat, and they had it too. After freedom, I remember these quiltin's where they would have big dinners. They would have me there, threadin' needles for 'em. We always had a big time Christmas. They had dances and dinners for a week. Yes'm, the cullud people did. They would celebrate the holidays out. That was all free too, and they all had plenty to eat. They would meet at one place one night and have a dance and supper and, the next night, meet over at another place and have the same thing.

"When I got to workin' for myself, it was cow work. I done horseback work for fifty years. Many a year passed that I never missed a day bein' in the saddle. I stayed thirteen years on one ranch. The first place was right below Hondo City. His name was Tally Burnett and I was gettin' $7.50 a month. Went to work for that and stayed about three or four months and he raised my wages to what the others was gettin' and that was $12.50. He said I was as good as they were. Then I went to Frio City. I done the same kind of work, but I went with the people that nearly raised me, the Rutledges.

"That's where I was give twice in the census. My mother gave me in and he gave me in. That was one time they had one man too many.

"I married when I was with them and I worked for him after that. That was when we would work away down on the Rio Grande, when Demp Fenley and Lee Langford and Tom Roland and the two Lease boys and one or two more was deliverin' cattle to the Gold Franks' ranch. He wanted 8,000 two-year-old heifers. He had 150,000 acres of land and wanted cattle to stock it. Some taken a contract to deliver so many and some taken a contract to deliver so many, so these men I was with went down below Laredo and down in there. We wound that up in '85. In '86, I went to Kerr County and taken a ranch out there on the head of the Guadalupe River. I stayed there two years and a half, till they sold out. This man I was workin' for was from Boston, and he leased the ranch and turned it over to me and I done all the hirin' and payin' off and buyin' and ever'thing. When he sold out, I left and went on the Horton ranch about thirteen months.

"My first wife died in 1892, but we had been separated about five or six years. I married again in Bandera and quit ranchin' and went to stock farmin' for Albert Miller, then leased a place from Charley Montague two years, then went over into Hondo Canyon and leased a place there in '98. We stayed there till 1906, then came to Uvalde. I leased a place out here, about two hundred acres, four miles from town, and had odd jobs around here too. Then, about 1907, we went to Zavala County and stayed till 1919. I leased a place here, then, and finally settled at this place I'm on now and have been here ever since.

"I've got 11 chillen livin'. One boy, Alfred, is in Lousiana and I don't know what he's doin', but he's been married about five times. I have a boy workin' in the post office in San Antonio named Mack, and the rest of the chillen are here. There's Sarah, Riley, Frank, James, Banetta, John, Theodore, Tommy, Annie Laurie. They all live here and work at different places.

"I know when we used to camp out in the winter time we would have these old-time freezes, when ever'thing was covered in ice. We would have a big, fat cow hangin' up and we could slice that meat off and have the best meals. And when we was on the cow hunts we would start out with meal, salt and coffee and carry the beddin' for six or eight men on two horses and carry our rations on another horse. I guess it would scare people now to hear 'em comin' with all them pots and pans and makin' all that racket.

"When we camped and killed a yearlin' the leaf fat and liver was one of the first things we would cook. When they would start in to gather cattle to send to Kansas, they would ride out in the herd and pick out a fat calf, and they would get the 'fleece' and liver and broil the ribs. The meat that was cut off the ribs was called the fleece. It was a terr'ble waste, for many a time, the hams wasn't even cut out of the hide, jes' left there. Old Man Alec Rutledge used to say, when they would throw out bread and meat, he would say, 'I'll tell you, Tom, he will have to walk alone sometimes because this willful waste will make woeful wants.' He was talkin' about his brother--they was two of 'em and sure 'nough, his brother finally lost all his cattle, quit the business, and never had nothin' left. There would be an awful lot of good meat wasted, and now we are payin' for it.

"The first fence I ever seen wasn't any larger then this addition here, and it was put up out of pickets. The Mexicans used to build lots of fences and we got the idea from them, mostly on these old-timey stake-and-rider fences. It was an awful pasture when they had eight mile of fence. The way they made the field fences was nothin' but brush. I remember when I was a little fellow at John Kanady's (Kennedy's), George Johnson would come over and stay with his sister, Mrs. Kanady, and he would keep the cattle out of the field. One day, he came there and put me on his horse. He had loosened up his girt, and I got out there a little ways and one of the cows turned back. The horse was a regular old cow pony and when that cow turned back, the old horse turned just as quick and the saddle slipped and I stayed there.

"Oh, pshaw! they turn so quick you have to be on the lookout. You have to watch the horse as well as the cow. Some of them horses get pretty smart. One time they were cuttin' cattle and a fellow brought a cow to the edge of the herd and the cow turned back and when she did, the horse cut back too and left him there. When he went from under him, that fellow's spurs left a mark clear across the saddle as he went over. It was my saddle he was ridin' and that mark never did leave it, where the spurs cut across it.

"We've done some ridin' even after my wife, here, and I were married. She's seen 'em breakin' horses and all that pitchin' and bawlin'. But, I never was no hand to show off. If I kep' my seat, that was all I wanted. You see lots of fellows ridin' just to show off, but I never was for anything like that.

"No, I never did go up on the trail. I've helped prepare the herd to take. Usually, there would be one owner takin' his cattle up on the trail. They had no place to hold the cattle, only under herd. Usually, they would start with a thousand or fifteen hundred head, but they didn't put 'em all together till they got away out on the divide. They would have 'em shaped up as they gathered 'em and jes' hold what they wanted to send. It didn't take so many men, either, because they all understood their business.

"I was jes' thinkin' about when Mr. Demp Fenley and Rutledge was here. They had about nine hundred head of cattle. We brought 'em right in below Pearsall, right about the Shiner ranch, and delivered 'em there. But before we got there at a little creek they called *Pato*, they was hardly any place to bed the cattle because they was so much pear[TR: cactus]. Mr. Rutledge and I always bedded the cattle down, and then I would go on the last relief, usually about the time to get up, anyway. He used me all the time when they would get ready to go to camp in the evenin', and we'd spread 'em out and let 'em graze before beddin' 'em down. Sometimes he would give me a motion to come over there, and I knew that meant an animal to throw. He always got me to do the ropin' if one broke out. Well, we was comin on with those cattle and they was a steer that gave us trouble all the time. As soon as you got away, he would walk out of the herd. Well, we got the cattle all bedded down and they were quiet, but that steer walked out. I was ridin' Mr. Fenley's dun horse, and Mr. Rutledge says to me, 'I tell you what we'll do. We'll ketch that steer out here and give 'im a good whippin'.' I says, 'We'll get into trouble, too.' Well, he was to hold 'im away from the herd and I was to rope 'im, but the steer run in front of him and out-run 'im. If he would have run in behind him, I would 'a caught 'im, but that steer beat 'im to the herd and run right into the middle of 'em. And did he stampede 'em! Those cattle run right into the camp, and the boys all scramblin' into the wagon and gettin' on their horses without their boots on. One steer fell and rolled right under the chuck wagon. You know, we run those cattle all night, tryin' to hold 'em. It was a pear flat there, and next mornin' that pear was all beat down flat on the ground. They sure did run, and all because of that foolishness. Mr. Rutledge got to me and told me not to tell it, and I don't reckin to this day anybody knows what done that.

"I never told you about the panther about to get on to me, did I? Well, we was out on the Rio Grande, about thirty-one or thirty-two miles beyond Carrizo. It was at the *Las islas* (The Islands) Crossin'. I was about three days behind the outfit when they went out there. That was in July, and they was a law passed that we had to quit wearin' our guns the first day of July and hang 'em on the ho'n of our saddle. When I got to the outfit, the boys was gettin' pretty tired herdin'. They had to bring 'em out about six miles to grass and to this little creek. We would put 'em in the pen at night and feed 'em hay. We were waitin' there for them to deliver some cattle out of Mexico. The Mexican told me they was somethin' out there where they were herdin' sheep that was scarin' the sheep out of the pen at night. I had seen some bobcats, but I laid down under one of these huisache trees and went to sleep. I had my pistol on and was layin' there and about two o'clock, I woke up. I turned over and rested myself on my elbow and looked off there about 12 feet from me and there stood a big old female panther. She was kind of squattin' and lookin' right at me. I reached right easy and got my Winchester that was layin' beside me and I shot her right between the eyes. Why, I had one of her claws here for a long time. She had some young ones somewhere. I imagined, though, she was goin' to jump right on me. It wasn't no good feelin', I know. She was an awful large one.

"Oh, my goodness! I have seen lobos, eight or ten in a bunch. They're sure mean. I've seen 'em have cattle rounded up like a bunch of cow hands. If you heard a cow or yearlin' beller at night, you could go next mornin' and sure find where they had killed her. They would go right into the cow or calf and eat its kidney fat first thing. I tell you, one sure did scare me one time. I was out ridin', usually ropin' and brandin' calves, and I came across a den in the ground. I heard something whinin' down there in that hole. It was a curiosity to me and I wanted to get one of those little wolf pups. That was what I thought it was. I got down there and reached in there and got one of those little fellows. They was lovos (lobos). They are usually gray, but he was still black. They are black at first, then they turn gray. He was a little bit of a fellow. Well, I got him out and the old lovo wolf run right at me, snappin' her teeth, and my horse jerked back and came near gettin' away. But I hung to my wolf and got to my horse and got on and left there. I didn't have nothin' to kill her with. I was jes' a boy, then. I took that pup and give it to Mrs. Jim Reedes, down on the Hondo, and she kep' it till it began eatin' chickens.

"I had a bear scare, too. That was in '87, about fifty years ago. Well, Ira Wheat was sheriff at Leakey in Edwards County, then. I went down there, and I was ridin' a horse I broke for a sheriff in Kerr County. I came to Leakey to see Wheat--you see they was burnin' cattle (running the brands) all over that country then. As I was ridin' along, I seen some buzzards and I rode out there. Somethin' had killed a hog and eat on it. I knowed it was a bear afterwards, but then I went on down to Leakey and started back, I got up on the divide, at the head of a little canyon and I seen those buzzards again. I seen two black things and I jes' thought to myself them buzzards was comin' back and eatin' on that dead hog. I rode up and seen that it was two bears and I made a lunge at 'em and the old bear run off and the little cub ran up a tree. I thought, 'I'll ketch you, you little rascal.' So I tied my horse and I went up the tree after the cub and when I was near 'im, he squalled jes' like a child. I tell you, when it squalled that way, here came that old bear and begin snuffin' around the tree. My horse was jes' rearin' and tryin' to break loose out there. I tell you, when I *did* get down there and get to him, I had to lead him about two hundred yards before I could ever get on him. He sure was scared. Like it was when I was a boy down on the Hondo one time and I could hear horses comin' and thought it was Indians and after awhile, I couldn't hear nothin' but my heart beatin'."

————

Uncle Tom Mills is one of the most contented old darkies surviving the good old days when range was open and a livelihood was the easiest thing in the world to get. He lives in the western part of Uvalde, in a four-room house that he built himself. A peach orchard and a grape arbor shade the west side of the house. It is here that Uncle Tom spends many hours cultivating his little garden patch. Contented and well-fed milk cows lie in the shade of the oak trees in a little pasture east of the house, and he proudly calls attention to their full udders and sleek bodies. His wife, Hattie, laughs and joins him in conversation, helping to prod his memory on minor events. He smiles a lot and seems optimistic about most things. I did not hear him speak grudgingly toward anyone, or make a complaint about the old-age pension he gets. He is always busy about the place and claims that he can do a lot of work yet.

La San Mire

La San Mire, 86, aged French Negro of the Pear Orchard Settlement, near Beaumont, Texas, is alert and intelligent, and his long, well-formed hands gesture while he talks. He was born in Abbeville Parish, Louisiana, a slave of Prosper Broussard. His father was a Spaniard, his mother spoke French, and his master was a Creole. La San's patois is superior to that of the average French Negro. His story has been translated.

"The old war? No, I don't remember so much about it, because I was so young. I was ten years old at the beginning of the war. I was born the 13th of May, but I do not know of what year, in the Parish of Abbeville, on M'sieu Prosper's plantation between Abbeville and Crowley. My parents were slaves. My father a Spaniard, who spoke Spanish and French. My mother spoke French, the old master too, all Creoles. I, as all the other slaves, spoke French.

"During the war all the children had fear. I drove an old ox-cart in which I helped pick up the dead soldiers and buried them. A battle took place about 40 miles from the plantation on a bluff near a large ditch--not near the bayou, no. We were freed on July 4th. After the war I remained with my old master. I worked in the house, cooked in the kitchen. Early each morning, I made coffee and served it to my master and his family while they were in the bed.

"The old master was mean--made slaves lie on the ground and whipped them. I never saw him whip my father. He often whipped my mother. I'd hide to keep from seeing this. I was afraid. Why did he whip them? I do not remember. He did not have a prison, just 'coups de fault' (beatings). But not one slave from our plantation tried to escape to the north that I can remember.

"The slaves lived in little cabins. All alike, but good. One or two beds. Rooms small as a kitchen. Chimneys of dirt. Good floors. We had plenty to eat. Cornbread and grits, beef, 'chahintes'(coons), des rat bois (possum), le couche-couche, and Irish and sweet potatoes.

"Everyone raised cotton. In the evenings the slave women and girls seeded the cotton, carded it, made thread of it on the spinning wheel. They made it into cotton for dresses and suits. No shoes or socks. In winter the men might wear them in winter. Never the women or children.

"How many slaves? I do not recall. There were so many the yard was full. They worked from sun-up to sundown, with one hour for dinner. School? I hoed cotton and drove the oxen to plow the field.

"I never went to Mass before I was twenty years old. Yes, there were churches and the others went, but I did not want to go. There were benches especially for the slaves. Yes, I was baptized a Catholic in Abbeville, when I was big.

"Sunday the Negro slaves had round dances. Formed a circle--the boys and the girls--and changed partners. They sang and danced at the same time. Rarely on Saturday they had the dances. They sang and whistled in the fields.

"The marriages of the slaves were little affairs. Before the witnesses they'd 'sauter le balais'--the two--and they were married. No celebration, but always the little cakes.

"We had no doctor. We used 'vingaire' (an herb) for the fever; la 'chaspare' (sarsaparilla); la 'pedecha (an herb), sometimes called L'absinthe amer, in a drink of whiskey or gin, for the fever. Des regulateurs (patent medicines). On nearly all plantations there were 'traiteurs', (a charm-doctor, always a Negro).

"Noel we had the little cakes and special things to eat, but no presents.

Le San Mire

"I was married by the judge first, and after the marriage was blessed by the priest. I was 21 years old. I wore a new suit, because I had some money. I worked in the house during the day and at night I caught wild horses and sold them. I remember my wedding day. It was the Saturday before Mardi Gras. My wife came from Grand Chenier (Cameron) to Abbeville when she was small. We had 16 children, 11 boys and five girls. Three girls and two boys died when they were small.

"One year after my marriage I left the big house and made a home of my own. For an enclosure I made a levee of earth around. I planted cotton. I worked the place for a half or a third.

"I came to Beaumont 12 years ago, so my children could work, because I was sick. I could no longer work."

Charley Mitchell

Charley Mitchell, farmer in Panola Co., Texas, was born in 1852, a slave of Nat Terry, an itinerant Baptist preacher of Lynchburg, Virginia. Charley left the Terrys one year after he was freed. He worked in a tobacco factory, then as a waiter, until 1887, when he moved to Panola Co. For fifty years he has farmed in the Sabine River bottom, about twenty-five miles southeast of Marshall, Texas.

"I's born in Virginia, over in Lynchburg, and it was in 1852, and I 'longed to Parson Terry and Missy Julia. I don't 'member my pappy, 'cause he's sold when I's a baby, but my mammy was willed to the Terrys and allus lived with them till freedom. She worked for them and they hired her out there in town for cook and house servant.

"They hired me out most times as nuss for white folks chillen, and I nussed Tom Thurman's chillen. He run the bakery there in Lynchburg and come from the north, and when war broke they made him and 'nother northener take a iron clad oath they wouldn't help the north. Durin' the war I worked in Massa Thurman's bakery, helping make hard tack and doughnuts for the 'federate sojers. He give me plenty to eat and wear and treated me as well as I could hope for.

"Course, I didn't git no schoolin'. The white folks allus said niggers don't need no larnin'. Some niggers larnt to write their initials on the barn door with charcoal, then they try to find out who done that, the white folks, I mean, and say they cut his fingers off iffen they jus' find out who done it.

"Lynchburg was good sized when war come on and Woodruff's nigger tradin' yard was 'bout the bigges' thing there. It was all fenced in and had a big stand in middle of where they sold the slaves. They got a big price for 'em and handcuffed and chained 'em together and led 'em off like convicts. That yard was full of Louisiana and Texas slave buyers mos' all the time. None of the niggers wanted to be sold to Louisiana, 'cause that's where they beat 'em till the hide was raw, and salted 'em and beat 'em some more.

"Course us slaves of white folks what lived in town wasn't treated like they was on most plantations. Massa Nat and Missy Julia was good to us and most the folks we was hired out to was good to us. Lynchburg was full of pattyrollers, jus' like the country, though, and they had a fenced in whippin' post there in town and the pattyrollers sho' put it on a nigger iffen they cotch him without a pass.

"After war broke, Lee, you know General Lee himself, come to Lynchburg and had a campground there and it look like 'nother town. The 'federates had a scrimmage with the Yankees 'bout two miles out from Lynchburg, and after surrender General Wilcox and a big company of Yankees come there. De camp was clost to a big college there in Lynchburg and they throwed up a big breastworks out the other side the college. I never seed it till after surrender, 'cause us wasn't 'lowed to go out there. Gen. Shumaker was commander of the 'Federate artillery and kilt the first Yankee that come to Lynchburg. They drilled the college boys, too, there in town. I didn't know till after surrender what they drilled them for, 'cause the white folks didn't talk the war 'mongst us.

"Bout a year after the Yankees come to Lynchburg they moved the cullud free school out to Lee's Camp and met in one of the barracks and had four white teachers from the north, and that school run sev'ral years after surrender.

"Lots of 'Federate sojers passed through Lynchburg goin' to Petersburg. Once some Yankee sojers come through clost by and there was a scrimmage 'tween the two armies, but it didn't last long. Gen. Wilcox had a standin' army in Lynchburg after the war, when the Yankees took things over, but everything was peaceful and quiet then.

"After surrender a man calls a meetin' of all the slaves in the fairgrounds and tells us we's free. We wasn't promised anything. We jus' had to do the best we could. But I heared lots of slaves what lived on farms say they's promised forty acres and a mule but they never did git it. We had to go to work for whatever they'd pay us, and we didn't have nothing and no place to go when we was turned loose, but down the street and road. When I left the Terry's I worked in a tobacco factory for a dollar a week and that was big money to me. Mammy worked too and we managed somehow to live.

"After I married I started farmin', but since I got too old I live round with my chillen. I has two sons and a boy what I raised. One boy lives clost to Jacksonville and the other in the Sabine bottom and the boy what I raised lives at Henderson. I been gittin' $10.00 pension since January this year. (1937)

"I never fool round with politics much. I's voted a few times, but most the time I don't. I leaves that for folks what knows politics. I says this, the young niggers ain't bein' raised like we was. Most of them don't have no manners or no moral self-respect.

Charley Mitchell

"I don't 'lieve much in hants but I's heared my wife call my name. She's been dead four years. If you crave to see your dead folks, you'll never see them, but if you don't think 'bout them they'll come back sometime.

"Two nigger women died in this house and both of them allus smoked a pipe. My boy and me used to smell the pipes at night, since they died, and one mornin' I seed one of them. I jus' happened to look out the window and saw one of them goin' to the cow-pen. I knowed her by her bonnet.

"They's a nigger church and cemetery up the road away from my house where the dead folks come out by twos at night and go in the church and hold service. Me and the preacher what preaches there done seed and heared them.

"They's a way of keepin' off hants. That's done by tackin' an old shoe by the side the door, or a horseshoe over the door, or pullin' off part of the planks of your house and puttin' on some new boards."

Peter Mitchell

Peter Mitchell, in the late seventies, was born in Jasper, Texas, a slave of Thad Lanier. He has lived in or near Jasper all his life.

"Yes'm, I's Peter Mitchell and I was born right near here and my father and mother wasn't lawful married. De niggers wasn't in dem days. My pappy's name was Richard Lanier and my mammy's was Martha Mitchell, but us all taken mammy's name. She taken her name from de Mitchells, what owned her befo' de Laniers git her. My brothers named Lewis Johnson and Dennis Fisher, and William and Mose and Peter Mitchell. My sisters was Sukie and Louisa and Effie.

"Mammy was de house gal. She say de Mitchells done treat her hard but Massa Lanier purty good to us. In summer she kep' us chillen near de big house in de yard, but we couldn't go in de house. In winter we stays round de shack where we lives while mammy work.

"We gits plenty cornbread and soup and peas. On Sunday dey gives us jus' one biscuit apiece and we totes it round in de pocket half de day and shows it to de others, and says, 'See what we has for breakfast.'

"We wears duckin' dyed with indigo, and hickory shirts, and we has no shoes till we gits old 'nough to work. Den dey brogans with de brass toe. Mammy knitted de socks at night and weaves coats in winter. Many a night I sits up and spins and cards for mammy.

"Massa Lanier live in de fine, big house and have hundreds of acres in de plantation and has twenty-five houses for de slaves and dere families. He kep' jus' 'nough of de niggers to work de land and de extry he sells like hosses.

"Missy larned mammy to read and dey have de cullud preacher, named Sam Lundy. Dey have de big bayou in de field where dey baptises. De white people has de big pool 'bout 50 yard from de house, where dey baptise.

"Sometimes dey runs 'way but didn't git far, 'cause de patter rollers watches night and day. Some de men slaves makes hoe handles and cotton sacks at night and de women slaves washes and irons and sews and knits. We had to work so many hours every night, and no holidays but Christmas.

"Us plantation so big, dey kep' de doctor right on de place, and taken purty good care of de sick niggers, 'cause dey worth money. We was not so bad off, but we never has de fun, we jus' works and sleeps.

"When freedom come dey turn us loose and say to look out for ourselves. Mos' of de slaves jus' works round for de white folks den and gits pay in food and de clothes, but after while de slaves larns to take care demselves. I marries and was dress up in black and my wife wore de purple dress. De Rev. Sam Hadnot marry us.

"I farms all my life and it ain't been so bad. I's too old to work much now, but I makes a little here and there on de odd jobs."

Andrew Moody and wife Tildy

Andrew Moody was born in 1855, in Orange, Texas, a slave to Colonel Fountain Floyd, who owned a plantation of about 250 acres on Lacey's River. Andrew is said to be the oldest ex-slave in Orange County.

"I was ten year old when freedom come and I'm the oldest slave what was born in Orange County still livin' there. They called Orange, Green Bluff at the first, then they call it Madison, and then they call it Orange. I used to live on Colonel Fountain Floyd's plantation on Lacey's River, 'bout 17 miles from here. They had 'bout forty hands big enough to pick cotton.

"My grandmother was with me, but not my mother, and my father, Ball, he belong to Locke and Thomas. We lived in houses with home-made furniture. Yes, they had rawhide chairs and whenever they kilt a beef they kep' the skin offen the head to make seat for chairs.

"Colonel Floyd he treat us good, as if he's us father or mother. No, we didn' suffer no 'buse, 'cause he didn' 'low it and he didn' do it hisself.

"Parson Pipkin, he come 'round and preach to the white folks and sometimes he preach extry to the cullud quarters. Some of the cullud folks could read the hymns. Young missus, she larn 'em. They sing,
"Jerdon ribber so still and col',
Let's go down to Jerdon.
Go down, go down,
Let's go down to Jerdon.
"Every man had a book what carried his own niggers' names. The niggers' names was on the white folks' church book with the white folks' names and them books was like tax books. The tax collector, he come 'round and say, 'How many li'l darkies you got?' and then he put it down in the 'sessment book.

Andrew Moody and wife Tildy

"Folks had good times Christmas. Dancin' and big dinner. They give 'em two or three day holiday then. They give Christmas gif', maybe a pair stockin's or sugar candy. The white folks kill turkey and set table for the slaves with everything like they have, bread and biscuit and cake and po'k and baked turkey and chicken and sich. They cook in a skillet and spider. The cullud folks make hoe cake and ash cake and cracklin' bread and they used to sing, 'My baby love shortenin' bread.'

"When a hand die they all stop work the nex' day after he die and they blow the horn and old Uncle Bob, he pray and sing songs. They have a wake the night he die and come from all 'round and set up with the corpse all night. They make the coffin on the place and have two hands dig a grave.

"The way they done when 'mancipation come, they call up at twelve o'clock in June, 1865, right out there in Duncan Wood, 'twixt the old field and Beaumont. They call my mother, who done come to live there. They say, 'Now, listen, you and your chillen don' 'long to me now. You kin stay till Christmas if you wants.' So mother she stay but at Christmas her husban' come and they all go but me. I was the las' nigger to stay after freedom come, and the marster and I'd would go huntin and fishin' in the Naches River. We ate raccoon then and rabbit and keep the rabbit foot for luck, jus' the first joint. The 'Toby' what we call it, and if we didn' have no 'Toby' we couldn' git no rabbit nex' time we goes huntin'."

A.M. Moore

A.M. Moore, aged preacher and school teacher of Harrison Co., Texas, was born in 1846, a slave of W.R. Sherrad who, in the 1830's, settled a large plantation eight miles northeast of Marshall. Moore worked as a farmhand for several years after he left home, but later attended Bishop and Wiley Colleges, in Marshall, and obtained a teacher's certificate. He taught and preached until age forced him to retire to his farm, which is on land that was once a part of his master's plantation.

"My name is Almont M. Moore and I was born right here in Harrison County, in 1846, and belonged to Master W.R. Sherrad. My master was one of the first settlers in these parts and owned a big plantation, eight miles northeast of Marshall. My father was Jiles D. Moore and he was born in Alabama, and my mother, Anna, was born in Mississippi. They came to Texas as slaves. My grandmother on my mother's side was Cherry and she belonged to the Sherrads, too. She said the Indians gave them a hot time when they first came to Texas. Finally they became friendly to the white people.

"My mistress was Lucinda Sherrad and she had a world of children. They lived in a big, log house, but you wouldn't know it was a log house unless you went up in the attic where it wasn't ceiled. The slaves helped master build the house. The quarters looked like a little town, with the houses all in lines.

"They had rules for the slaves to be governed by and they were whipped when they disobeyed. Master didn't have to whip his slaves much, because he was fair to them, more than most of the slaveowners. Lots of masters wouldn't let the slaves have anything and wouldn't let them read or even look at a book. I've known courts in this county to fine slaveowners for not clothing and feeding their slaves right. I thought that was right, because lots of them were too stingy to treat the slaves right unless they made them do it.

"Corn shucking was a big sport for the Negroes and whites, too, in slavery time. Sometimes they gave a big dance when they finished shucking, but my master's folks always had a religious service. I went to a Methodist church and it had too floors, one for the slaves and one for the whites. Just before the war they began to let the Negroes preach and have some books, a hymn book and a Bible.

"After the war they treated the slaves fine in this part of the country. The industrious ones could work and save money. Down in Louisiana lots of owners divided syrup, meat and other things with the slaves. My brother and I saved enough to buy five hundred acres of land. Lots of white men took one or more slaves to wait on them when they joined the army, but my master left me at home to help there.

"Some owners didn't free their slaves and they soon put soldiers at Marshall and Shreveport and arrested the ones who refused to let the slaves go. My father died during the war and my mother stayed with Master Sherrad three years after surrender. I stayed with her till I was big enough and then hired out on a farm. They paid farmhands $10.00 to $15.00 a month then.

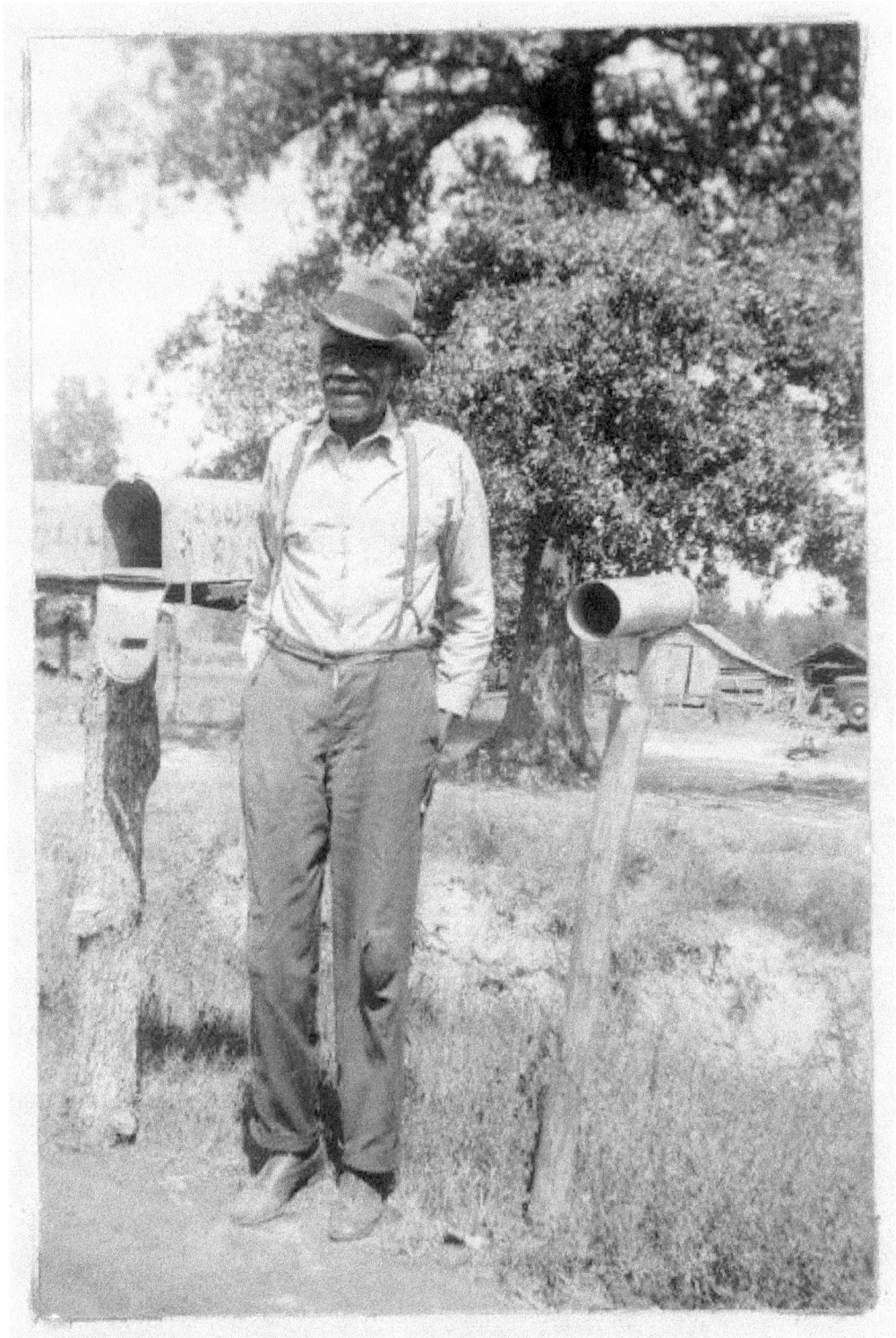

A.M. Moore

"Then I went to school at Wiley and Bishop Colleges here for four years and I hold a county teacher's certificate. I have taught school in Harrison and Gregg Counties and in Caddo Parish, in Louisiana. I started preaching in 1880 and for several years was District Missionary for the Texas-Louisiana Missionary Baptist Association. I have preached in and organized churches all over East Texas.

"We raised six children and two boys and two girls are still living. The girls live in Longview and one boy farms. The other boy is a preacher here in Harrison County.

"I have voted in county and other elections. I think they should instruct the Negroes so they can vote like white folks. The young Negroes now have a better chance than most of us had. They have their schools and churches, but I don't think they try as hard as we did. We learned lots from the white folks and their teaching was genuine and had a great effect on us. I attribute the Christian beliefs of our people to the earnest, faithful teaching of white people, and today we have many educated Negro teachers and preachers and leaders that we are not ashamed of."

Jerry Moore

Jerry Moore, a native of Harrison County, Texas, was born May 28, 1848, a slave of Mrs. Isaac Van Zandt, who was a pioneer civic leader of the county. Jerry has always lived in Marshall. For fifty years after he was freed he worked as a brick mason. He now lives alone on the Port Caddo road, and is supported by a $15.00 per month pension from the government.

"My name is J.M. Moore, but all the white and cullud folks calls me Uncle Jerry, 'cause I has lived here mos' since Marshall started. I was born on the 28th of May, in 1848, up on the hill where the College of Marshall is now, and I belonged to the Van Zandts. That was their old home place.

"I never did see Col. Isaac Van Zandt, my mistresses' husband, but has heared her and the older folks talk lots o' him. They say he was the one who helped set up Marshall and name it. They say he run for Governor and had a good chance, but was never honorated as Governor, 'cause he died 'fore election.

"My mistress was named Fanny and was one sweet soul. She had five children and they lived here in town but have a purty big farm east of town. My mother sewed for Mistress Fanny, so we lived in town. There were lots of niggers on the farm and everybody round these parts called us 'Van Zandt's free niggers,' 'cause our white folks shared with their darkies and larned 'em all to read and write. The other owners wouldn't have none of Van Zandt's niggers.

"My mother was Amy Van Zandt Moore and was a Tennessian. My father was Henry Moore and he belonged to a old bachelor named Moore, in Alabama. Moore freed all his niggers 'fore 'mancipation except three. They was to pay a debt and my father was Moore's choice man and was one of the three. He bought hisself. He had saved up some money and when they went to sell him he bid $800.00. The auctioneer cries 'round to git a raise, but wouldn't nobody bid on my father 'cause he was one of Moore's 'free niggers'. My father done say after the war he could have buyed hisself for $1.50. So he was a free man 'fore the 'mancipation and he couldn't live 'mong the slaves and he had to have a guardian who was 'sponsible for his conduct till after surrender. They was lots of niggers here from the free states 'fore the war, but they wasn't 'lowed to mix with the slaves.

"Mistress Fanny allus give the children a candy pullin' on Saturday night and the big folks danced and had parties. She allus gave the children twenty-five cents apiece when the circus come to town. The patterrollers wasn't 'lowed 'bout our place and her darkies went mos' anywhere and wasn't ever bothered. I never seed a slave whipped on our place. She give her darkies money along for doin' odd jobs and they could spend it for what they wanted. She was a Christian woman and read the Bible mos' all the time. She give my mother two acres of land at 'mancipation.

"The first thing I seed of the war was them musterin' and drillin' sojers here in Marshall, back in Buchanan's time. Politics was hot in '59 and '60. I 'member 'em havin' a big dinner and barbecue and speakin' on our place. They had a railroad to Swanson's Landing on Caddo Lake and the train crew brung news from boats from Shreveport and New Orleans. Soon as the train pulled into town it signaled. Three long, mournful whistles meant bad news. Three short, quick whistles meant good news. I went to town for the mail with my sister durin' the war. She'd say to me, 'Jerry, the sooner the war is over, the sooner we'll be free. All the Van Zandt Negroes wanted to be free.' They didn't understand how well they was bein' treated till after they had to make their own livin'.

"I rec'lect the time the cullud folks registered here after the war. They outnumbered the whites a long way. Davis was governor and all the white folks had to take the Iron Clad oath to vote. Carpetbaggers and Negroes run the government. In the early days they held the election four days. They didn't vote in precints but at the court house. The Democratic Party had no chance to 'timidate the darkies. The 'publican party had a 'Loyal League' for to protect the cullud folks. First the Negroes went to the league house to get 'structions and ballots and then marched to the court house, double file, to vote. My father was a member of the 11th and 12th legislature from this county. He was 'lected just after the Constitutional Convention, when Davis was elected governor. Two darkies, Mitch Kennel and Wiley Johnson, was 'lected from this county to be members of that Convention.

"Durin' the Reconstruction the Negroes gathered in Harrison County. The Yankee sojers and 'Progoe' law made thousands of darkies flock here for protection. The Ku Klux wasn't as strong here and this place was headquarters for the 'Freedman'. What the 'Progoe' Marshal said was Gospel. They broke up all that business in Governor Hogg's time. They divided the county into precints and the devilment was done in the precints, just like it is now.

Jerry Moore

"My father told me about old Col. Alford and his Kluxers takin' Anderson Wright out to the bayou. They told him, 'You'd better pray.' Wright got down on his knees and acted like he was prayin' till he crawled to the bank and jumped off in the bayou. The Klux shot at him fifty or sixty times, but he got away. The Loyal League give him money to leave on and he stayed away a long time. He came back to appear against Alford at his trial and when the jury gave Alford ninety-nine years, Anderson was glad, of course.

"I left the Van Zandts two years after I was freed and worked in hotels and on the railroad and saved up money and went in business, helping people ship cotton. I've seen a thousand cotton wagons in town at one time. I stayed in business till I was burnt out. I came back to Marshall and took up the brick mason trade and worked at it till I got too old to hold out.

"I've sat on the jury in the county, justice and federal courts. I know enough to vote or set on a jury but I think the restriction on colored folks votin' is all right in this State. The white folks has a good government system. Our leaders ain't hard-hearted people and the cullud folks is well off or better as if they voted. I've lived here in Marshall most all the time since I was born and ain't had no trouble. As long as the Negroes treat the white folks right, the white folks will treat them right."

John Moore

John Moore, 84, was born a slave to Duncan Gregg, in Vermillionville, La., where he lived until he was freed. In 1876 he came to Texas and now lives in Beaumont.

"I was twelve year old when freedom broke up. I lives 'tween Vermillionville and Lafayette in Louisiana and my massa's name Duncan Greggs and he have purty big farm and lots of cullud people. His house was two, three hun'erd yard from de nigger quarters. De old grammas, dey took care of de chillen when dere mothers was in de fields and took dem up to de big house so de white folks could see 'em play.

"We chillens was dress in a shirt and we was barefoot. Sometime dey make what dey call moccasin out of rawhide. Shoes was skeerce.

"Dey raise de food and have grits ground in de grits mill. Dey raise hawgs and make syrup and farm and raise chickens. Marster didn' 'low de niggers to have big garden patch but sometime he 'low 'em have place raise watermillion.

"Marster have purty good house, a box-house, and have good furniture in it. De cullud folks have house with chimbly in de middle of two rooms and one fambly live on one side de chimbly and 'nother fambly on de other side de chimbly. De chillen have pallets on de floor.

"After freedom my daddy die with cholera. I don' know how many chillen in us fambly. My daddy's name Valmore Moore and mamma's name Silliman.

"Dey have niggers in de fields in different squads, a hoe squad and a plow squad, and de overseer was pretty rapid. Iffen dey don' do de work dey buck dem down and whip dem. Dey tie dey hands and feet togedder and make 'em put de hands 'tween de knees, and put a long stick 'tween de hands to dey can't pull 'em out, and den dey whip dem in good fashion.

"When war starts, dey have a fight at Penock Bridge, not far from a place dey call La'fette. Dey burn de bridge and keep de Yankees from takin' de town. But de Yankees gits floatin' bridges and gits 'cross de bayou dat way. De Yankees comes to our place and dey go to de sugarhouse and takes barrels of sugar and syrup, and corn and meat and de white folks hides de chickens under de bed, but de old rooster crow and den de Yankees hear dem.

"Young marster say he gwine to war to kill a Yankee and bring he head back and he take a servant 'long. He didn' bring no Yankee head back but he brung a shot up arm, but dat purty soon git well.

"Iffen us sick dey make med'cine out of weeds, mos' bitter weed, boneset dey calls it. Dey bile Jerusalem oak and give it to us.

"We has dances sometimes and sings

'Run, nigger, run,

De patterroles git you;

Run, nigger run,

It almos' day.'

Or we sings

'My old missus promise me

Shoo a la a day,

When she die she set me free

Shoo a la a day.

She live so long her head git bald,

Shoo a la a day.

She give up de idea of dyin' a-tall

Shoo a la a day.'

"Sometimes we hollers de corn hollers. One was somethin' like this: 'Rabbit gittin' up in a holler for niggers kotch for breakfast.' Sometimes my mudder jump up in de air and sing,

'Sugar in de gourd,

Sugar in de gourd,

Iffen you wanter git

De sugar out--

R-o-o-l-l de gourd over.'

"And all de time she shoutin' dat, she jumpin' right straight up in de air.

"I heered lots about de Klu Klux. Sometimes dey want a nigger's place and dey put up notice he better sell out and leave. Iffen he go see a lawyer, de lawyer wouldn' take de case, 'cause mos' dem in with de Klux. He tell de nigger he better sell.

"I come to Texas in '76 and been here ever since. I's had 13 chillen. I owns eight acres in dis place now and I got de purties' corn in de country but de insecks give it de blues."

Van Moore

Van Moore, now living at 2119 St. Charles St., Houston, Tex., was born on a plantation owned by the Cunningham family, near Lynchburg, Virginia. While Van was still a baby, his owner moved to a plantation near Crosby, Tex. Van is about 80 years old.

"Like I say, I's born on de first day of September, near Lynchburg, in Virginy, but I's reared up here in Texas. My mammy's name was Mary Moore and my pappy's name was Tom Moore. Mammy 'longed to de Cunninghams but Pappy 'longed to de McKinneys, what was Missy Cunningham's sister and her husban'. That's how my mammy and pappy come together. In dem days a slave man see a slave gal what he wants and he asks his old massa, kin he see her. Iffen she owned by someone else, de massa ask de gal's massa iffen it all right to put 'em together, and iffen he say so, dey jus' did. Twa'nt no Bible weddin', like now.

"Mammy had 19 chillen, 10 boys and 9 gals, but all of 'em dead 'cept me. Dey was call' Matthew and Joe and Harris and Horace and Charley and Sam and Dave and Millie and Viney and Mary and Phyllis, and I forgit de others.

"While I jus' a baby Massa Cunningham and he family and he slaves, and Massa McKinney and he slaves comes to Texas. I never did 'member old Massa Cunningham, 'cause dey tells me he kilt by a rarin' beef, right after we gits to Texas. Dey say he didn't take up 'nough slack on dat rope when he tryin' brand de beef and de critter rared over and broke massa's back.

"But I 'members Missy Mary Ellen Cunningham, he wife, from de time I's a little feller till she die. She sho' was de good woman and treated de slaves good.

"Mammy told me it dis-a-way how come de Cunninghams and de McKinneys to come to Texas. When war begin most folks back in Virginny what owns slaves moved further south, and lots to Louisiana and Texas, 'cause dey say de Yankees won't never git dat far and dey won't have to free de slaves iffen dey come way over here. 'Sides, dey so many slaves runnin' 'way to de north, back dere. Mammy say when dey starts for here in de wagons, de white folks tells de po' niggers, what was so ig'rant dey 'lieve all de white folks tell 'em, dat where dey is goin' de lakes full of syrup and covered with batter cakes, and dey won't have to work so hard. Dey tells 'em dis so dey don't run away.

"Well, mammy say dey comes to de lake what has round things on top de water. Course, dey jus' leaves, but de niggers thinks here is de lake with de syrup and one runs to de edge and takes de big swallow, and spits it out, and say 'Whuf!' I reckon he thinks dat funny syrup.

"De plantation at Crosby was a great big place, and after old Massa Cunningham kilt by dat beef Missy Cunningham couldn't keep it up and we goes to Galveston. Dere she has de great big house with de beautiful things in it, de mirrors and de silk chairs and de rugs what soft 'nough to sleep on. Missy Cunningham mighty good to us niggers and on Sunday she'd fill up de big wood tray with flour and grease and hawg meat, so we could have de biscuit and white bread. Mammy say back in Virginny dey called biscuits 'knots' and white bread 'tangle-dough.'

"Iffen old Missy Cunningham ain't in heaven right now, den dere ain't none, 'cause she so good to us we all loved her. She never took de whip to us, but I heered my mammy say she knowed a slave woman what owned by Massa Rickets, and she workin' in de field, and she heavy with de chile what not born yet, and she has to set down in de row to rest. She was havin' de misery and couldn't work good, and de boss man had a nigger dig a pit where her stomach fit in, and lay her down and tie her so she can't squirm 'round none, and flog her till she lose her mind. Yes, suh, dat de truf, my mammy say she knowed dat woman a long time after dat, and she never right in de head 'gain.

"When de war broke, de Union soldiers has a camp not so far from we'uns and I slips down dere when old missy not lookin', 'cause de soldiers give me black coffee and sugar what I takes to my mammy. I had to walk in de sand up to de knees to git to dat camp. Lots more chillen went, too, but I never seed no cruelness by de soldiers. Dey gives you de sugar in de big bucket and when you puts de hand in it you could pinch de water out it, 'cause it not refined sugar like you gits now, but it sure tasted good.

"Mammy wrops me in both de Yankee and de 'federate flags when I goes to dat camp, and de soldiers takes off de 'federate flag, but I allus wears it 'round de house, cause old missy tell me to.

"When freedom come, old missy tell my mammy, 'You is free now, and you all jus' have to do de best you kin.' But mammy she never been 'way from old missy in her life, and she didn't want no more freedom dan what she had, so we jus' stays with old missy till she moved back to Crosby.

Van Moore

"When pappy's set free by Massa Albert McKinney, he didn't have nothin'--not even a shirt, so Massa Albert 'lowed him stay and work 'round de plantation. One day 'fore we goes back to Crosby, pappy come down to Galveston to see mammy and us chillen, 'cause he wants to take us back with him. He rid all de way on a mule, carryin' a wallet what was thrown over de back of de mule like de pack saddle, and he gives it to mammy. You know what was in dat wallet? He brung a coon and possum and some corn dodger, 'cause he thinks we don't have 'nough to eat down there. Mammy she give one look at de stuff and say, 'You, Tom, I's stayin' right here with old Missy Cunningham, and we has white folks eats,' and she throw de whole mess 'way. I sho' 'member dat happenin'.

"But old missy gittin' poorly and, like I told you, we move back to Crosby and mammy and pappy lives together 'gain. I gits me some small work here and there till I grows up, and I's worked hard all my life.

"All de old folks is gone now. Old missy, she die in Crosby, and mammy and pappy die, too, and is buried there. Doctor say I got dis and dat wrong and can't work no more, so I guess I go, too, 'fore long. But I still has love for my old missy, 'cause she loved us and sho' was good to us, and it make me feel kinda good to talk 'bout her and de old times."

William Moore

William Moore was born a slave of the Waller family, in Selma, Alabama, about 1855. His master moved to Mexia, Texas, during the Civil War. William now lives at 1016-1/2 Good Street, Dallas, Texas.

"My mammy done told me the reason her and my paw's name am Moore was 'cause afore they 'longed to Marse Tom Waller they 'longed to Marse Moore, but he done sold them off.

"Marse Tom heared they gwine 'mancipate the slaves in Selma, so he got his things and niggers together and come to Texas. My mammy said they come in covered wagons but I wasn't old 'nough to 'member nothin' 'bout it. The first 'lections I got is down in Limestone County.

"Marse Tom had a fine, big house painted white and a big prairie field front his house and two, three farms and orchards. He had five hundred head of sheep, and I spent mos' my time bein' a shepherd boy. I starts out when I'm li'l and larns right fast to keep good 'count of the sheeps.

"Mammy's name was Jane and paw's was Ray, and I had a brother, Ed, and four sisters, Rachel and Mandy and Harriet and Ellen. We had a purty hard time to make out and was hongry lots of times. Marse Tom didn't feel called on to feed his hands any too much. I 'members I had a cravin' for victuals all the time. My mammy used to say, 'My belly craves somethin' and it craves meat.' I'd take lunches to the field hands and they'd say, 'Lawd Gawd, it ain't 'nough to stop the gripe in you belly.' We made out on things from the fields and rabbits cooked in li'l fires.

"We had li'l bitty cabins out of logs with puncheon beds and a bench and fireplace in it. We chillun made out to sleep on pallets on the floor.

"Some Sundays we went to church some place. We allus liked to go any place. A white preacher allus told us to 'bey our masters and work hard and sing and when we die we go to Heaven. Marse Tom didn't mind us singin' in our cabins at night, but we better not let him cotch us prayin'.

"Seems like niggers jus' got to pray. Half they life am in prayin'. Some nigger take turn 'bout to watch and see if Marse Tom anyways 'bout, then they circle theyselves on the floor in the cabin and pray. They git to moanin' low and gentle, 'Some day, some day, some day, this yoke gwine be lifted offen our shoulders.'

"Marse Tom been dead long time now. I 'lieve he's in hell. Seem like that where he 'long. He was a terrible mean man and had a indiff'ent, mean wife. But he had the fines', sweetes' chillun the Lawd ever let live and breathe on this earth. They's so kind and sorrowin' over us slaves.

"Some them chillun used to read us li'l things out of papers and books. We'd look at them papers and books like they somethin' mighty curious, but we better not let Marse Tom or his wife know it!

"Marse Tom was a fitty man for meanness. He jus' 'bout had to beat somebody every day to satisfy his cravin'. He had a big bullwhip and he stake a nigger on the ground and make 'nother nigger hold his head down with his mouth in the dirt and whip the nigger till the blood run out and red up the ground. We li'l niggers stand round and see it done. Then he tell us, 'Run to the kitchen and git some salt from Jane.' That my mammy, she was cook. He'd sprinkle salt in the cut, open places and the skin jerk and quiver and the man slobber and puke. Then his shirt stick to his back for a week or more.

"My mammy had a terrible bad back once. I seen her tryin' to git the clothes off her back and a woman say, 'What's the matter with you back?' It was raw and bloody and she say Marse Tom done beat her with a handsaw with the teeth to her back. She died with the marks on her, the teeth holes goin' crosswise her back. When I's growed I asks her 'bout it and she say Marse Tom got mad at the cookin' and grabs her by the hair and drug her out the house and grabs the saw off the tool bench and whips her.

"My paw is the first picture I got in my mind. I was settin' on maw's lap and paw come in and say Marse Tom loaned him out to work on a dam they's buildin' in Houston and he has to go. One day word come he was haulin' a load of rocks through the swamps and a low-hangin' grapevine cotched him under the neck and jerked him off the seat and the wagon rolled over him and kilt him dead. They buried him down there somewheres.

"One day I'm down in the hawg pen and hears a loud agony screamin' up to the house. When I git up close I see Marse Tom got mammy tied to a tree with her clothes pulled down and he's layin' it on her with the bullwhip, and the blood am runnin' down her eyes and off her back. I goes crazy. I say, 'Stop, Marse Tom,' and he swings the whip and don't reach me good, but it cuts jus' the same. I sees Miss Mary standin' in the cookhouse door. I runs round crazy like and sees a big rock, and I takes it and throws it and it cotches Marse Tom in the skull and he goes down like a poled ox. Miss Mary comes out and lifts her paw and helps him in the house and then comes and helps me undo mammy. Mammy and me takes to the woods for two, three months, I guess. My sisters meets us and grease mammy's back and brings us victuals. Purty soon they say it am safe for us to come in the cabin to eat at night and they watch for Marse Tom.

"One day Marse Tom's wife am in the yard and she calls me and say she got somethin' for me. She keeps her hand under her apron. She keeps beggin' me to come up to her. She say, 'Gimme you hand.' I reaches out my hand and she grabs it and slips a slip knot rope over it. I sees then that's what she had under her apron and the other end tied to a li'l bush. I tries to get loose and runs round and I trips her up and she falls and breaks her arm. I gits the rope off my arm and runs.

"Mammy and me stays hid in the bresh then. We sees Sam and Billie and they tell us they am fightin over us niggers. Then they done told us the niggers 'clared to Marse Tom they ain't gwine be no more beatin's and we could come up and stay in our cabin and they'd see Marse Tom didn't do nothin'. And that's what mammy and me did. Sam and Billie was two the biggest niggers on the place and they done got the shotguns out the house some way or 'tother. One day Marse Tom am in a rocker on the porch and Sam and Billie am standin' by with the guns. We all seen five white men ridin' up. When they gits near Sam say to Marse Tom, 'First white man sets hisself inside that rail fence gits it from the gun.' Marse Tom waves the white men to go back but they gallops right up to the fence and swings off they hosses.

"Marse Tom say, 'Stay outside, gen'man, please do, I done change my mind.' They say, 'What's the matter here? We come to whip you niggers like you done hire us to.'

"Marse Tom say, 'I done change my mind, but if you stay outside I'll bring you the money.'

"They argues to come in but Marse Tom outtalk them and they say they'll go if he brings them they three dollars apiece. He takes them the money and they goes 'way.

"Marse Tom cuss and rare, but the niggers jus' stay in the woods and fool 'way they time. They say it ain't no use to work for nothin' all them days.

"One day I'm in a 'simmon tree in middle a li'l pond, eatin' 'simmons, and my sister, Mandy, come runnin'. She say, 'Us niggers am free.' I looks over to the house and seen the niggers pilin' they li'l bunch of clothes and things outside they cabins. Then mammy come runnin' with some other niggers and mammy was head runner. I clumb down out that tree and run to meet her. She say Marse Tom done told her he gwine keep me and pay her for it. She's a-scared I'll stay if I wants to or not and she begs me not to.

"We gits up to the house and all the niggers standin' there with they li'l bundles on they head and they all say, 'Where we goin'?'

"Mammy said, 'I don't know where you all gwine but me, myself, am gwine to go to Miss Mary.' So all the niggers gits in the cart with mammy and we goes to Miss Mary. She meets us by the back door and say, 'Come in, Jane, and all you chillen and all the rest of you.

You can see my door am open and my smokehouse door am open to you and I'll bed you down till we figurates a way for you.'

"We all cries and sings and prays and was so 'cited we didn't eat no supper, though mammy stirs up some victuals.

William Moore

"It warn't long afore we found places to work. Miss Mary found us a place with a fine white man and we works on sharance and drifts round to some other places and lives in Corsicana for awhile and buys mammy a li'l house and she died there.

"I got married and had three chillen, cute, fetchin' li'l chillen, and they went to school. Wasn't no trouble 'bout school then, but was when 'mancipation come. My brother Ed was in school then and the Ku Klux come and drove the Yankee lady and gen'man out and closed the school.

"My chillen growed up and my wife died and I spent mos' my days workin' hard on farms. Now I'm old and throwed 'way. But I'm thankful to Gawd and praiseful for the pension what lets me have a li'l somethin' to eat and a place to stay."

Mandy Morrow

Mandy Morrow, 80, was born a slave of Ben Baker, near Georgetown, Texas. Mr. Baker owned Mandy's grandparents, parents, three brothers and one sister. After she was freed, Mandy was Gov. Stephen Hogg's cook while he occupied the Governor's Mansion in Austin. She married several times and gave birth to eight children. Two of her sons were in the World War and one was killed in action. She now receives a $11.00 Old Age Pension check each month, and lives at 3411 Prairie Ave., Fort Worth, Texas.

"Massa, I don' know 'zactly how old I is, 'cause I never gits de statement from my massa. My daddy keep dat record in he Bible and I don't know who has it. But I's old 'nough for to 'member de war 'cause I carries uncle's lunch to him and sees de 'federate sojers practicin'.

"One day I stops a li'l while and watch de sojers and dey am practicin' shootin', and I seed one sojer drap after de shot. Den dere lots of 'citement, and sho' 'nough, dat sojer dead. Dey says it's a accident.

"I's born in Burnet County on Massa's farm, and I has three brothers call Lewis and Monroe and Hale, and one sister, Mollie. Most de time Massa am in de town, 'cause he have blacksmith shop dere. From what I's larnt by talk with other slaves, we's lucky slaves, 'cause dere no sich thing as whippin' on our farm. Sho', dere's spankin's, and I's de one what gits dem from my mammy, 'cause I's de pestin' chile, into something all de time. I gits in de devilment.

"Massa smoked and I 'cides to try it, so I gits one old pipe and some home-cured tobaccy and goes to de barn and covers up with de hay. Mammy miss me, 'cause everything am quiet 'round. She look for me and come to de barn and hears de crinklin' of de hay. She pulls me out of dat and den dere am plenty of fire put on my rear and I sees lots of smoke. I sho' 'members dat 'sperience!

"We all lives in one big family, 'cept us have dinin' room for de cullud folks. Grandpappy am de carpenter and 'cause of dat us quarters fixed fine and has reg'lar windows and handmade chairs and a real wood floor.

"Mammy and my grandma am cooks and powerful good and dey's larnt me and dat how I come to be a cook. Like everybody dem times, us raise everything and makes preserves and cure de meats. De hams and bacons am smoked. Dere am no hickory wood 'round but we uses de corncobs and dey makes de fine flavor in de meat. Many's de day I watches de fire in dat smokehouse and keeps it low, to git de smoke flavor. I follows de cookin' when I gits big and goes for myself and I never wants for de job.

"When surrender breaks all us stay with Massa for good, long spell. When pappy am ready to go for hisself, Massa gives him de team of mules and de team of oxen and some hawgs and one cow and some chickens. Dat give him de good start.

"My uncle gits de blacksmith shop from de Massa and den him and pappy goes together and does de blacksmithin' and de haulin'. I stays in Georgetown 'bout 20 year and den I goes to Austin and dere I works for de big folks. After I been dere 'bout five year, Gov'nor James Stephen Hogg sends for me to be cook in de Mansion and dat de best cook job I's ever had. De gov'nor am mighty fine man and so am he wife. She am not of de good health and allus have de misery, and befo' long she say to me, 'Mandy, I's gwineter 'pend on you without my watchin'.' Massa Hogg allus say I does wonders with dat food and him proud fer to have him friends eat it.

"Yes, suh, de Gov'nor am de good man. You knows, when he old nigger mammy die in Temple, him drap all he work and goes to de fun'ral and dat show him don't forgit de kindness.

"No, suh, I don't know de names of de people what comes to de Mansion to eat. I hears dem talk but how you 'spose dis igno'mus nigger unnerstan what dey talks 'bout. Lawd A-mighty! Dey talks and talks and one thing make 'pression on my mind. De Gov'nor talk lots 'bout railroads.

"I works for de Gov'nor till he wife die and den I's quit, 'cause I don't want bossin' by de housekeeper what don't know much 'bout cookin' and am allus fustin' 'round.

"I cooks here and yonder and den gits mixed up with dat marriage. De fust hitch lasts 'bout one year and de nex' hitch lasts 'bout two year and 'bout four years later I tries it 'gain and dat time it lasts till I has two chillen. Three year dat hitch lasts. After 'while I marries Sam Morrow and dat hitch sticks till Sam dies in 1917. I has six chillen by him.

"My two oldes' boys jines de army and goes to France and de young one gits kilt and de other comes home. All my chillen scattered now and I don't know where they's at. In 1920 I's married de last time and dat hitch lasts ten years and us sep'rate in 1930, 'cause dat man am no good. What for I wants a man what ain't of de service to me? If I wants de pet, den I gits de dawg or de cat. Shucks! It didn't take me long. When dey don't satisfy dis nigger, I transports dem.

"De last five and six year I does li'l work, 'cause I don't have no substance to me no more. I's jus' 'bout wore out. I gits dat pension from de state every month and with dat $11.00 I has to git on."

Patsy Moses

Patsy Moses, 74, was born in Fort Bend Co., Texas, a slave of the Armstrong family. She tells of charms and "conjure," many learned from ex-slaves. Patsy lives at Mart, Texas.

"I was born in Fort Bend County, about de year 1863. My daddy's old master by name of Armstrong brung my folks from Tennessee. My own daddy and mammy was named Preston and Lucy Armstrong. Mammy's grand-dad was Uncle Ned Butler, and he 'longed to Col. Butler, in Knoxville, in Tennessee. Old master sold he plantation and come to Texas jes' befo' freedom, 'cause nobody thunk dey'd have to free de slaves in Texas.

"My great grand-dad fit in de Rev'lutionary War and my own daddy fit in de war for freedom, with he master, for bodyguard. He had some fingers shot off in de battle and was tooken pris'ner by dem Yankees, but he run 'way and come back to he master and he master was wounded and come home. Den he moved to Texas befo' I's born.

"My old grand-dad done told me all 'bout conjure and voodoo and luck charms and signs. To dream of clear water lets you know you is on de right side of Gawd. De old voodoo doctors was dem what had de most power, it seem, over de nigger befo' and after de war. Dey has meetin' places in secret and a voodoo kettle and nobody know what am put in it, maybe snakes and spiders and human blood, no tellin' what. Folks all come in de dark of de moon, old doctor wave he arms and de folks crowd up close. Dem what in de voodoo strips to de waist and commence to dance while de drums beats. Dey dances faster and faster and chant and pray till dey falls down in a heap.

"De armour bearers hold de candles high and when dey sways and chants dey seize with power what sends dem leapin' and whirlin'. Den de time dat old doctor work he spell on dem he wants to conjure. Many am de spell he casts dem days. Iffen he couldn't work it one way, he work it 'nother, and when he die, do he stay buried? No, sir! He walks de street and many seed he ghost wavin' he arms.

"De conjure doctor, old Dr. Jones, walk 'bout in de black coat like a preacher, and wear sideburns and used roots and sich for he medicine. He larnt 'bout dem in de piney woods from he old granny. He didn't cast spells like de voodoo doctor, but uses roots for smallpox, and rind of bacon for mumps and sheep-wool tea for whoopin' cough and for snake bite he used alum and saltpeter and bluestone mix with brandy or whiskey.

"He could break conjure spells with broth. He take he kettle and put in splinters of pine or hickory, jes' so dey has bark on dem, covers dem with water and puts in de conjure salt.

"A good charm bag am make of red flannel with frog bones and a piece of snakeskin and some horse hairs and a spoonful of ashes. Dat bag pertect you from you enemy. Iffen dat bag left by de doorstep it make all kind misfortune and sicknesses and blindness and fits.

"De big, black nigger in de corn field mos' allus had three charms round he neck, to make him fort'nate in love, and to keep him well and one for Lady Luck at dice to be with him. Den if you has indigestion, wear a penny round de neck.

"De power of de rabbit foot am great. One nigger used it to run away with. His old granny done told him to try it and he did. He conjures hisself by takin' a good, soapy bath so de dogs can't smell him and den say a hoodoo over he rabbit foot, and go to de creek and git a start by wadin'. Dey didn't miss him till he clear gone and dat show what de rabbit foot done for him.

"'O, Molly Cottontail,

Be sho' not to fail,

Give me you right hind foot,

My luck won't be for sale.'

"De graveyard rabbit am de best, kilt by a cross-eyed pusson. De niggers all 'lieved Gen. Lee carried a rabbit foot with him. To keep de rabbit foot's luck workin', it good to pour some whiskey on it once in a while.

Patsy Moses

"If you has a horseshoe over you door, be sho' it from de left, hind foot of a white hoss, but a gray hoss am better'n none.

"Conjures am sot with de dark or light of de moon, to make things waste or grow. Iffen a hen crow, it best to wring her neck and bake her with cranberry sauce and gravy and forgit 'bout her crowin'. Everybody know dat.

"I larnt all dem spells from my daddy and mammy and de old folks, and most of dem things works iffen you tries dem."

Andy Nelson

Andy Nelson, 76, is leader of a small rural settlement of negroes known as Moser Valley, ten miles east of Fort Worth on State Highway #15. He was born a slave to J. Wolf, on a Denton County farm, and his mother belonged to Dr. John Barkswell, who owned an adjoining farm. At the death of his father he was sold to Dr. Barkswell. When freed, he and his mother came to Birdville and later moved to Moser Valley, which derives it name from Telley Moses, who gave his farm to his slaves, and sold parcels to other negroes.

"I don' 'member much 'bout de war, but I was bo'n in slavery near de line of Tarrant County, in 1861. My master was named Wolf, but 'bout de end of de war he sells me to Dr. Barkswell, who owns my mammy.

"When de war is over we gits out and comes to Birdville and after three years Master Moser gives my mammy 17 acres of lan'. He owned lots of slaves and gives 'em all some land for a home.

"For ten, twelve years after de war, de Klux gits after de niggers who is gittin' into devilment. De cullud folks sho' quavered when they thought de Klan was after them. One nigger crawls up de chimney of de fireplace and that nigger soon gits powerful hot and has to come out. You should of seen that nigger. He warn't human lookin'. He is all soot, fussed up, choked and skeered. Dey warn't after him but wants to ask him if he knows whar other niggers is hidin'. I was too young to git in no picklement with de Klux.

"Years after dat, I'se married and have four, five chillens, and I'se comin' home. I'se stopped by seven men on hosses and dey all has rifles and pistols. I says to myself, 'De Klux sho' have come back and dey is gwine to git me. It sho' looks like troublement.'

"One of dem weighs 'bout 135 pounds and has dark hair and complexiun, and he says to me, 'Nigger, whar's de lower Dalton crossin'? Dere was two crossin's of de Trinity River, de upper and de lower. I says, 'De upper crossin' is back yonder.'

"He says, 'I knows whar de upper crossin' is, I'se askin' you whar de lower one is. Don' fool with us, nigger.'

"Dere was a big fellow, 'bout 250, settin' in de saddle and sorta ant goglin', with his gun pointin' at me. De hole in de end of dat gun looked big as a cannon. He was mean lookin' and chewin' a quid of terbaccy. He says, 'You is goin' with us to de crossin'. Lead de way.' Den I gits de quaverment powerful bad. I knows I'se a gone nigger.

"I says to dem, 'I done nothin',' and de big fellow raises his gun and says, 'Git goin', nigger, to dat lower crossin', or you'll be a dead nigger.'

"On de way I never says a word, but I'se prayin' de good Lawd to save dis nigger. When we reached de crossin' I says to myself, 'Dis am de end.'

"De little fellow says, 'Do you know who I is?' I says, 'No.'

"He says, 'I'se Sam Bass.'

"I'se heered of Sam Bass, everybody had in dem days. He was leader of a band.

"He says, 'We don' want nobody to know we been here. Which you ruther be, a dead nigger befo' or after tellin'?'

"De big fellow says, 'Make a sno' job. A dead nigger cain't talk,' and den starts raisin' de gun.

"I wants to talk, but I'se so skeered I can' say one word.

"Den Sam Bass says, 'No, no! Let him go,' and den I knows de Lawd has heered dis nigger's prayers.

"Dey tells me dey's comin' back if I tells and I promised not to tell. I'se skeered for a week after dat.

"In a few weeks, I hears dat Sam Bass is killed at Round Rock. Den I tells.

"Dat's de las' troublement I'se been in. Since dat I'se been busy earnin' vittles for de family. I'se been married 40 years and we'uns has 14 chillen and 10 of 'em are livin'. If it warn't for dis farm and de work white folks give me, I don' know how I could of got on. We gits a pension of $21 every month from de state and dat helps a heap.

"I'se never had no schoolin'. Dey used to think us cullud folks has no use for edumacation. I thinks diff'rent and sends my chillen to school. Dey reads to me from de papers and sich."

Virginia Newman

Virginia Newman was freeborn, the daughter of a Negro boat captain and a part Negro, part Indian mother. When a young girl, Virginia apprenticed herself, and says she was nursegirl in the family of Gov. Foster, of Louisiana. She does not know her age, but says she saw the "Stars fall" in 1833. She has the appearance of extreme old age, and is generally conceded to be 100 years old or more. She now lives in Beaumont, Texas.

"When de stars fall I's 'bout six year old. They didn' fall on de grou'. They cross de sky like a millions of firebugs.

"My fus' name Georgia Turner, 'cause my pappy's name George Turner, and he a freeborn nigger man. He's captain of a boat, but they call 'em vessels them days. It have livin' quarters in it and go back and forth 'tween dis place and dat and go back to Africy, too.

"My grandmudder, she an Africy woman. They brung her freeborn from Africy and some people what knowed things one time tol' us we too proud but us had reason to be proud. My grandmudder's fambly in Africy was a African prince of de rulin' people. My udder grandmudder was a pure bred Indian woman and she raise all my mudder's chillen. My mudder name Eli Chivers.

"When I's small I live with my grandmudder in a old log cabin on the ribber, 'way out in de bresh jus' like de udder Indians live. I's born on my fadder's big boat, 'way below Grades Island, close by Franklin, in Louisiana. They tells me he carry cargo of cotton in de hull of de boat, and when I's still li'l they puts out to sea, and grandmudder, Sarah Turner her name, tuk us and kep' us with her in de cabin.

"Us didn' have stick of furniture in de house, no bed, no chair, no nothin'. Us cut saplings boughs for bed, with green moss over 'em. Us was happy, though. Us climb trees and play. It was hard sometime to git things to eat so far in de woods and us eat mos' everything what run or crawl or fly outdoors. Us eat many rattlesnake and them's fine eatin'. We shoot de snake and skin him and cut him in li'l dices. Den us stew him slow with lots of brown gravy.

"They allus askin' me now make hoe-cake like we et. Jus' take de cornmeal and salt and water and make patties with de hands and wrop de sof' patties in cabbage leafs, stir out de ashes and put de patties in de hot ashes. Dat was good.

"One my grandfadders a old Mexican man call Old Man Caesar. All de grandfolks was freeborn and raise de chillen de same, but when us gits big they tell us do what we wants. Us could stay in de woods and be free or go up to live with de white folks. I's a purty big gal when I goes up to de big house and 'prentice myself to work for de Fosters. Dey have big plantation at Franklin and lots of slaves. One time de Governor cripple in de leg and I do nothin' but nuss him.

"I's been so long in de woods and don' see nobody much dat I love it up with de white folks. Dey 'lowed us have dances and when dat old 'cordian starts to play, iffen I ain't git my hair comb yit, it don't git comb. De boss man like to see de niggers 'joy demselves. Us dance de quadrille.

"Us have 'ceptional marsters. My fadder sick on Marster Lewis' plantation and can't walk and de marster brung him a 'spensive reclinin' chair. Old Judge Lewis was his marster.

"I git marry from de plantation and my husban' he name Beverly Newman and he from de Lewis plantation in Opelousas. They read out'n de Book and after de readin' us have lots of white folks to come and watch us have big dance.

"When a nigger do wrong den, they didn' send him to de pen. They put him 'cross a barrel and strop him behin'.

"When fightin' 'gin, all our white folks and us slaves have to go 'way from Louisiana. Opelousas and them place was free long time 'fore de udders. Us strike out for Texas and it took mos' a year to walk from de Bayou la Fouche to de Brazos bottoms. I have to tote my two li'l boys, dat was Jonah and Simon. They couldn' neither walk yit. Us have de luggage in de ox cart and us have to walk. Dey was some mo' cullud people and white and de mud drag de feetses and stick up de wheels so dey couldn' even move. Us all walk barefeets and our feets break and run they so sore, and blister for months. It cold and hot sometime and rain and us got no house or no tent.

"De white folks settles in Jasper county, on a plantation dere. After while freedom come to Texas, too, but mos' de slaves stay round de old marsters. I's de only one what go back to Louisiana. After de war my fambly git broke up and my three oldes' chillen never see de li'l ones. Dose later chillen, dey's eight livin' now out'n nine what was born since slavery and my fourth chile die seven year ago when she 75 year old.

Virginia Newman

"When I git back to Louisiana I come to be a midwife and I brung so many babies here I can't count. De old priest say I ought to have a big book with all their names to 'member by.

"It were 'bout dis time I have my fur' bought dress and it was blue guinea with yaller spots. It were long at de ankle and make with a body wais'. Us wore lots of unnerwear and I ain't take 'em off yit.

"I never been sick, I's jus' weak. I almos' go blin' some time back but now I git my secon' sight and I sees well 'nough to sew."

Margrett Nillin

Margrett Nillin, 90, was born a slave to Charles Corneallus, at Palestine, Texas. After they were freed, Margrett and her mother moved to Chamber's Creek, Texas. She now lives with one of her children at 1013 W. Peach St., Fort Worth, Texas.

"Yas, sar, I's de old slave, and 'bout my age, I am young woman when de War started. Mus' be 90 for sure and maybe more. My marster's name was Charles Corneallus and hims owned a small farm near Palestine and him had jus' four slaves, my mammy, my sister and my cousin and me. I don' know 'bout my pappy, for reason he's sold 'fore I's born and I ain' never seed him.

"I tell you 'bout de place. Dere was a cabin with bunks for to sleep on and fireplace for to cook in. No window was in dat cabin, jus' a hole with a swingin' door and dat lets flies in durin' de summer and col' in durin' de winter. But if you shut's dat window dat shut out de light.

"De marster ain' de boss of dis nigger, 'cause I 'longs to Missy Corneallus and she don' 'low any other person boss me. My work was in de big house, sich as sewing, knitting and 'tending Missy. I keeps de flies off her with de fan and I does de fetching for her, sich as water and de snack for to eat, and de likes. When she goes to fix for sleep I combs her hair and rubs her feet. I can't 'member dat she speak any cross words to dis nigger.

"Our marster, he good to us and take we'uns to church. And whuppin', not on him place. De worst am scoldin'. Not many have sich a good home, 'cause lots gits 'bused powerful bad. Marster's neighbor, he's mean to his niggers and whups 'em awful. De devil sho' have dat man now!

"My mammy git de p'sentment lots of times. Often in de mornin' she say to me, 'Chile, dere am gwine be someone die, I seed de angels last night and dat am sho' sign.' Sho' 'nough, 'fore long we heered someone has died. Some says de haunts brings p'sentment to mammy.

"Fore de War I hears de white folks talking 'bout it. I 'members hearin' 'bout someone fires on de fort and den de mens starts jinin' de army. De marster didn' go and his boy too young. We didn' hear lots 'bout de War and de only way we knows it goin' on, sometimes we'uns couldn' git 'nough to eat.

Margrett Nillin

"After freedom we'uns see de Klux and dey is round our place but dey not come after us. Dey comes across de way 'bout a nigger call Johnson, and him crawls under him house, but dey makes him come out and gives him some licks and what de bellow come from dat nigger! Him had git foolishment in him head and dey come to him for dat.

"After de war mammy and me goes to Chamber's Creek and takes de sewin' for make de livin'. We gits 'long all right after awhile, and den I marries Ben Nillin. He dies 'bout fifteen year ago and now I lives with my son, Tom, and don' work 'cause I's too old.

"What I likes bes, to be slave or free? Well, it's dis way. In slavery I owns nothin' and never owns nothin'. In freedom I's own de home and raise de family. All dat cause me worryment and in slavery I has no worryment, but I takes de freedom."

John Ogee

John Ogee, 96 years old, was born in Morgan City, La., in 1841, the property of Alfred Williams. John ran away to join the Union Army and served three years. He recalls Sherman's march through Georgia and South Carolina and the siege of Vicksburg. He came to Jefferson County in 1870, and has lived there since.

"I was born near Morgan City, Louisiana in a old log cabin with a dirt floor, one big room was all, suh. My mother and father and four chillen lived in that room.

"The marster, he live in a big, old house near us. I 'member it was a big house and my mudder done the cleanin' and work for them. I jus' played round when I's growin' and the fus' work I done, they start me to plowin'.

"I haven't got 'lection like I used to, but I 'members when I's in the army. Long 'bout '63 I go to the army and there was four of us who run away from home, me and my father and 'nother man named Emanuel Young and 'nother man, but I disremember his name now. The Yankees comed 'bout a mile from us and they took every ear of corn, kilt every head of stock and thirteen hawgs and 'bout fifteen beeves, and feed their teams and themselves. They pay the old lady in Confed'rate money, but it weren't long 'fore that was no money at all. When we think of all that good food the Yankees done got, we jus' up and jine up with them. We figger we git lots to eat and the res' we jus' didn't figger. When they lef' we lef'. My father got kilt from an ambush, in Miss'ippi--I think it was Jackson.

"We went to Miss'ippi, then to South Carolina. I went through Georgia and South Carolina with Sherman's army. The fus' battle lasts two days and nights and they was 'bout 800 men kilt, near's I kin 'member. Some of 'em you could find the head and not the body. That was the battle of Vicksburg. After the battle it took three days to bury them what got kilt and they had eight mule throw big furrows back this way, and put 'em in and cover 'em up. In that town was a well 'bout 75 or 80 feet deep and they put 19 dead bodies in that well and fill her up.

"After the war we went through to Atlanta, in Georgia and stay 'bout three weeks. Finally we come back to Miss'ippi when surrender come. The nigger troops was mix with the others but they wasn't no nigger officers.

"After the war I come home and the old marster he didn' fuss at me about going to war and for long time I work on the old plantation for wages. I 'member then the Klu Klux come and when that happen I come to Texas. They never did git me but some they got and kilt. I knowed several men they whip purty bad. I know Narcisse Young, they tell him they was comin'. He hid in the woods, in the trees and he open fire and kilt seven of them. They was a cullud man with them and after they goes, he comes back and asks can he git them dead bodies. Narcisse let him and then Narcisse he lef' and goes to New Orleans.

John Ogee

"I thinks it great to be with the Yankees, but I wishes I hadn't after I got there. When you see 1,000 guns point at you I knows you wishes you'd stayed in the woods.

"The way they did was put 100 men in front and they git shoot and fall down, and then 100 men behin' git up and shoot over 'em and that the way they goes forward. They wasn't no goin' back, 'cause them men behin' you would shoot you. I seed 'em fightin' close 'nough to knock one 'nother with a bay'net. I didn' see no breech loaders guns, they was all muskets, muzzle loaders, and they shoot a ball 'bout big as your finger, what you calls a minnie-ball.

"I come to Taylor's Bayou in '70 and rid stock long time for Mister Arceneaux and Mister Moise Broussard and farms some too. Then I comes to Beaumont when I's too old to work no more, and lives with one of my girls."

Annie Osborne

Annie Osborne, 81, was born in Atlanta, Georgia, a slave of Tom Bias. She was 'refugeed' to Louisiana by the Bias family, before the Civil War, and remained there with them for two years after she was freed. She has lived in Marshall, Texas, since 1869.

"Yes, suh, I's a Georgia nigger. I 'longed to Massa Tom Bias, and he lived in Atlanta. I couldn't state jus' how old I is, but I knows I was eleven years old when we come to Marshall, and that's in 1869.

"Mammy was Lizzie and born in Atlanta, and I's heared her say she was give to Tom Bias to settle a dept her owner owed. I don't know nothin' 'bout my daddy, 'cept he am named Tom Bias, and that am massa's name. So I guess he's my daddy. But I had two brothers, Frank and James, and I don't know if Massa Bias was they daddy or not.

"Massa Bias refugees me and my mammy to Mansfield, in Louisiana when I's jus' a baby. They come in wagons and was two months on the way, and the big boys and men rode hossback, but all the niggers big 'nough had to walk. Massa Bias opens a farm twelve mile from Mansfield. My mammy plowed and hoed and chopped and picked cotton and jus' as good as the menfolks. I allus worked in the house, nussin' the white chillen and spinnin' and housework. Me and my brother, Frank, slep' in Missy Bias house on a pallet. No matter how cold it was we slep on that pallet without no cover, in front the fireplace.

"Old man Tom never give us no money and half 'nough clothes. I had one dress the year round, two lengths of cloth sewed together, and I didn't know nothin' 'bout playin' neither. If I made too much fuss they put me under the bed. My white folks didn't teach us nothin' 'cept how they could put the whip on us. I had to put on a knittin' of stockin's in the mornin' and if I didn't git it out by night, Missy put the lash on me.

"My mammy was sceered of old Tom Bias as if he was a bear. She worked in the field all day and come in at night and help with the stock. After supper they made her spin cloth. Massa fed well 'nough, but made us wear our old lowel clothes till they most fell off us. We was treated jus' like animals, but some owners treated they stock better'n old Tom Bias handled my folks. I still got a scar over my right eye where he put me in the dark two months. We had a young cow and when she had her first calf they sent me to milk her, and she kicked me and run me round a li'l pine tree, fightin' and tryin' to hook me. Massa and missy standin' in the gate all the time, hollerin' to me to make the cow stand still. I got clost to her and she kicked me off the stool and I run to the gate, and massa grab me and hit me 'cross the eye with a leather strap and I couldn't see out my right eye for two months. He am dead now, but I's gwine tell the truth 'bout the way we was treated.

"I could hear the guns shootin' in the war. It sound like a thunder storm when them cannons boomin'. Didn't nary one our menfolks go to war. I know my brother say, 'Annie, when them cannons stops boomin' we's gwine be all freed from old Massa Tom's beatin's.

"But massa wouldn't let us go after surrender. My mammy pretends to go to town and takes Frank and goes to Mansfield and asks the Progoe Marshal what to do. He say we's free as old man Tom and didn't have to stay no more. Frank stays in town and mammy brings a paper from the progoe, but she's sceered to give it to Massa Tom. Me and James out in the yard makin' soap. I's totin' water from the spring and James fetchin' firewood to put round the pot. Mammy tells James to keep goin' next time he goes after wood and her and me come round 'nother way and meets him down the road. That how we got 'way from old man Bias. Me and mammy walks off and leaves a pot of soap bilin' in the backyard. We sot our pails down at the spring and cuts through the field and meets James down the big road. We left 'bout ten o'clock that mornin' and walks all day till it starts to git dark.

"Then we comes to a white man's house and asks could we stay all night. He give us a good supper and let us sleep in his barn and breakfast next mornin' and his wife fixes up some victuals in a box and we starts to Mansfield. We was sceered most to death when we come to that man's house, fear he'd take us back to old man Bias. But we had to have somethin' to eat from somewheres. When mammy tells him how we left old man Bias, he says, 'That damn rascal ought to be Ku Kluxed.' He told us not to be 'fraid.

"We come to Mansfield and finds Frank and mammy hires me and James out to a white widow lady in Mansfield, and she sho' a good, sweet soul. She told mammy to come on and stay there with us till she git a job. We stayed with her two years.

"Then old man Charlie Stewart brung us to Marshall, and when I's eighteen I marries and lives with him twenty-six years. He worked on the railroad and helped move the shops from Hallsville to Marshall. He laughed and said the first engine they run from here to Jefferson had a flour barrel for a smokestack. He died and I married Tom Osborne, but he's dead eight years.

"I raises a whole passel chillen and got a passel grandchillen. They allus brings me a hen or somethin'. My boy is cripple and lives with me, and my gal's husband works for Wiley College. Old man Bias' son got in jail and sent for me. He say, 'Annie, you is my sister, and help me git out of jail.' I told him I didn't help him in and wouldn't help him out. I washed and ironed and now gits $9.00 pension. My boy got his leg cut off by the railroad. He can't do much."

Horace Overstreet

Horace Overstreet was born in Harrison Co., Texas, in 1856, a slave of M.J. Hall. He was brought to Beaumont when a youth and still lives there.

"I born near Marshall what was de county seat and my master was call' Hall. My mother name Jennie and my father's name Josh. He come back from de 'federate War and never got over it. He in de army with he young massa.

"Dat old plantation must have been 'bout 200 acres or even mo', and 'bout 500 head of slaves to work it. Massa Hall, he big lawyer and bought more niggers every year. He kep' a overseer what was white and a nigger driver. Sometime dey whip de slaves for what dey call dis'bedjonce. Dey tie 'em down and whip 'em. But I was raise' 'round de house, 'cause I a fav'rite nigger.

"De niggers didn't have no furniture much in dere houses, maybe de bedstead nail up to de side de house, and some old seats and benches. De rations was meat and meal and syrup 'lasses. Dey give 'em de shirt to wear, made out of lowers. Dat what dey make de cotton sack out of. De growed people has shoes, but de chillen has no need.

"Christmas time and Fourth July dey have de dance, jus' a reg'lar old breakdown dance. Some was dancin' Swing de Corner, and some in de middle de floor cuttin' de chicken wing. Dey has banjo pickers. Seem like my folks was happy when dey starts dancin'. Iffen dey start without de permit, de patterroles run up on dem and it 150 lashes. Law, dem niggers sho' scatter when de patterroles comes. Jus' let a nigger git de start and de patterrole sho' got to git a move on hisse'f to git dat nigger, 'cause dat nigger sho' move 'way from dat place!

"When de war comes, I seed plenty soldiers and if dey have de uniform I could tell it jus' in spots, for dey so dirty. Dey was Yankee soldiers and some stops in Marshall and takes charge of de court martial.

Horace Overstreet

"Fore long time come to go up and hear de freedom. We has to go up and hear dat we's free. Massa Hall, he say we kin stay and he pay us for de work. We didn' have nothin' so most of us stays, gatherin' de crop. Some of dem gits de patch of land from massa and raises a bale of cotton. Massa buy dat cotton and den he sell it.

"After 'while they slips away, some of 'em works for de white folks and some of 'em goes to farmin' on what they calls de shares. I works nearly everywhere for de white folks and makes 'nough to eat and git de clothes. It was harder'n bein' de slave at first, but I likes it better, 'cause I kin go whar I wants and git what I wants.

"Dey was conjure men and women in slavery days and dey make out dey kin do things. One of 'em give a old lady de bag of sand and told her it keep her massa from shippin' her. Dat same day she git too uppity and sass de masaa, 'cause she feel safe. Dat massa, he whip dat nigger so hard he cut dat bag of sand plumb in two. Dat ruint de conjure man business."

Mary Overton

Mary Overton, 117 W. Heard St., Cleburne, Texas, was born in Tennessee, but moved when very young to Carroll Co., Arkansas, where her parents belonged to Mr. Kennard. Mary does not know her age.

"I'se born in Tennessee but I don' 'member where, and I don' know how ole I is. I don' 'member what de marster's name was dere. My mother's name was Liza and my father's name was Dick. When I was 'bout four year ole, my marster and mistis give me to dere daughter, who married a Dr. James Cox and dey come to Texas and brought me with 'em. The marster in Arkansas, which give me to his daughter, was named Kennard. I never seed him but one time. Dat when he was sick and he had all his little niggers dressed up and brought in to see him.

"Dr. Cox and his wife and me come to Fort Graham, in Hill County, Texas, from Arkansas. We was 'bout two weeks comin'. Fort Graham wasn' no reg'lar fort. Dere was jus' some soldiers campin' dere and dere was a little town. Lots of Indians come in to trade. Den de doctor got a farm on Nolan river, not far from whar Cleburne is now, and we went there.

"While we was on de farm, I got married. My husban' was Isaac Wright. I had seven chillen by him. My second husban' was Sam Overton. Him and me had two chillen. I wasn't married to Isaac by a preacher. De slaves wasn' jin'rally married dat way. Dey jus' told dey marsters dey wanted to be husban' and wife and if dey agreed, dat was all dere was to it, dey was said to be married. I heered some white folks had weddin's for dere niggers, but I never did see none.

"My marster had 'bout four slaves. He sold and bought slaves sev'ral times, but he couldn' sell me, 'cause I belonged to de mistis, and she wouldn' let him sell me. I cooked and washed and ironed and looked after de chillen, mostly. Dey had three chillen, but de mistis died when the least one was 'bout six months ole and I raised de two older ones. Dey was two boys, and dey was 'bout grown when I lef' after freedom.

"We slaves had good 'nuf houses to live in. We didn' have no garden. I wore cotton dresses in summer and linsey dresses and a shawl in de winter. I had shoes most of de time. My white folks was pretty good to keep me in clothes. I gen'rally went to church wid mistis.

"Didn' have no special clothes when I got married. I slep' in de kitchen gen'rally, and had a wooden bed, sometimes with a cotton mattress and sometimes it was a shuck mattress.

"My mistis teached me to read and write, but I wouldn' learn. I never went to school neither. She would read de Bible to us.

"I didn' know no songs when I was in slavery. I didn' know 'bout no baptizin'. I didn' play no certain games, jus' played roun' de yard.

"I wasn' at no sale of slaves, but saw some bein' tuk by in chains once, when we lived at Reutersville. Dey was said to be 'bout 50 in de bunch. Dey was chained together, a chain bein' run 'tween 'em somehow, and dey was all man and women, no chillen. Dey was on foot. Two white men was ridin' hosses and drivin' de niggers like dey was a herd of cattle.

"Lots of slaves run away, but I don' know how dey got word 'round 'mong de niggers.

"I don' 'member much 'bout de war. Dere wasn' no fightin' whar we was, on de farm on Nolan river. On de day we was made free, de marster come and called us out one at a time and tol' us we was free. He said to me, 'Mary, you is free by de law. You don' belong to me no more. You can go wherever you wan' to. I ain't got no more to say 'bout you.' He tol' us if we'd stay awhile he'd treat us good and maybe we'd better stay, as de people was pretty much worked up. De rest of 'em stayed 'bout a week, den dey went off, and never come back, 'cept Isaac. I didn' go, but I stayed a long time after we was made free. I didn' care nothin' 'bout bein' free. I didn' have no place to go and didn' know nothin' to do. Dere I had plenty to eat and a place to stay and dat was all I knowed 'bout.

"When I lef' I hired out as cook. I got ten dollars a month and all my food and clothes and a place to sleep. I didn' spend but one dime of my pay for eight months. I bought candy wid dat dime, like a walkin' stick.

"I sure wish I knew how old I is, but I ain' sure. I don' even know my birthday!" (According to some white persons who have known Mary for a long time, calculated from information Mary had given them as to her younger days, when her memory was better than it is now, she is probably more than one hundred years old.)

George Owens

George Owens, medium in height and weight, seated comfortably under the shade of an old oak tree, was clad in a blue shirt and overalls, and brogan shoes with a few slits cut in them to prevent hurting his feet. He has kinky gray hair, a bit of gray hair on his chin and a nicely trimmed mustache on his upper lip. George's right eye is completely closed from an injury which he received while in railroad service. Born near Marshall, Texas, the slave of Dave Owens, he told his story with great interest and enjoyed the opportunity to tell about the old days.

"I was bo'n right close to de ol' powder mill up in Marshall, Texas, where dey uster mek powder. Understan'? Dey call it Mills Quarters. I was a right sizeable boy twel' year' ol' when freedom come."

"Dave Owens, dat was my ol' marster' name, and dat was my daddy' name too. My name' George William David Owen. I use dat William 'cause one of dem other Owens uster git my mail."

"Ol' marster he had a big farm plantation. Dey uster raise cotton, and co'n and 'taters and sich like. My daddy was de shoemaker for de plantation."

"One day me and my daddy was talkin'. Dat was de fus' Crismus atter freedom. He say to me, 'Son, does you know how ol' you is?' I say, 'No, suh.' He say, 'Well, you is 12 year' ol'.' I 'member dat and dat was de fus' Crismus atter freedom."

"Williams was my fus' marster but he sel' us to Owens. He live in Marshall, but he hab a plantation 'bout t'ree or fo' mile' out. Atter dat Owens he buy out Mills Quarters from Williams."

"My wuk was jis' de odds and en's 'roun' de yard. When ol' mistus call me and tell me to pick up chips, or pull up weeds or bring in weed and sich, I hafter do it. You knew how wimmen is, allus havin' you do fus' one t'ing and den anudder. I neber did wuk in de fiel'."

"It was a big plantation. Dey was in de neighborhood of 25 or 30 slaves on de place. Us had a good marster and I 'speck us was pretty lucky. Ol' marster see to it dat us have plenty to eat. Dey feed us milk and 'taters and peas, and bread and meat. No sir, we didn' sit down at no trough for to eat. Dey had tables in de slaves' houses. Us sit down to us meals like human bein's. My mammy was de cook on de place. Her name was Sarah Owens."

"Dey give de little ones what couldn' come to de table, a pan and spoon for dem to have at meal time. Dem what so little dey can't eat outer a pan, dey have suck bottles for dem."

"Dey milk 'bout 12 or 14 head of cow' on de place. Dey had plenty of milk and butter. Dey had a big safe what dey put de milk and butter in to keep it fresh. Dere was a trough wid water in it and dey set de milk and butter in it in de summer time. Dey had a peg of wood in a hole at de en', and when dey want to change de water dey pull out de peg and dreen de water out and put some cool fresh water in."

"When I was a boy us uster play wid spools, and puppies and stick hosses. Us uster have bows and arrers. Sometime us go out in de wood huntin' wid de bows and arrers. Us shoot at birds and sich, but us neber did had no luck at it."

"De grown up folks uster go huntin' at night and kill deers and 'possums. Dey had to have a permit transfer iffen dey go huntin' or go from one plantation to annuder. Iffen dey didn' have a permit de patterrollers would git 'em."

"De patterrollers neber git me. I see 'em chase slaves. When dey ketch 'em dey whip 'em, and tell 'em nex' time be sho' to have a pass from ol' marster."

"I neber see ol' marster beat nobody. What whippin' he done he done it wid his mout'. He mighty keen speakin' den, but when he speak rough to a nigger he need it."

"De kind of chu'ch dey have in dem days on dat place was fence-corner chu'ch. Dey go off down in de fence corner and sing and pray. Dey feerd for anybody to see 'em."

"Dey was some cullud preacher' 'roun' but dey warn't on us plantation. I jine' de Baptis' Chu'ch but dat was way atter slavery. I uster be pro tem deacon."

"De fus' money I earn' was wukkin' on the T&P Railroad. I jis' blow it in, you know like boys do. I los' dis eye railroadin'. I was spikin' on a col' frosty mornin'. I hit dat spike and it broke up in t'ree piece' and de middle piece hit me in de eye and put it out."

"Seems like I 'members de sojers. I couldn' specify wedder dey was Yankees or not. You know dat ol' battle fo't (fort) was dere at Marshall, two or t'ree mile' from Mills Quarters."

"Dem sojers had on long blue overcoats wid brass buttons on 'em. Dey was a eagle on dem button. De way I 'member dat, I find one in de road like it was tore off and I pick it up and make me a play toy outer it."

"Dey uster keep two cannons at de co't house and dey shoot dem cannon eb'ry Friday. I 'member dey uster stick a rod in 'em and el'vate 'em. Dey had a U.S. flag on de mas'-pole and dey shoot de cannon when dey tek down de flag."

"I dunno nuthin' 'bout conjur' men. I see people sick or cripple' and dey say conjure' man done it, but I dunno. I ain't neber see no ghos' needer. People try to show 'em to me but I ain't see 'em. One time I see sumpin' white in de wood and I go up to see what it was and it warn't nuthin' 'cep'n' a pillow what somebody lef' in a swing 'tween two tree'. Iffen I hadn' had a li'l "coffee" in me I don' guess I'd been brave 'nuff to go see what it was."

"I allus pronounced de patterrollers and de Klu Kluxers 'bout de same. Fur as seein' 'em, I ain't. I t'ink dey done good to de country. Dey didn' bodder nobody 'cep'n' dem what was out of dere place. Iffen dey had some now it mought do good."

"If you all keep on you gwineter hab a book outer my testimony."

"Dey had a gin on de plantation and dey mek de clo's on a spinnin' wheel and loom. I see my mammy mek many a bolt of clo'f on a loom befo' she die."

"It mighter slip' my 'membrance how dey tol' us we free, but I 'members my daddy say we free. Us stay on ol' marster's place a while den he buy a li'l place de other side of Marshall. He do odd jobs 'roun', too."

"Fus' time I marry Mary Harper at Gilmer. Dey was two darters, Gettys and Alice Owens. I lef' her and I marry my secon' wife, Betty Cheatham in 1913. I been 'roun' dese parts 'bout 46 or 47 year' and I been in Kountze 25 year'."

"I don't t'ink I commit to mem'ry anyt'ing else. I ain't gwine to tell no mo' 'cause I ain't to make statement and testify 'bout sumpin' I ain't know 'bout."

Mary Anne Patterson

Mary Anne Patterson, who now lives with her daughter, Elizabeth Lee, in Austin, Texas, was born in Louisiana, but she does not know exactly where. She is between 97 and 102 years old. Mary and her mother belonged to Col. Aaron Burleson of Rogers' Hill, Travis County, Texas.

"Way back yonder my name was Mary Anne Burleson and I's born in Louisiana somewhere. I knows I's told dey brung me and my mammy to Texas when I's eighteen months old, and dat Massa Turner what brung us, sold us to Col. Aaron Burleson. Massa Burleson buy both of us, 'cause he a good man and didn't 'lieve in separatin' a chile from de mammy. I do think dat man gone to Heaven.

"When I growed up it was my job to wet nuss Rufe Burleson, 'cause he mammy didn't have 'nough milk for him. Beside dat, I helped in de loom room and have to spin five cuts de day, but I's fast 'nough to make eight cuts.

"Durin' cotton pickin' time I larns to count a little, 'cause I picks de cotton, brung it to de wagon and listen to 'em countin' on dem scales. Purty soon I could of counted my own cotton.

"Massa Burleson good to we'uns and when a woman have a chile and no husband to take care of her, he make a man go out and chop wood for her, and dat slave had better act like he wants to. Massa so good to us he have lumber hauled clear from de Bastrop pineries and builds us good wood dwellin's. He have de plantation on Rogers' Hill what am east of Austin.

"Now, let me tell you 'bout de cooks. Massa Burleson have de cook for de big house and de cook for de slaves. Dere a kitchen in de big house for de white folks and dere a kitchen with a long table for de hands. We had purty good victuals and I 'member we have so much hawg meat we'd throw de hog's head and feet 'way. Massa raised he own hawgs and everythin' he et, we had it, too. Sometimes we et deer meat and dere times we had bear meat and honey, 'cause Massa Burleson have he own bees, too.

"I 'member how at sweet 'tater time my mammy'd sneak out to de patch and scratch up some sweet 'taters. When Massa Burleson finds de 'taters gone, he jes' say, 'Now, I know nobody done dis but de Lawd!'

"I seed many a Injun and seed 'em in droves. Dem Injuns never bothered us. A old Injun call Placedo and he son come on down to massa's place and he give 'em plenty food.

When de Injuns come near de cattle'd bellow and cut up, 'cause dey knowed it was Injuns 'round.

Mary Anne Patterson

"When I's 'bout 20 years old I marries Alex Patterson and he was brung from Tennessee to Texas and owned by Massa Joshua Patterson. After freedom we rents land from Massa Patterson and lives dere and farms 'bout seven years.

"Me and Alex has 15 chillen and six of dem is still livin'. Dere is two here in Texas and two in California and one in Oklahoma and one in Kansas. My husband am dead now and I's alone.

"I owns a little farm of 36 acres out near Rogers' Hill and I gits sixty dollars de year for de rentin' of dat land and now de folks wants me to sell it. But my husband bought dat place and I wants to keep it. I don't git no pension. I know dis much, I's worked harder since after freedom den I ever worked befo' freedom."

Martha Patton

Martha Patton was born 91 years ago in Alabama, slave to the Lott family, who came to Texas about 1847 and settled near Goliad. After marrying and bearing two children, surviving a famine and scarcity of water, she was freed. She, her husband and others of her family leased farm land on the San Antonio River near La Bahia Mission, at Goliad.

"Yes'm, I was bo'n befo' de war. Best I kin remember, I'll be 91 years old come June 15, 1937. I was bo'n in Alabama, but was brought to Texas when I was nine months old. My folks stopped at Goliad, on de creek near to Goliad.

"I 'member seein' de soldiers, but t'weren't no fightin' 'round us no closer den Corpus Christi. One day one of my uncles went to Corpus Christi. He say, 'Dey done tol' all de women and chillen to git outta town.' We done heard 'em shootin' bombs. De smoke was so thick it looked like it were cloudy. De soldiers come through and took anything dey wanted outta de stores. Pretty soon nothin' was left in de stores and dey couldn' git no more.

"My mother was a cook. We chillen brought in wood and water. My uncles had cotton patches. My master sol' dere cotton for dem and dey had money to buy shoes or anything dey needed. We picked cotton and picked peas. We had a spinnin' wheel and a weave(loom). We made cloth, blankets and our own stockin's. We made dye outta live oak bark, mesquite bark, pecan leaves. They made a dark brown and it dyed the cloth and blankets pretty.

"I never saw any slaves whipped, nor any with chains on. Our white people were very good to us. Their name was Lott, Jim Lott, yes'm, me and Jim Lott was chillen together. He sure was a good boy. He died over at Goliad las' yea'.

"We made cotton and wool cloth both, yes'm, we made both. We raised cotton. The sheep were so po' they would die. We would go through de woods and find de dead sheep and pick de wool offen 'em. Then we would wash de wool and spin it into thread and weave it into cloth to make wool clothes.

"My man, he worked in de tan ya'd. He fixed de hides to make us all de shoes we had, and dey made harness and saddles fo' de gov'nment--fo' de soldiers. To make de lime to take de hair off of de hides, dey would burn limestone rocks. Then dey would hew out troughs and soak de hides in lime water till all the hair come off. Den dey would take 'ooze' made from red oak bark and rub the hides till dey were soft and dry.

"Dey sho was hard times after de war, and durin' de war too. Our white folk was good to us, but we had a time to get pervisions. Sometimes we had co'n meal and sometimes we would have flour. We would pa'ch co'n meal and make coffee. When we could git 'em we used pertater peelings, pa'ched, for coffee. Sometimes we drank wild sage tea.

"When we could, we would go over on de Brazos to de molasses mills and get molasses and brown sugar; when we couldn't, we had to do widout de sweetenin'.

"Water sho was sca'ce. We had to tote it about half a mile from de hole. De creeks just dried up, only 'long in holes. De wells was all dried up. There would be dead cows lyin' on t'other side of de hole and grasshoppers thick on de water, but we jist skimmed de water off and went on. Didn't make us sick, lady, 'twas all we had and de good Lo'd took ca'e of us.

"De grasshoppers sho was bad 'long 'bout fo' or five in de ebenin'; dey would be so thick de sun would be cloudy lookin'. Dey was a little speckled grasshopper. Yes'm, red and speckled. De chickens and hawgs et 'em. Dey et so many grasshoppers de meat was bright red. You couldn't eat it.

"Twa'n't no use to send fo' a docta, no'm, 'cause dey didn't have no medicine. My grandmother got out in de woods and got 'erbs. She made sage ba'm (balm). One thing I recomember, she would take co'n shucks--de butt end of de shucks--and boil 'em and make tea. 'Twould break de chills and fever. De Lo'd fixed a way. We used roots for medicine too.

"Dey was salt lakes. De men would get a wagonbed full of salt and take it to town and trade it for flour. De men would take de old ox wagons and go down to Mexico towa'ds Brownsville to git pervisions. Coffee--real coffee--was a dollar a poun'. De men what used terbaccer had to pay a dollar a plug. Cotton cloth was fifty and sixty cents a ya'd.

"Durin' de war de white people had church in their homes. Dey would have church in de mornin' and in de afternoon dey would preach to de slaves.

"After de war, we all leased land on de ribbah fum de white folks--my uncles, my brothers and alls. We leased de land fo' six years. At de end of dat time most of us bought places.

"When de war was over and we moved, de men put up a picket house. Dr. McBride, a soldier, taught school. When de crops was laid by, all de men and women went to school. De chillen went all de time. We had log seats and a dirt flo'. We would have meetin's in de school house. Twasn't fine, but we had good times.

"We lived clost to de old mission, built during Santa Anna's war, I think it were.

"I has ten chillen; seven of them are living. I have fifteen or nineteen grandchillen, but I don't know where dey all are or what dey are doing."

Ellen Payne

Ellen Payne, 88, was born a slave of Dr. Evans, pioneer physician of Marshall, Texas, and father-in-law of former Governor Clark. She married Nelson Payne when she was twenty-five, and they farmed in Marshall for fifty-two years. Since Nelson's death eleven years ago, Ellen has operated the farm herself and has always made a crop. She lives alone on the Port Caddo Road.

"My name is Ellen Payne now, but in slave times it was Ellen Evans, and I was born on the old Mauldin place right here at Marshall and belonged to old Dr. Evans. Dr. Evans loans the Bible what had all our ages in it and never got it back, so when he freed us they guessed our ages. My mistress say I was 'bout sixteen years old when surrender come, and my daddy and mammy was Isom and Becky Lewis. Mammy come from Tennessee and they was seventeen of us chillen.

"Master Evans lived in a big brick house on the north side of Marshall and run his farm four miles from town, and I stayed on the farm, but come in town some with my mammy to work for Mistress Nancy. The niggers on other farms had to sleep on 'Damn-it-to Hell' beds, but we didn't have that kind. We had good wood beds and hay mattresses with lowell covers.

"I mostly minded the calves and chickens and turkeys. Master Evans had a overseer but he didn't 'low him to cut and slash his niggers and we didn't have no hard taskmaster. They was 'bout thirty slaves on the farm, but I is the only one livin' now. I loved all my white folks and they was sweet to us.

"The hands worked from sun to sun and had a task at night. Some spinned or made baskets or chair bottoms or knit socks. Some the young'uns courted and some jest rambled round most all night. On Saturday was the prayer meetin' in one house and a dance in another. On Sunday some went to church and visitin', but not far, 'cause that was in patterroller times.

"They was allus plenty to eat and one nigger didn't do nothin' but raise gardens. They hunted coon and possum and rabbits with dogs and the white folks kilt deer and big game like that. My daddy allus had some money, 'cause he made baskets and chair bottoms and sold them, and Master Evans give every slave a patch to work and they could sell it and keep the money.

"We didn't know nothin' but what went on at the place. Us slaves didn't carry news 'cause they wasn't none to carry and if the white folks want to send news anywhere, they put a boy on a mule to take it.

"Master Evans had a old woman what tended to us when we was sick, and he give us quinine and calomel and castor oil and boneset tea. That tea was 'nough to kill a mule, but it done us good. Some wore esfidity bags round they necks to keep off sickness.

"My young mistress married Master Clark and they lived close, and my mammy and me used to spent part the time workin' for her. Master Clark got to be governor 'bout time war started and moved to Austin. I still got the Bible he give me.

Ellen Payne

"I 'member the white southern men folks run off to the bottoms to git 'way from war, but I never seed nothin' of the war. When we was freed my old master calls us up and say, 'You is free, and I'm mighty glad, but I'm mighty sad.' We stays on till Christmas, then mammy and me leaves and hires out. I stays workin' with her till I'm twenty-five and then I marries Nelson Payne.

"My young mistress sends me a blue worsted dress to marry in, and we's married at mammy's house and she give us a nice supper. He was a farmer and we kep' on livin' on the farm fifty-two years, till he died. We loved farm life. I raised four boys but none of them is livin' now. When Nelson died first one then 'nother holps me and I has made a crop every year till now. I'm too old now, but I still raises some corn and peas and garden stuff. They gives me a $15.00 month pension, but I likes to be doin' somethin'.

"I still shouts at meetin's. I don't have nothin' to do with it. It hits me jes' like a streak of lightning, and there ain't no holdin' it. I goes now to camp meetin's clost to Karnack and tries to 'have, but when I gits the spirit, I jest can't hold that shoutin' back. The young folks makes fun of me, but I don't mind. Style am crowded all the grace out of 'ligion, today."

Henderson Perkins

Henderson Perkins, about 85, was born a slave to John Pruitt, near Nashville, Tenn., who owned Henderson's mother and about 20 other slaves. Prior to the Civil War, Mr. Pruitt moved to Centerville, Leon Co., Texas, and sold Henderson and his mother to Tom Garner, of Centerville. When the war began, Henderson was old enough to be trusted with taking grain to the mill and other duties. After they were freed, Henderson and his mother worked in Mr. Garner's tavern until he sold it. He then placed the two on a piece of land and gave them tools to work it. Henderson later married and moved to Waco, where he reared 14 children. After they were grown he moved to Fort Worth and now lives at 610 Penn St.

"I'se tells you de truth 'bout my age, I'se too ol' for any good, but from what de white folks says, I'se bo'n 'bout 1839 in Ten'see, near Nashville. In dem days, 'twarn't so partic'lar 'bout gettin' married, and my mammy warn't before I'se bo'n, so I'se don' know my father. Dat's one on dis nigger.

"After I'se ol' enough to tote water, pick up kindlin' and sich, Marster Pruitt moves to Texas, near Centerville and sol' me and my mammy to Marster Garner. My mammy gits married seven times after we comes to Texas.

"Marster Garner runs a tavern, dey calls 'em hotels now. My mammy was cook for de tavern. De other nigger's named Gib, and I'se to do de work 'roun de place and take grist to de water mill for to grin'. Marster have de farm, too, and have seven niggers on dat place and sometimes I goes dere for to he'p.

"Well, 'bout treatment, you can say Marster Garner am de bestest man ever lived. I'se jus' says he am O. K. I'se never hears him say one cross word to my mammy. Back in Tennessee, Marster Pruitt was good, too. Hims have him's own still and gives de toddy to we'uns lots of times. I'se gits a few whuppin's, but 'twas my fault. I'se cause de devilment. I tells you 'bout some. I drives de oxen and de two-wheel cart for to go to de water mill and sich. In dem days, it was great insult to say, 'You'uns has bread and rotten egg for supper.' I'se gwine to de mill one day, past de school and I say's dat to de chillens. I thinks de teacher won't let 'em come out, but I makes a mistake, for it am like yellow jackets pourin' outta de hive. Dey throws sticks and stones at we'uns and dat 'sprise de ox and he runs. De road am rough and dat cart have no springs and de co'n made scatterment on de road. Marster whups us for dat. Not hard, just a couple licks.

"Did you's ever drive de ox? Dey's de devil sometimes and de angel sometimes. When dey's gwine home, you can go to sleep and dey takes you dere. If dey's dry and you comes near water, de devil can't stop 'em, dey goes in de water wid de cart and all dat's in it.

"When de war starts Marster's girl gits married to Charles Taylor, and dey have big weddin'. Befo' de war am over, we'uns have hard time. De soldiers comes and takes all de co'n, all de meat, every chicken and all de t'baccy. You couldn' buy t'baccy for a dollar a pound. But we makes it. We takes de leaves and cures dem, den place dem on de board and put honey 'tween 'em. We place a log on top and leave it 'bout a month. White man, dat am t'baccy!

"After de army took de food, it am scarce for awhile. Short time after de army come, de pigeons goes north. If you's never see dat, it am hard to believe. Dey am so thick and so many dey cuts off de sun like de cloud. We'uns gits lots of 'em and dat helps with de food. I'se sho' glad de army don' come any more, once was 'nuff. I'se seen squirrels travelin' on de groun' so thick it look like de carpet. Dey was all runnin' 'way from de army.

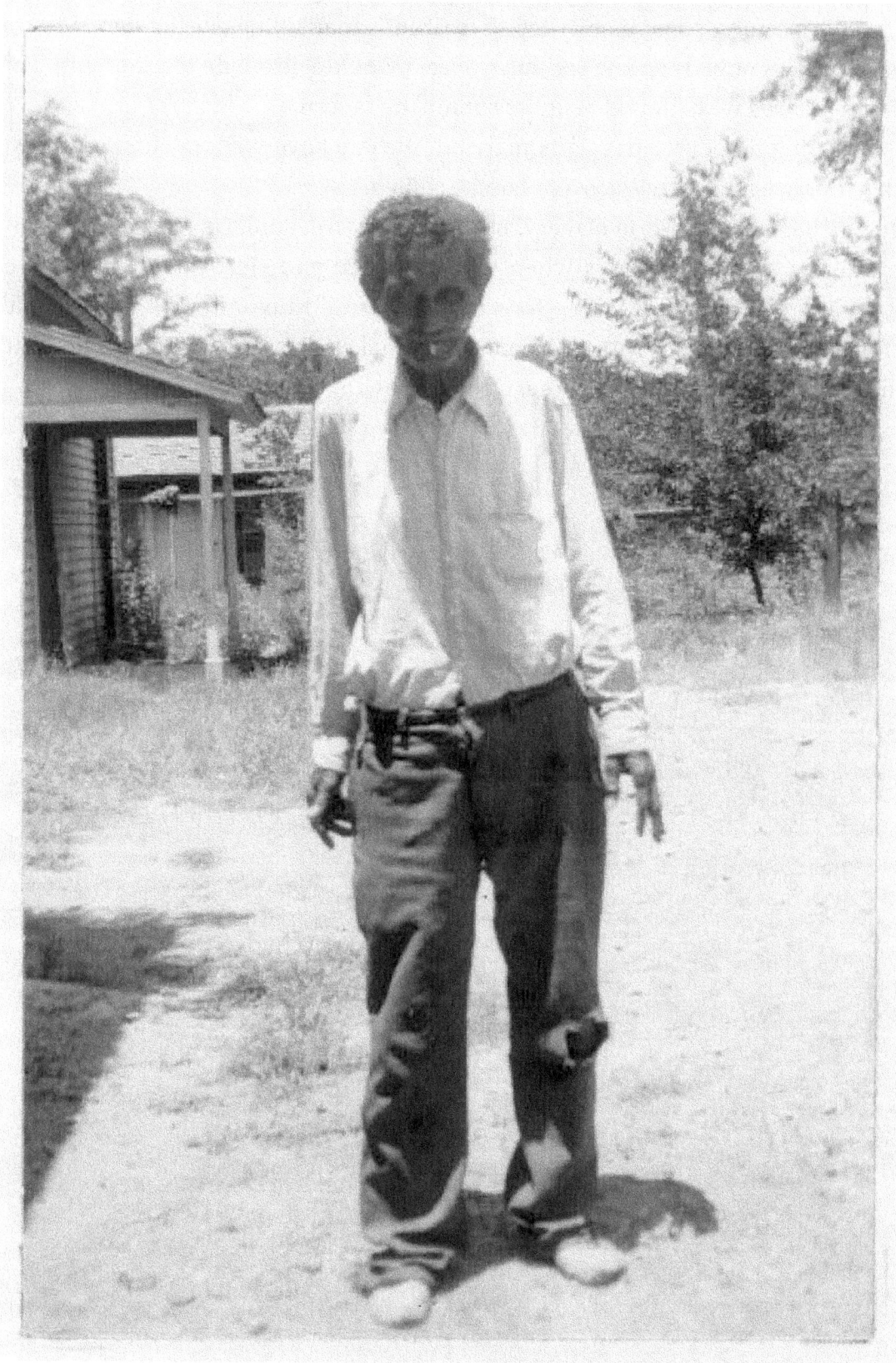

Henderson Perkins

"When freedom comes, some mans--dey says Grant's mans--lines we'uns up side de house and says, 'Yous am now free,' and we'uns is free. I wouldn' leave de Marster, him am sich a gran' man, so I stays with him till he quits runnin' de tavern.

"It am a long time after dat I gits married. We'uns have weddin' supper and sho' am happy den. Den we moves to Waco and has 14 chillen.

"We'uns had good times in slavery, but I likes my freedom. De Marster allus give us a pass on Sunday and some nights when we has dance and sich. But iffen you went out without a pass, den de patterollers--'fore de War--or de Klux--after de War--would come lookin' for you. Dem niggers without de pass sho' makes de scatterment, out de window or up de chimney. But when we'uns is free, we'uns goes anywhere we wants to."

Daniel Phillips

Daniel Phillips, Sr., 704 Virginia Street, San Antonio, Texas. Born 1854 at Stringtown, five miles south of San Marcos, Texas. Big framed, good natured. Never has worn glasses.

"I was a slave to Dr. Dailey and his son, Dr. Thomas Dailey. They brought my mother and father from Georgia and I was born in Stringtown just after they arrived, in 1854. I calls him Mr. Tommy. Dey has a plantation at Stringtown and a ranch on de Blanco River. We come from Georgia in wagons.

"Marse Dailey raised cotton and co'n on de plantation. On de ranch dey ketches wild horses and I herds dem. When I'm on de ranch I has to drive de wild horses into de pen. De men cotches de wild horses and I has to drive 'em so's dey won't git wild agin.

"Lots of dem wild horses got colts and I has to brand dem. Marse Dailey he helps to cotch de wild horses but I has to drive 'em. In de mornin' I drives dem out and in de evenin' I drives dem back. Dere's sure a lot of dem wild horses.

"Marse Dailey brings twenty-five slaves from Georgia but he sells some after we comes to San Marcos. No suh, we niver gits paid. We lives in log houses built on de side of a hill. De houses has one room. My mother has a wooden bed with a cotton mattress. My sister Maria was housewoman. My younger sister married a man named Scott.

"We feeds good. Dere's cornbread and beef. Plenty milk, 'cause Marse Dailey's got plenty cows. Dere's gardens with peas, cabbage, beans and beets. We makes de clothes ourself. My father is handy man. He builds a loom and a spinnin' wheel. No suh, we didn't do no huntin'. Marse Dailey didn' let us have guns.

"We's treated all right. My uncle is overseer. When de war's over I didn't know about it. Marse Tommy comes to de ranch when I's herdin' de wild horses. He says, 'Dan, you'se free now.' I say, 'Wha' dat mean, Marse Tommy?' He say, 'Dat mean you can live with you mammy and you pappy, and what you makes you kin keep.'

"And I leaves de wild horses and comes to de plantation. Yas suh, we goes to church. We walks fo' mile to de church. De w'ite folks sits in front and de cullud folks sits back by de do'.

"Yassuh, we's glad de slav'ry is over. My mother would go to milk cows and I was sent to kill a calf. And dere was my mother in de corner of de fence and she was prayin', 'O, Lawd, set us free!'

Daniel Phillips

"I was too young for de army. My brother was a cook in de Confederate Army, and de Yankees run dem 60 miles in one night. And my brother is ridin' one horse and front of him is a pack horse, and he cut de traces of de pack horse and dat horse run so he didn't see him again. Yassuh, my brother was 108 years ole. He died two years ago.

"We gits along better after we's free. Often de Yankees comes down to San Marcos. Dey wants to buy milk.

"One time on de plantation a cullud preacher wants to hold a service. De marster say 'all right'. De preacher must tell how much he collects. Dat so de marster fin' out if we's got any money."

Lee Pierce

Lee Pierce, 87, was born a slave of Evans Spencer, in Marshall, Texas. Lee was sold to a trader in 1861, and bought by Henry Fowler, of Sulphur Springs, Texas. Lee remained with his master until 1866, then returned to Marshall. When he became too old to work, he went to live with a son, in Jefferson, Tex.

"My name am Lee Anderson Pierce, borned on the fifteenth of May, in 1850, up in Marshall, and 'longin' to Marse Evans Spencer, what was a surveyor. I never knowed my pappy. He died 'fore I was borned. Mammy was Winnie Spencer and Old Marse's folks fetched her to Texas from Greenwood, what am over in Mississippi.

"When I was 'bout eleven year old, Marse Spencer done got in debt so bad he had to sell me off from mammy. He sold me to a spec'lator named Buckley, and he taken me to Jefferson and drapped me down there with a man called Sutton. I had a hard time there, had to sleep on the floor on hot ashes, to keep warm, in wintertime. I nussed Marse Sutton's kids 'bout a year, den Buckley done got me 'gain and taken me to de nigger trader yard in Marshall. I was put on de block and sold jes' like a cow or horse, to Marse Henry Fowler, what taken me to Sulphur Springs. I lived with him till after surrender.

"Marse Fowler worked 'bout a hundred and fifty acres of land and had sev'ral cullud families. He done overseeing hisself, but had a black man for foreman. I seed plenty niggers whopped for not doin' dey tasks. He'd whop 'em for not pickin' so many hundreds of cotton a day, buckle 'em down hawg fashion and whop 'em with a strap. Us never stopped work no day, lessen Sunday, and not then iffen grass in the field or crops sufferin'.

"Most time we et bacon and cornbread and greens. Sometimes we'd git deer meat to eat, 'cause a old man named Buck Thomas am clost friend to Marse Fowler and a big hunter. We got our own fish when we wasn't workin'.

"The first work I done was herdin' sheep. I never done much field work, but I was kep' busy with them sheep and other jobs round the place. The cullud folks had big breakdowns Saturday night and a good time then and on Christmas, but all the res' the time us jus' worked.

"On Christmas we never got nothin but white shorts. Them was for biscuits and they was jus' like cake to the niggers in slavery time. Marse Fowler didn't have too much regard for he black folks. Two families of them was stolen niggers. A spec'lator done stole them in Arkansas and fotch them to Texas.

"I didn't know much 'bout the war, 'cause I'm only ten year old when it starts, and the white folks didn't talk it with us cullud folks. Long 'bout the end of the war a big Yankee camp was at Jefferson right where the courthouse is now, but I wasn't 'lowed to go there and never did know nothin' 'bout it.

"I stayed with Marse Fowler till the Ku Klux got to ragin'. The Yankees run it out of business. That Ku Klux business started from men tryin' to run the niggers back to they farms. They near all left they masters and didn't have nothin' or nowheres to go. The cullud folks was skeered of them Kluxers. They come round the house and had some kind of riggin' so's they could drink sev'ral buckets of water.

"A cullud man at Jefferson, named Dick Walker, got up a cullud militia to keep the Klux off the niggers. The militia met here in the old African Methodist Church. Marse Fowler done git up a bunch of thirty men to break up that cullud militia, and he org'ized his bunch at our place. I helped saddle the hosses the night they went to take the church. Ben Biggerstaff, he was one the main white leaders. They kilt sev'ral of the militia and wounded lots more. That's after the Yankees done leave.

"I hired out to Col. King, a Yankee officer in Sulphur Springs, and works for him one year. I was makin' $25.00 a month. Land was sellin' for twenty-five cents an acre but I wouldn't buy none. That same land am worth a fortune now. But I left and come back to Jefferson.

"I never found my mammy until 1870. She was workin' in a cafe in Terrell. Judge Estes of Jefferson and some white men done been to Dallas and stopped where she was workin'. She asked 'em if they knowed Lee Pierce and the Judge said he did. When she done tell him how long it am since she seed me, he put her on the train and sent her to Jefferson.

"I was here when Jay Gould tried to git them to let him put his railroad through this town and they told him they didn't need a railroad. Then they done somethin' on Red River what done take all the water out of Big Cypress and the town went down to nothin'. Cullud folks run this town 'bout them times. Paul Matthews, a cullud man, was county judge, and Bill Wisham was sheriff.

"I think the younger race of our folks has more 'vantages for prosper'ty than what we had. Most of them am makin' good use of it. Some ain't got no principle or ambition, but lots of them are 'spectable people."

Ellen Polk

Ellen Polk, born in Gonzales County, Texas. Age, 83. Lives at 724 Virginia Blvd., San Antonio, Texas. Her hair is only slightly grey at the temples and forehead and her eyesight is good.

"I was a slave to Jim and Hannah Nations, Gonzales County, Texas. Marse Jim was a fine looker, a heavy set man. He and Missis lived in a big lumber house with a shingle roof. Dere was a nice yard with lots of pecan trees and de plantation fields had rail fences aroun' dem. Dere were fields of cotton and co'n and a purty river and all kind of wild flowers.

"Marse Jim sho was good to his slaves, but his foremens twern't. He bought my mudder and some other slaves in Mississippi and dey walked frum Mississippi to de Nations plantation in Gonzales.

"Marse Jim had nigh a hundred slaves. De quarters was built of logs and de roofs was river bottom boards. Some of de houses was built of logs like de columns on dis house.

"It was a fine, big plantation. De young women slaves wukked in de fields and de ole women slaves made de cloth on de spinnin' wheels and de looms. Den de women would go in de woods and take de bark frum de trees and pursley frum de groun' and mix dem wid copperas and put it all in a big iron pot and boil it. Den dey would strain de water off and dye de cloth. De color was brown and, O Lawd, all de slaves wore de same color clothes. Dey even made our socks on de plantation.

"Ole Missy Hannah was sho good to me. I had to feed de children while dere mudders was in de fields. Missy Hannah would have de cooks fix de grub in a big pan and I would take it to de cullud quarters and feed 'em.

"De plantation was on de Guadalupe River and when dere was no meat de slaves went to de river and killed wild hogs and turkeys and ketched fish. We groun' de co'n for cornbread and made hominy. And, O Lawd, de sugar cane, and what good 'lasses we used to make. De slaves had purty good times and de ole boss was awful good to 'em. We drank well water. In dry times we toted de water frum de river for washin'.

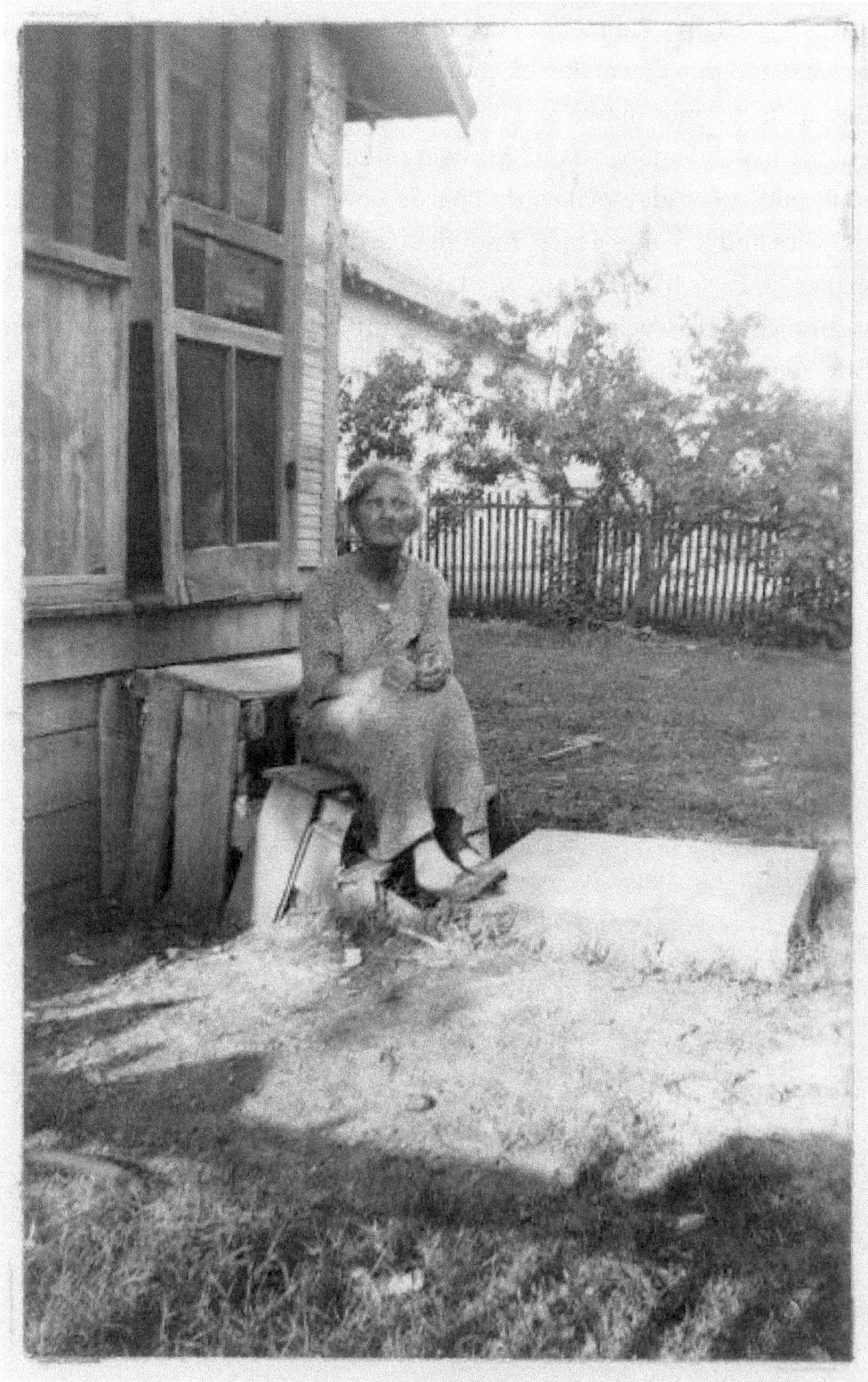

Ellen Polk

"De houses was log cabins. De men slaves built 'em. Dey goes into de woods and chops down de big trees and den dey make 'em square. Did dey have tools? Sho, dey had a ax and a hatchet. Dey splits de trees in two and dat makes de sides of de house and de roun' side is outside. How dey make dem logs tight? Jus' wid mud. Den dey puts de boards over de mud so it cain't fall out. When dey makes de boards dey splits de end of de log and puts de hatchet in de place and it makes a nice, smooth board.

"Dey makes de beds like dat too. Dey takes four sticks and lays poles in de crotches, den dey puts branches crossways. No suh, dey never had no springs. For a mattress dey had hay and straw, sometimes corn shucks or cobs. Dey slep' good, too.

"After de war we lived on de plantation a long time, den we moved to San Marcos, den back to de plantation. I was married on de plantation and moved here 24 years ago. I liked de slavery days de best."

Betty Powers

Betty Powers, 80, was born a slave of Dr. Howard Perry, who owned Betty's family, several hundred other slaves and a large plantation in Harrison Co., Texas. Betty married Boss Powers when she was only thirteen. She now lives at 5237 Fletcher St., Fort Worth, Texas.

"What for you wants dis old nigger's story 'bout de old slavery days? 'Tain't worth anythin'. I's jus' a hard workin' person all my life and raised de fam'ly and done right by 'em as best I knowed. To tell the truf 'bout my age, I don't know 'zactly. I 'members de war time and de surrender time. I's old 'nough to fan flies off de white folks and de tables when surrender come. If you come 'bout five year ago, I could telt you lots more, but I's had de head mis'ry.

"I's born in Harrison County, 'bout twenty-five miles from Marshall. Mass's name am Dr. Howard Perry and next he house am a li'l buildin' for he office. De plantation an awful big one, and miles long, and more'n two hundred slaves was dere. Each cabin have one family and dere am three rows of cabins 'bout half a mile long.

"Mammy and pappy and us twelve chillen lives in one cabin, so mammy has to cook for fourteen people, 'sides her field work. She am up way befo' daylight fixin' breakfast and supper after dark, with de pine knot torch to make de light. She cook on de fireplace in winter and in de yard in summer. All de rations measure out Sunday mornin' and it have to do for de week. It am not 'nough for heavy eaters and we has to be real careful or we goes hongry. We has meat and cornmeal and 'lasses and 'taters and peas and beans and milk. Dem short rations causes plenty trouble, 'cause de niggers has to steal food and it am de whippin' if dey gits cotched. Dey am in a fix if dey can't work for bein' hongry, 'cause it am de whippin' den, sho', so dey has to steal, and most of 'em did and takes de whippin'. Dey has de full stomach, anyway.

"De babies has plenty food, so dey grow up into strong, portly men and women. Dey stays in de nursery whilst dey mammies works in de fields, and has plenty milk with cornbread crumble up in it, and pot-licker, too, and honey and 'lasses on bread.

"De massa and he wife am fine, but de overseer am tough, and he wife, too. Dat woman have no mercy. You see dem long ears I has? Dat's from de pullin' dey gits from her. De field hands works early and late and often all night. Pappy makes de shoes and mammy weaves, and you could hear de bump, bump of dat loom at night, when she done work in de field all day.

"Missy know everything what go on, 'cause she have de spies 'mongst de slaves. She purty good, though. Sometimes de overseer tie de nigger to a log and lash him with de whip. If de lash cut de skin, dey puts salt on it. We ain't 'low to go to church and has 'bout two parties a year, so dere ain't much fun. Lawd, Lawd, most dem slaves too tired to have fun noway. When all dat work am finish, dey's glad to git in de bed and sleep.

"Did we'uns have weddin's? White man, you knows better'n dat. Dem times, cullud folks am jus' put together. De massa say, 'Jim and Nancy, you go live together,' and when dat order give, it better be done. Dey thinks nothin' on de plantation 'bout de feelin's of de women and dere ain't no 'spect for dem. De overseer and white mens took 'vantage of de women like dey wants to. De woman better not make no fuss 'bout sich. If she do, it am de whippin' for her. I sho' thanks de Lawd surrender done come befo' I's old 'nough to have to stand for sich. Yes, sar, surrender saves dis nigger from sich.

"When de war am over, thousands of sojers passes our place. Some camps nearby, and massa doctors dem. When massa call us to say we's free, dere am a yardful of niggers. He give every nigger de age statement and say dey could work on halves or for wages. He 'vises dem to stay till dey git de foothold and larn how to do. Lots stays and lots goes. My folks stays 'bout four years and works on shares. Den pappy buys de piece of land 'bout five miles from dere.

Betty Powers

"De land ain't clear, so we'uns all pitches in and clears it and builds de cabin. Was we'uns proud? There 'twas, our place to do as we pleases, after bein' slaves. Dat sho' am de good feelin'. We works like beavers puttin' de crop in, and my folks stays dere till dey dies. I leaves to git married de next year and I's only thirteen years old, and marries Boss Powers.

"We'uns lives on rent land nearby for six years and has three chillen and den he dies. After two years I marries Henry Ruffins and has three more chillen, and he dies in 1911. I's livin' with two of dem now. I never took de name of Ruffins, 'cause I's dearly love Powers and can't stand to give up he name. Powers done make de will and wrote on de paper, 'To my beloved wife, I gives all I has.' Wasn't dat sweet of him?

"I comes to Fort Worth after Ruffins dies and does housework till I's too old. Now I gits de $12.00 pension every month and dat help me git by."

Tillie R. Powers

Tillie R. Powers was born free in Oklahoma, near the Washita River. Her mother had been kidnapped by a band of raiding Indians, one of whom was her father. Her mother, desiring to prevent her from living among the Indians, wrapped her in a buffalo robe and laid her on the road near the Washita, where she was found by Joseph Powers, an army officer, who took her to his plantation in Edgecombe Co., North Carolina. She lives at 1302 E. 11th St. Fort Worth, Texas.

"I don' 'member my mammy or pappy, and all I knows 'bout my early life was tol' me by Marster Powers. He says him and he wife takin' soldiers back to some fort and dey sees a bundle side de road near de Washita River, wropped in a buffalo robe. He gits off his hoss and picks de bundle up and in dat bundle am de piccaniny, dis nigger. Dat 77 year ago. Dey took me to Edgecombe Co., over in North Car'lina, whar him owns a plantation and 'bout 50 slaves. Dere I's 'dopted.

"Dey raises de cotton and tobaccy and corn and sich. Den dere am hawgs and chickens and sheep, and sich a orchard with peaches and pears and sich. Mos' de work I done in slavery was eat de food, 'cause I's only six year old when de war am over. But I 'members 'bout de plantation.

"De treatment am good and bad. If de nigger gits onruly, him gits a whippin', but de marster's orders is for not to draw de blood like I heered dey do on other places. De food is plenty, 'cept for de shortage cause by de War. When de food gits short, some of de niggers am sent a-hustlin' for game, sich as de turkey and de squirrel, but we'uns allus has plenty cornmeal and 'lasses and fruit.

"Did we'uns see sojers? Lawd-a-massy! Towards de las', jus' 'fore surrender and after, we'uns see dem by thousands, de Yanks and de 'federates, dey's passin' and repassin'. When de War am over, de marster come home and he calls all us cullud folks to de house and him reads a paper and says, 'All yous niggers am free, and you can go whar you wants, but I 'vises yous not to go till yous has a place for work and make de livin'. All de niggers stay at fust, den leave one after 'nother.

Tillie R. Powers

"I jus' de chile and de orphan, so I has to stay and it was bes' for me. Marster pays me when I big enough to work, and gives me $5.00 a month, and I works for him till I's 18 years old. Den de missy die and I leaves. Dat was de break-up of de place. I cries now when I thinks of de missy, 'cause she allus good to me and I feels for her.

"After dat, I works 'round a while and gits married to John Daniels in 1880. Dis nigger was better off in slavery dan with dat nigger. Why, him won't work and whips me if I complains. I stood dat for six year and den I's transported him. Dat in Roberts County. Marster Race Robinson brought dat no good nigger and me, with 'bout 50 other niggers, here to Texas. We 'uns share cropped for him till I transported dat ornery husban'.

"I makes a livin' workin' for white folks till 'bout three years ago and now I gits $15.00 every month from de State to live on, 'cause I has high blood now and I can't work no more."

Allen Price

Allen Price was born in a covered wagon in Fannin Co., Texas, in 1862. His master was John Price. Allen remembers many incidents of pioneer days, and stories of the Civil War told him by the Price family. Allen now lives in Mart, Texas.

"De way I comes to be born in Texas am my pappy and mammy is in de covered wagon, comin' to Texas with dere master, what am John Price, what was a Virginny man. Dey stops in Fannin County awhile and dere I'm born. Dat in 1862, dey tells me.

"De Price and Blair families was first ones to come to Texas. Dey had to use ox teams and ford creeks and rivers and watch for Indians. I done hear dem talk 'bout all dis, 'cause course I can't 'member it. Once de Indians done 'tack dem and dey druv 'em off, and every night near dey hears de howl of de wolves and other wild animals. Some folks went by boat and dey had river boat songs, one like dis:

"I'm drinkin' of rum and chawin' tobaccy,

Hi! Oh! The rollin' river!

I'm drinkin' of rum and chawin' tobaccy,

I'm boun' for the wide Missouri."

"Dese things am handed down to me by de Price family and my granddaddy. De Price family done fight for de Confed'racy all de way down de line of de family, to my own pappy, who went with he master when dey calls for volunteers to stop de blockade of Galveston.

"My master think he gwine 'scape de worst of de war when he come to Texas and dey am livin' peaceable de year I'm born, raisin' cotton. Dey had a gin what my pappy worked in, and makes dey own clothes, too, when de Yankees has de Texas ports blockade so de ships can't git in. When dey blockades Galveston, our old master done take my pappy for bodyguard and volunteers to help. Fin'ly Gen. Magruder takes Galveston from de Yankees with two old cotton steamers what have cotton bales on de decks for breastworks.

"De last battle Master Price and my pappy was in, was de battle of Sabine Pass, and de Yankee general, Banks, done send 'bout five thousand troops on transports with gunboats, to force a landin'. Capt. Dick Dowling had forty-seven men to 'fend dat Pass and my pappy helped build breastworks when dem Yankees firin'. Capt. Dowling done run dem Yankees off and takes de steamer Clinton and 'bout three hundred and fifty prisoners. My pappy told me some de Captain's men didn't have real guns, dey have wood guns, what dey call cam'flage nowadays.

"My pappy helped at de hospital after dat battle, and dey has it in a hotel and makes bandages out of sheets and pillow cases and underwear, and uses de rugs and carpets for quilts.

"I 'member dis song, what dey sing all de time after de war:
"O, I'm a good old Rebel, and dat's jus' what I am,
And for dis land of freedom, I do not give a damn;
I'm glad we fought again 'em, and only wish we'd won,
And I ain't asked no pardon for anything I've done.

"I won't be reconstructed, I'm better dan dey am,
And for a carpetbagger I do not give a damn.
So I'm off to de frontier, soon as I can go--
I'll fix me up a weapon and start for Mexico!

"I can't get my musket and fight dem now no more,
But I'm not goin' to love dem, dat am certain sho'--
I don't want no pardon for what I was or am,
I won't be reconstructed, and I don't give a damn.
"I has mighty little to say 'bout myself. I's only a poor Baptist preacher. De her'tage handed down to me am de proudes' thing I knows. De Prices was brave and no matter what side, dey done fight for dey 'lief in de right."

John Price and wife Mirandy

John Price, nearing 80, was born a slave of Charles Bryan, in Morgan City, Louisiana. The Bryans brought him to Texas about 1861, and he now lives in Liberty. Mirandy, his wife, was also a slave, but has had a paralytic stroke and speaks with such difficulty that she cannot tell the story of her life. Their little home and yard are well cared for.

"I's five year old when de Lincoln war broke up and my papa was name George Bryan in slavery time and he come from St. Louis, what am in Missouri. After freedom de old boss he call up de hands and say, 'Iffen you wants to wear my name you can, but take 'nother one iffen you wants to.' So my daddy he change he name to George Price and dat why my name John Price.

"My old massa name George Bryan and he wife name Felice. Dey buy my papa when he 18 year old boy and dey take him and raise him and put all dey trust in him and he run de place when de old man gone. Dat in Morgan City, in Louisiana on de Berwick side.

"De year I's one year old us come to Texas and settle in Liberty. I wes a-layin' in my mammy's arms and her name Lizette but dey call her Lisbeth. She mos'ly French. I got three sister, Sally Hughes and Liza Jonas and Celina, and two brothers, Pat Whitehouse and Jim Price.

"De white folks have a tol'able fair house one mile down south of Raywood and it were a long, frame house and a pretty good farm. Us quarters was log houses built out of li'l pine poles pile one top de other. Dey have nail up log, country beds and home-made tables and rawhide bottom chairs and benches. Dem chair have de better weight dan de chair today. Iffen you rare back now, de chair gone, but de rawhide stay with you.

"De old massa pretty fair to us all. Iffen my papa whip me I slips out de house and runs to de big house and crawls under de old massa's bed. Sometime he wake up in de middle de night and say, 'Boy,' and I not answer. Den he say 'gain, 'Boy, I know you under dat bed. You done been afoul your papa 'gain,' and he act awful mad. Den he throw he old sojer coat under de bed for to make me a pallet and I sleep dere all night.

"Us chillen have lots of time to play and not much time to work. Us allus ridin' old stick hosses and tie a rope to de stick and call it a martingale. Us make marbles out of clay and dry 'em and play with 'em. De old boss wouldn't 'low us have no knife, for fear us cut each other. Us never sick much dem days, but us have de toothache. Dey take white tree bark what taste like peppermint and stew it up with honey and cure de toothache.

"Us never go to church. Some my wife's people say dey used to have a church in de hollow and dey have runners for to watch for de old boss man and tell 'em de massa comin'.

"Us old massa say Christmas Day am he day to treat and he tell us 'bout Santy Claus. Us taken us socks up to he house and hang dem 'round de big fireplace and den in de mornin' us find candy and cake and fruit and have de big time. New Year Day was old missy time. She fix de big dinner on dat day and nobody have to work.

"When de war is breakin' old massa come by ship to Galveston up de Trinity River to Liberty by boat to try to save he niggers, but it wasn't no use. Us see lots of tents out by Liberty and dey say it sojers. I tag long with de big boys, dey sneaks out de spades and digs holes in de prairie in de knolls. Us plannin' to live in dem holes in de knolls. When dey say de Yankees is comin' I sho' is 'fraid and I hear de cannon say, 'Boom, boom,' from Galveston to Louisiana. De young white missy, she allus sing de song dat go:

"We are a band of brothers, native to de soil,

Fightin' for our liberty with treasure, blood and toil,

And when us rights was threaten', de cry rise far and near,

Hurrah for the Bonnie Blue Flag what bears a single star.

"After freedom my papa move away but de old massa come after him and worry him till he 'most have to come back. When my li'l sister have de whoopin' cough, old massa come down in a hurry and say, 'You gwineter kill dem chillen,' and he puts my sister and brother on de hoss in front of him and takes 'em home and cures 'em hisself. It were years after dat 'fore my papa leave him 'gain.

"Dey driv beefs and have two rivers to cross to git dere, de Sabine and de Neches. Dey 'liver 'em by so many head and iffen dey ain't have 'nough, other mens on de prairie help 'em fill out de number what dey needs. I's rid many a wild hoss in my day and dat's where I make my first money for myself.

John Price and wife Mirandy

"I's workin' in Hyatt when I 'cide to git marry and I marry dis gal, Mirandy, 'bout 52 year ago and us still been together. Us marry in Moss Bluff and Sam Harris, he a cullud man, he de preacher what marry us. I have on pretty fair suit of clothes but one thing I 'member, de gal I marry, she have $5.00 pair of shoes on her feet what I buys for her.

"Us done have five sons and three daughters and I been a pretty 'fluential man 'round Liberty. One time dey a man name Ed Pickett what was runnin' for Clerk of de Court in Liberty County and he come 'round my place 'lectioneering, 'cause he say whatever way I votes, dey votes.

"Did you ever hear a old coon dog? Old coon dog, he got a big, deep voice what go, 'A-woo-o-o, a-woo-o-o.' You can hear him a mile. Well, dat Ed Pickett he say to me, 'John Price, you know what I wants you to do? I wants you put dat other feller up a tree. I wants you put him so fur up a tree he can't even hear dat coon dog beller.' And I does it, 'cause I's pretty 'fluential 'round here."

Reverend Lafayette Price

Reverend Lafayette Price, ancient and venerable minister of a small, dilapidated church on the outskirts of Beaumont, received his education under his old master, a plantation owner of the South. He was born a slave of the Higginbotham family, in Wilcox County, Alabama, but after the death of his original master, he became known as "orphan children property" and went to Louisiana to live with Robert and Jim Carroll, brothers-in-law of Sam Higginbotham. During the Civil War, LaFayette, then about 12 years old (he does not know his exact age) served as water boy for young Robert Carroll at the battle of Mansfield. When the slaves were freed he came to Texas and has been a minister since that time. He lives with his one daughter in a small, ramshackle house near the church and conducts Baptist services each Sunday. LaFayette is small and very dark, and with his crop of almost white hair and his Van Dyke beard, he has facial characteristics much like those of the patriarch who played the part of "De Lawd" in the "Green Pastures" picture. His conversation is that of a devout person, well informed in the Scriptures.

"I had a statement when I was bo'n, but I don' 'member jus' now. When de war fus' start I was water toter for my marster. Well, now den, I wan' to say dat my marster whar I was bo'n in Wilcox County, Alabama, his name was Higginbotham. When Mr. Higginbotham die, his son, Mr. Sam Higginbotham, was my young marster. When he married, he marry in de Carroll family. My father and mother belong to Mr. Higginbotham. Mr. Sam, he move to Louisiana. When he went back to Alabama, he tuk sick wid de cholera and die dere. Mr. Sam, he marry Miss Ca'line Carroll. Later on after Mr. Sam die Miss Ca'line marry Mr. Winn. I become orphan chillen property. Mr. Winn was de overseer. When I was a small boy I had playtime. I allus had good owners. When I get bigger I had some time off after work in de evenin's and on Sundays. Den I want to say I was hired out an' dey claimed dey was goin' to be a war. The north and de south was goin' to split apart. In 1861 war commence and my mistress die. I was den stayin' wid de Carroll family. De Carrolls were brothers of my owner. Mr. Jim and Mr. Robert was soldiers in de war. Mr. Robert was in de infantry and Mr. Jim they took him along to drive. When dey was goin' to Barn Chest (evidently the name of a place) Mr. Robert he say to me, 'Fay, you go back home and tell ma she need not be oneasy 'bout me, 'cause de Yankees is retreatin' to Nachitoches.' So I driv back but I didn' put up de team. When I was tellin' her, it was 'bout three mile over to Mosses Fiel' (Mosses'

Field was the local name for the tract of land on which the battle of Mansfield was fought, in part). When I was tellin' her, a big cannon shot overhead--'Boom'. She jus' shook and say, 'Oh, Fay, git some co'n and throw it to de hogs and go to Chicet.' I got some co'n and start to git out de crib. Dey shot another cannon. She say to me, 'Go back and give de co'n to de pigs.' When I put my feets through de crib do', dey shoot another shot, and I pull my feets back. She tell me to go back and feed de pigs, but I don' know if I ever did git de co'n to de pigs.

"Mr. Carroll say dat at Mansfiel' where dey was shootin' de big guns de ladies was cryin'. He told 'em dey needn' to cry now, when dey was shootin' de big guns dey wasn't killin' men, but when dey hear de little guns shoot, den dey could start cryin', 'cause dat mean dat men was gittin' kill. I dunno if you ever parch popco'n. Dat de way de little guns soun'. He say dat den dey could begin cryin'. Our w'ite people (the Confederates) was comin' from Shreveport to meet de Yankees from Nachitoches, aimin' to go to Shreveport. If anything was a wunnerful consideration it was den. Mr. Robert Carroll was stood up by a big tree there at Mansfiel' and de captain, he said, "Is anybody here dat know de neighborhood?" Here's de ting dey want to know: When de soldiers start out dey didn' want 'em to launch out and git mix up. Dey sent for Mr. Carroll, 'cause he live 'bout a mile away. He was order to stan' by de tree and de captain went by wavin' a sword, and purty soon de captain was kill. Dey kep' on fightin' and after awhile a soldier come by and ax what he doin' there. He said he had orders to stan' dere. De soldier say dat de captain was kill and for him to go and help wid de wounded soldiers. When de big General come from Shreveport and holler, 'Charge,' de Yankees git in de corner of a rail fence. Dey broke right through dat fiel' o' prairie and 60 men git kill dead befo' dey git across. Nex' day, comin' home, I want to tell you de hosses didn' lay on dis side nor on dat side, dey jus' squat down, dey was dead. I think it was a wunnerful consideration to bring up in mem'ry.

"One night right w'ere de battle was fought we had to camp. It was rainin' and sleetin' and snowin! I said, 'What you goin' to do tonight?' Mr. James Carroll said, 'We jus' hafta stan' w'ere we camp. Jus' stack de guns and put out what you call de watchman.' I said, 'Sentinel,' and he said, 'Yes.' Dey had what you call de relief. Dey wasn't in bed, dey was out under a tree in de col'. Ev'ry hour dey'd walk 'em out 'long a runway to walk guard. It was a wunnerful distressin' time. De soldiers had a little song dey sung:
"'Eat when you're hungry,
Drink when you're dry,
Iffen a tree don' kill you,
You'll live 'til you die.'

"Dis was 'cause dey had to stan' under trees and when de Yankees shoot cannon dey'd knock off limbs and tops of trees and them under de trees might git kill from de fallin' branches. Another song was:

"'Hit was on de eighth of April,

Dey all 'member well,

When fifes and drums were beatin'

For us all to march away.'

"In slavery times de slaves went to church wid dere w'ite folks and heard de w'ite preacher. I never knew of cullud baptisms. Dey'd have camp meetin' and when cullud people wanted to jine de church dey'd take 'em in den. I didn' quite git through 'bout de Mansfiel' battle. Dem 60 men dat was kill, dey jus' dig a big hole and put 'em in and threw dirt on 'em. I went back after two or three days and de bodies done swell and crack de groun'. Marster's plantation comin' from Shreveport was on de eas' side of Mosses Fiel'. We was 'bout one and a half or two mile' from Mosses Fiel'. I wasn't acquaint' wid many w'ites 'cause I was wid de Carrolls and dey was allus kind. I heard dey was people dis way and dat, but I don' know 'bout dat. My w'ite folks see dat I was not abused. When news of de surrender come lots of cullud folks seem to be rejoicin' and sing, "I's free, I's free as a frog" 'cause a frog had freedom to git on a log and jump off when he please. Some jus' stayed on wid dere w'ite folks. One time dey say dey sen' all de niggers back to Africa. I say dey never git me. I bin yere, and my w'ite folks bin yere, and yere I goin' to stay. My young marster say he want me for a nigger driver, so he teach me how to read and spell so I could ten' to business. In time of de war Miss Ca'line say de soldiers been dere and take de bes' hoss. Dey sent me off wid Ball, a little hoss. When I come back I meet some soldiers. Dey say dey goin' take de hoss, if dey don' de Yankees come take 'em. I tell 'em dey done got Marster Carroll other hoss, to leave dis one. Dey say, "Git down, I goin' give you a few licks anyhow." I fall down but dey never hit me and dey say, "Maybe dat Mr. Carroll whose hoss we tuk, let dis boy go on wid de hoss." Miss Ca'line say she wish she'd let me take Dandy, dey was de bes' hoss.

"I wan' to tell you one story 'bout de rabbit. De rabbit and de tortus had a race. De tortus git a lot of tortuses and put 'em long de way. Ever now and den a tortus crawl 'long de way, and de rabbit say, "How you now, Br'er Tortus?" And he say, "Slo' and sho', but my legs very short." When dey git tired, de tortus win 'cause he dere, but he never run de race, 'cause he had tortuses strawed out all 'long de way. De tortus had other tortuses help him."

Henry Probasco

Henry Probasco, 79, was born a slave of Andrew McGowen, who owned a plantation and 50 slaves in Walker County, Texas. Henry lived with his family, in Waco, until 1875, when he became a stock hand on Judge Weakly's ranch in Ellis County. In 1902 he came to Fort Worth and worked in packing plants until 1932. Since that time he has supported himself by any little work he could find and now has an $8.00 per month pension. He lives at 2917 Cliff St., Fort Worth, Texas.

"I's born on Massa McGowen's plantation. He name was Andrew McGowen and us lived near Huntsville, down in Walker County. All my folks and grandfolks was dere. Grandpap am carpenter, grandma am nuss for cullud chillen, and pappy and mammy does de shoemakin' and de cookin'.

"In de days I's a boy even de plows was made on de place. De blacksmith do de iron work and de wood work am done by pappy, and de plows am mostly wood. Jus' de point and de shear am iron. My grandpap made de mouldboards out of wood. No, sar, 'twarnt no steel mouldboards den. I's watch grandpap take de hard wood block and with de ax and de drawshave and de plane and saw and rule, him cut and fit de mouldboard to de turnin' plow. De mouldboard las' 'bout one year.

"Now, with de shoes it am dif'rent and dem last more'n twict de time as store shoes. Gosh for 'mighty! We'uns can't wear dem out. De leather am from cattle raise on de place and tan right dere. It am real oak tan, and strong as steel. We'uns grease de shoes with mutton tallow and dat make dem waterproof shoes.

"Cotton am main crop and corn for feed. De corn feed both de critters and de niggers, 'cause de main food for de niggers am de corn and de cornbread and de corn mush. Course, us have other victuals, plenty meat and veg'tables. De hawgs allus run in de woods and find dere own food, sich as nuts and acorns. Dey allus fat and when massa want meat he hitch de mules to de wagon and go to de woods. Dere him catch de hawg with massa's mark on it and fotch it in.

"De quarters am not mansions, dey am log cabins with dirt floors, but good 'nough. Dey am fixed tight for de winter. If you am used to sleepin' in de bunks with straw ticks, it's jus' good as de spring bed. De fust time I sleeps on de spring bed, I's 'wake most all night.

"When surrender come, massa told we'uns dat all us am free folks and he reads from de paper. 'Now,' him say, yous am free and dem what wants to go, let me know. I'll 'range for de pay or to work de land on shares.'

"Some goes but all my folks stays, but in 'bout a year pappy moves to Waco and run a shoe shop. I stays with him till I 17 year old, den I goes to Ellis County and works on de cattle ranch of Judge Weakly. His brand am 111 and him place clost to Files Valley. I's larnt to ride some on de plantation and soon I's de good rider and I likes dat work best.

"We has lots of fun when we goes to town, not much drinkin', like some people says, but its mostest mischievious de boys am. We gits de joke on de preacher once. Him tellin' 'bout harm of drink and one of us say, 'Read from de Bible, Proverbs 31, 6 and 7. Him reads and it am like dis:

'Give de strong drink to dem dat am ready to perish and wine to dem what am heavy of heart.' Dat de last time him talk to us 'bout drink.

"We'uns holds de Kangaroo Court. If we'uns been on de party and someone do something what ain't right, den charges am file 'gainst you. If dem charges file, it's sho' you's found guilty, 'cause de fine am a drink for de bunch. If you don't buy de drink it's a lickin' with a pair of leggin's. If you 'low de hoss to throw you, dat am cause for charges.

"De last round-up I works am at Oak Grove, near Fort Worth and dat 'bout 40 year ago. After dat, I goes to Mulesfoot and works for T.D. Myers for 'bout five year, den I's done a little farmin' on de plains for awhile.

"I'll tell you 'bout my married life. I marries de fust time when I's 24 year old to Bertha Ellers and we'uns live togedder 20 year and sep'rates. We'uns have 11 chillen. Couple year after dat I goes to de cotton patch for de short spell and meets a woman. We'uns right off married and dat hitch lasts till de pickin' season am over. Den, 'bout two year after dat cotton pickin' hitch I marries Mary Little and we'uns lives togedder two year and dat am two year too many. Dat de last of de marriage business.

"Now I jus' fools de time away and I has no one to fuss at me 'bout where I goes and sich. Sich am my joyment now."

Jenny Proctor

Jenny Proctor was born in Alabama in 1850. She was a slave of the Proctor family and began her duties about the house when a very young girl. As soon as she was considered old enough to do field labor she was driven with the other slaves from early morning until late at night. The driver was cruel and administered severe beatings at the slightest provocations. Jenny remained with her owners after the close of the Civil War, not from choice but because they had been kept in such dense ignorance they had no knowledge of how to make their own living. After the death of her master several years later, she and her husband, John Proctor, came to Texas in a mule drawn covered wagon and settled in Leon County near the old town of Buffalo. There they worked as share croppers until the death of her husband. She then came to San Angelo, Texas with her son, with whom she has made her home for many years.

Jenny, who was ill at the time she was interviewed, shook her old white head and said,

"I's hear tell of dem good slave days but I ain't nev'r seen no good times den. My mother's name was Lisa and when I was a very small chile I hear dat driver goin' from cabin to cabin as early as 3 o'clock in de mornin' and when he comes to our cabin he say, 'Lisa, Lisa, git up from dere and git dat breakfast.' My mother, she was cook and I don't recollect nothin' 'bout my father. If I had any brothers and sisters I didn' know it. We had ole ragged huts made out of poles and some of de cracks chinked up wid mud and moss and some of dem wasn't. We didn' have no good beds, jes' scaffolds nailed up to de wall out of poles and de ole ragged beddin' throwed on dem. Dat sho' was hard sleepin' but even dat feel good to our weary bones after dem long hard days work in de field. I 'tended to de chillun when I was a little gal and tried to clean de house jes' like ole miss tells me to. Den soon as I was 10 years ole, ole marster, he say, 'Git dis yere nigger to dat cotton patch.' I recollects once when I was tryin' to clean de house like ole miss tell me, I finds a biscuit and I's so hungry I et it, 'cause we nev'r see sich a thing as a biscuit only some times on Sunday mornin'. We jes' have co'n braid and syrup and some times fat bacon, but when I et dat biscuit and she comes in and say, 'Whar dat biscuit?'

"I say, 'Miss, I et it 'cause I's so hungry.' Den she grab dat broom and start to beatin' me over de head wid it and callin' me low down nigger and I guess I jes' clean lost my head 'cause I know'd better den to fight her if I knowed anything 'tall, but I start to fight her and de driver, he comes in and he grabs me and starts beatin' me wid dat cat-o'-nine-tails, and he beats me 'til I fall to de floor nearly dead. He cut my back all to pieces, den dey rubs salt in de cuts for mo' punishment. Lawd, Lawd, honey! Dem was awful days. When ole marster come to de house he say, 'What you beat dat nigger like dat for?' And de driver tells him why, and he say, 'She can't work now for a week, she pay for several biscuits in dat time.' He sho' was mad and he tell ole miss she start de whole mess. I still got dem scars on my ole back right now, jes' like my grandmother have when she die and I's a-carryin' mine right on to de grave jes' like she did.

[1]   A big leather whip, branching into nine tails.

"Our marster, he wouldn' 'low us to go fishing, he say dat too easy on a nigger and wouldn' 'low us to hunt none either, but some time we slips off at night and ketch 'possums and when ole marster smells dem 'possums cookin' way in de night he wraps up in a white sheet and gits in de chimney corner and scratch on de wall and when de man in de cabin goes to de door and say, 'Who's dat?' He say, 'It's me, what's ye cookin' in dere?' and de man say, 'I's cookin' 'possum.' He say, 'Cook him and bring me de hind quarters and you and de wife and de chillun eat de rest.' We nev'r had no chance ter git any rabbits 'cept when we was a-clearin' and grubbin' de new grounds, den we ketch some rabbits and if dey looks good to de white folks dey takes dem and if dey no good de niggers git dem. We nev'r had no gardens. Some times de slaves git vegetables from de white folks' garden and sometimes dey didn'.

"Money? Umph um! We nev'r seen no money. Guess we'd a bought sumpin' to eat wid it if we ev'r seen any. Fact is, we wouldn' a knowed hardly how to bought anything, 'cause we didn' know nothin' 'bout goin' to town.

"Dey spinned de cloth what our clothes was made of and we had straight dresses or slips made of lowel. Sometimes dey dye 'em wid sumac berries or sweet gum bark and sometimes dey didn'. On Sunday dey make all de chillun change, and what we wears 'til we gits our clothes washed was gunny sacks wid holes cut for our head and arms. We didn' have no shoes 'ceptin' some home made moccasins and we didn' have dem 'til we was big chillun. De little chillun dey goes naked 'til dey was big enough to work. Dey was soon big enough though, 'cordin' to our marster. We had red flannel for winter under clothes. Ole miss she say a sick nigger cost more den de flannel.

"Weddin's? Ugh um! We jes' steps over de broom and we's married. Ha! Ha! Ha!

"Ole marster he had a good house. De logs was all hewed off smooth like and de cracks all fixed wid nice chinkin', plum 'spectable lookin' even to de plank floors, dat was sumpin'. He didn' have no big plantation but he keeps 'bout 300 slaves in dem little huts wid dirt floors. I thinks he calls it four farms what he had.

"Sometimes he would sell some of de slaves off of dat big auction block to de highest bidder when he could git enough fer one.

"When he go to sell a slave he feed dat one good for a few days, den when he goes to put 'em up on de auction block he takes a meat skin and greases all 'round dat nigger's mouth and makes 'em look like dey been eatin' plenty meat and sich like and was good and strong and able to work. Sometimes he sell de babes from de breas' and den again he sell de mothers from de babes and de husbands and de wives, and so on. He wouldn' let 'em holler much when de folks be sold away. He say, 'I have you whooped if you don't hush.' Dey sho' loved dere six chillun though. Dey wouldn' want no body buyin' dem.

"We might a done very well if de ole driver hadn' been so mean, but de least little thing we do he beat us for it, and put big chains 'round our ankles and make us work wid dem on 'til de blood be cut out all around our ankles. Some of de marsters have what dey call stockades and puts dere heads and feet and arms through holes in a big board out in de hot sun, but our old driver he had a bull pen, dats only thing like a jail he had. When a slave do anything he didn' like he takes 'em in dat bull pen and chains 'em down, face up to de sun and leaves 'em dere 'til dey nearly dies.

"None of us was 'lowed to see a book or try to learn. Dey say we git smarter den dey was if we learn anything, but we slips around and gits hold of dat Webster's old blue back speller and we hides it 'til way in de night and den we lights a little pine torch[2], and studies dat spellin' book. We learn it too. I can read some now and write a little too.

[2]   Several long splinters of rich pine, of a lasting quality and making a bright light.

"Dey wasn't no church for de slaves but we goes to de white folks' arbor on Sunday evenin' and a white man he gits up dere to preach to de niggers. He say, 'Now I takes my text, which is, nigger obey your marster and your mistress, 'cause what you git from dem here in dis world am all you ev'r goin' to git, 'cause you jes' like de hogs and de other animals, when you dies you ain't no more, after you been throwed in dat hole.' I guess we believed dat for a while 'cause we didn' have no way findin' out different. We didn' see no Bibles.

"Sometimes a slave would run away and jes' live wild in de woods but most times dey ketch'em and beats 'em, den chains 'em down in de sun 'til dey nearly die. De only way any slaves on our farm ev'r goes anywhere was when de boss sends him to carry some news to another plantation or when we slips off way in de night. Sometimes after all de work was done a bunch would have it made up to slip out down to de creek and dance. We sho' have fun when we do dat, most times on Sat'day night.

"All de Christmas we had was ole marster would kill a hog and give us a piece of pork. We thought dat was sumpin' and de way Christmas lasted was 'cordin' to de big sweet gum back log what de slaves would cut and put in de fireplace. When dat burned out, de Christmas was over. So you know we all keeps a lookin' de whole year 'round for de biggest sweet gum we could find. When we jes' couldn' find de sweet gum we git oak, but it wouldn' last long enough, 'bout three days on average, when we didn' have to work. Ole marster he sho' pile on dem pine knots, gittin' dat Christmas over so we could git back to work.

"We had a few little games we play, like Peep Squirrel Peep, You Can't Catch Me, and sich like. We didn' know nothin' 'bout no New Year's Day or holidays 'cept Christmas.

"We had some co'n shuckin's sometimes but de white folks gits de fun and de nigger gits de work. We didn' have no kind of cotton pickin's 'cept jes' pick our own cotton. I's can hear dem darkies now, goin' to de cotton patch way 'fore day a singin':

"'Peggy, does you love me now?'

"One ole man he sing:

"'Sat'day night and Sunday too
Young gals on my mind,
Monday mornin' way 'fore day
Ole marster got me gwine.

Chorus:

Peggy, does you love me now?'
"Den he whoops a sort of nigger holler, what nobody can do jes' like dem ole time darkies, den on he goes,
"'Possum up a 'simmon tree,
Rabbit on de ground
Lawd, Lawd, 'possum,
Shake dem 'simmons down.
Peggy, does you love me now?
Holler
Rabbit up a gum stump
'Possum up a holler
Git him out little boy
And I gives you half a dollar.
Peggy, does you love me now?'

Jenny Proctor

"We didn' have much lookin' after when we git sick. We had to take de worst stuff in de world fer medicine, jes' so it was cheap. Dat ole blue mass and bitter apple would keep us out all night. Sometimes he have de doctor when he thinks we goin' to die, 'cause he say he ain't got any one to lose, den dat calomel what dat doctor would give us would purty nigh kill us. Den dey keeps all kinds of lead bullets and asafoetida balls 'round our necks and some carried a rabbit foot wid dem all de time to keep off evil of any kind.

"Lawd, Lawd, honey! It seems impossible dat any of us ev'r lived to see dat day of freedom, but thank God we did.

"When ole marster comes down in de cotton patch to tells us 'bout bein' free, he say, 'I hates to tell you but I knows I's got to, you is free, jes' as free as me or anybody else what's white.' We didn' hardly know what he means. We jes' sort of huddle 'round together like scared rabbits, but after we knowed what he mean, didn' many of us go, 'cause we didn' know where to of went. Ole marster he say he give us de woods land and half of what we make on it, and we could clear it and work it or starve. Well, we didn' know hardly what to do 'cause he jes' gives us some ole dull hoes an' axes to work with but we all went to work and as we cut down de trees and de poles he tells us to build de fence 'round de field and we did, and when we plants de co'n and de cotton we jes' plant all de fence corners full too, and I never seen so much stuff grow in all my born days, several ears of co'n to de stalk and dem big cotton stalks was a layin' over on de ground. Some of de ole slaves dey say dey believe de Lawd knew sumpin' 'bout niggers after all. He lets us put co'n in his crib and den we builds cribs and didn' take long 'fore we could buy some hosses and some mules and some good hogs. Dem mangy hogs what our marster give us de first year was plum good hogs after we grease dem and scrub dem wid lye soap. He jes' give us de ones he thought was sho' to die but we was a gittin' goin' now and 'fore long we was a buildin' better houses and feelin' kind of happy like. After ole marster dies we keeps hearin' talk of Texas and me an' my ole man, I's done been married several years den and had one little boy, well we gits in our covered wagon wid our little mules hitched to it and we comes to Texas. We worked as share croppers around Buffalo, Texas 'til my ole man he died. My boy was nearly grown den so he wants to come to San Angelo and work, so here we is. He done been married long time now and got six chillun. Some of dem work at hotels, and cafes and fillin' stations and in homes."

A.C. Pruitt

A.C. Pruitt was born about 1861, a slave of the Magill family, in St. Martinville, La. He lives in a settlement of Negroes, on the road leading from Monroe City to Anahuac, in a shanty made of flattened tin cans, odd pieces of corrugated iron and scrap lumber, held together with rope, nails and tar paper. Pruitt migrated from Beaumont to Monroe City when the oil boom came and ekes out an existence doing odd jobs in the fields. He is a small, muscular man, dressed in faded work clothes and heavy brogans, laced with string.

"I really does live in Beaumont, but when dey start dat talk 'bout makin' sich good money in de oil fields I done move out here to git some of dat. It ain't work so good, though, and I been tearin' down part my house dis week and plannin' to move back.

"I ain't 'lect much 'bout slavery time, 'cause I jes' too li'l but I can tell some things my mama and grannma done told me.

"I's born in St. Martinville, over in Louisiana. I done go back to de old plantation onct but it start to change den. Dave Magill he was de old massa and Miss Frances de missy. My mama name Rachel Smith and she born and raise right dere, and my daddy I ain't never seed, but mama say he name Bruford Pruitt. Dey brudders and sisters but only one livin' and dat Clementine James in Beaumont.

"Jes' 'fore freedom us done move to Snowball, Texas, what was somewheres clost to Cold Springs. Dey told us dey tryin' keep us slaves 'way from de Yankees. Dey everywhere, jes' like dem li'l black ants what gits in de sugar, only dey blue. I's jes' de li'l chile den, runnin' 'round in my split shirt tail. Dem was sho' fancy shirt tails dey make us wore in dem days. Dey make 'em on de loom, jes' in two pieces, with a hole to put de head through and 'nother hole at de bottom to put de legs through. Den dey split 'em up de side, so's us could run and play without dem tyin' us 'round de knees and throw us down. Even at dat, dey sho' wasn't no good to do no tree climbin', less'n you pull dem mos' up over you head.

"Us chillen run down to de rail gate when us see dus' clouds comin' and watch de sojers ridin' and marchin' by. Dey ain't never do no fightin' 'round us, but dey's gunboats down de bayous a ways and us could hear de big guns from de other fights. Us li'l niggers sho' like to wave to dem sojers, and when de men on hosses go by, dey seem like dey more enjoyin' deyselves dan de others.

"I have de old gramma what come from Virginny. Her name Mandy Brown. Dey 'low her hire her own time out. She wasn't freeborn but dey give her dat much freedom. She could go git her a job anywhere jes' as long as she brung de old missy half what she done make. Iffen she make $5.00, she give Miss Frances $2.50 and like dat.

"De old massa he plumb good to he slaves. He have a good many but I ain't knowed of but one dem mens what he ever whip. He have a church right on de place and cullud preachers. Dey old Peter Green and every evenin' us chillen have to go to he cabin and he teach us prayers. He teach us to count, too. He de shoemaker on de plantation.

"My mama done told me 'bout de dances dey have in de quarters. Dey take de big sugar hogshead and stretch rawhide over de top. Den de man straddle de barrel and beat on de top for de drum. Dat de onlies' music dey have.

"Us allus have good things to eat, cabbage greens and cornbread and bacon. Jes' good, plain food. Dey have a sugarhouse and a old man call de sugar boiler. He give us de cane juice out de kittles and 'low us tote off lots dem cane jints to eat. Dat in June.

"De field hands stay up in de big barn and shuck corn on rainy days. Dey shuck corn and sing. Us chillen keep de yard clean and tie weeds together to make brooms for de sweepin'. Us sep'rate de seed from de cotton and a old woman do de cardin'. Dey have 'nother old woman what do nothin' on de scene but weave on de loom.

"One old, old lady what am mos' too old to git 'round, she take care de chillen and cook dere food sep'rate. She take big, black iron washpots and cook dem plumb full of victuals. Come five in de evenin' us have de bigges' meal, dat sho' seem long time 'cause dey ain't feed us but two meal a day, not countin' de eatin' us do durin' de day.

"After freedom come us leave Snowball and go back to Louisiana. Old massa ain't give us nothin'. I marry purty soon. I never go to school but one month in my life and dat in New Iberia. I can sign my name and read it, but dat all.

"I works fust for Mr. William Weeks as de yardboy and he pay me $7.00 de month. De fust money I gits I's so glad I runned and take it to my mama. I have de step-pa and he nearly die of de yellow fever. I's hardly able wait till I's 21 and can vote. Dat my idea of somethin', mos' as good as de fust time I wears pants.

"I tries farmin awhile but dat ain't suit me so good. Den I gits me de job firin' a steamboat on de Miss'sip River, de steamer Mattie. She go from New Orleans through Morgan City. I fire in de sawmills, too.

"My fust wife name Liny and us marry and live together 43 year and den she die. In 1932 I marry a gal call Zellee what live in Beaumont and she still dere. I ain't never have no chile in dis world.

"I larns all dese things 'bout slavery from my mama and gramma, 'cause I allus ask questions and dey talks to me lots. Dat's 'cause dey's nobody but me and I allus under dey feets."

Harre Quarls

Harre Quarls, 96, was born in Flardice, Missouri, a slave of John W. Quarls, who sold him to Charley Guniot. The latter owner moved to Texas, where Harre lived at the time of emancipation. Harre now lives in Madisonville, Texas. His memory is very poor, but he managed to recall a few incidents of early days.

"Massa Quarls he live in Missouri. Place call Flardice. He done give me to he son, Ben, and he sold me to Massa Charley Guniot. Massa Charley come to Texas but I don't know when. It's befo' de freedom war, dat all I knows.

"My daddy name Dan and mammy Hannah. She was blind. I 'member us have small room in back of dere house, with de bed make from poles and cowhide or deerhide. Our massa good to us.

"I must be purty big when us come to Texas, 'cause I plows and is stockman back in Missouri. I don't know 'xactly how old I is, but it am prob'bly 'bout 96. I think dat 'bout right.

"Sir, us got one day a week and Christmas Day, was all de holiday us ever heered of, and us couldn't go anywhere 'cept us have pass from our massa to 'nother. If us slips off dem patterrollers gits us. Patterroller hits 39 licks with de rawhide with de nine tails. Patterroller gits 50 cents for hittin' us 39 licks. Captain, here am de words to de patterroller song:

"'Run, nigger, run, patterroller cotch you,
How kin I run, he got me in de woods
And all through de pasture?
White man run, but nigger run faster.'

"Sir, us have everything to eat what's good, but here in Texas everybody eat beef and bread and it am cooked in oven in de fireplace and in washpot out in de open. Sir, de great day am when massa brung in de great, fat coon and possum.

"Captain, us has no weddin' dem days 'mong de slaves. I'd ask massa could I have a gal, if she 'long to 'nother massa, and she ask her massa could I come see her. If dey says yes, I goes see her once de week with pass. Boss, say, I had three wives. When I's sot free dey wouldn't let me live with but one. Captain, that ain't right, 'cause I wants all three.

"My missus larned me readin' and writin'. After freedom I taught de first nigger school. Dat in Madison and Leon Counties. I's de only nigger what can read and write in two settlements. They was thousands couldn't read and write.

"I 'lieve it's 1861 when us come to Texas. Us camps at Neasho in Arkansas and then come through the Indian Nation. Massa was purty good. He treated us jus' 'bout like you would a good mule.

"Us wore horseshoes and rabbit feet for good luck. Then us have de hoodoism to keep massa from bein' mean. Us git de stick and notch so many notches on it and slip up to massa's front steps, without him seein' us, and put this stick under his doorsteps. Every night us go back to de stick and drive it down one notch. By time de last notch down in de ground, it make massa good to us. Dat called hoodoism.

"Massa tells us we's free on June 'teenth. I leaves. I made a fiddle out of a gourd 'fore freedom and larns to play it. I played for dances after I's free.

"I marries Emily Unions and us have de home weddin' but not any preacher. Us jus' 'greed live together as man and wife and that all they was to it. Us have one gal and one boy.

"Emily leaves and I marries Lucindy Williams. Preacher marries us. Us have three boys and two gals. Dey all farms' now. I has some sixty odd grand and great grandchillen.

"Say, boss, I wants to sing you 'nother song 'fore you goes:
"Walkin' in de parlor,
Lightnin' is a yaller gal.
She live up in de clouds.

"Thunder he is black man,
He can holler loud,
When he kisses lightnin'.

"She dart up in wonder,
He jump up and grate de clouds;
That what make it thunder."

Eda Rains

Aunt Eda Rains, 94, was born a slave in Little Rock, Arkansas, in 1853. In 1860 Eda, her brothers and mother, were bought by a Mr. Carter and brought to Texas. She now lives in Douglasville, Texas.

"I don't 'member my first marster, 'cause my mammy and Jim and John who was my brothers, and me was sold when I was seven and brought to Douglass, in Texas, to hire out. Befo' we lef' Little Rock, whar I was born, we was vaccinated for smallpox. We came through in a wagon to Texas and camped out at night and we slep' on the groun'.

"When I's hired out to the Tomlins at Douglass I sho' got lonesome for I's jus' a little girl, you know, and wanted to see my mother. They put me to work parchin' coffee and my arm was still sore, and I'd pa'ch and cry, and pa'ch and cry. Finally Missus Tomlin say, 'You can quit now.' She looked at my arm and then put me to tendin' chillen. I was fannin' the baby with a turkey wing fan and I fell to sleep and when the missus saw me she snatched the fan and struck me in the face with it. This scar on my forehead is from that quill stuck in my head.

"I slep' on a pallet in the missus' room and she bought me some clothes. She had nine chillen, two boys and seven girls. But after awhile she sol' me to Marster Roack, and he bought my mother and my brothers, so we was togedder again. We had our own cabin and two beds. Every day at four they called us to the big house and give us milk and mush. The white chillen had to eat it, too. It was one of marster's ideas and he said he's raised that-away.

"Now, I mus' tell you all 'bout Christmas. Our bigges' time was at Christmas. Marster'd give us maybe fo'-bits to spend as we wanted and maybe we'd buy a string of beads or some sech notion. On Christmas Eve we played games, 'Young Gal Loves Candy,' or 'Hide and Whoop.' Didn' know nothin' 'bout Santa Claus, never was larned that. But we allus knowed what we'd git on Christmas mornin'. Old Marster allus call us togedder and give us new clothes, shoes too. He allus wen' to town on the Eve and brung back our things in a cotton sack. That ole sack'd be crammed full of things and we knewed it was clothes and shoes, 'cause Marster didn' 'lieve in no foolishness. We got one pair shoes a year, at Christmas. Most times they was red and I'd allus paint mine black. I's one nigger didn' like red. I'd skim grease off dishwater, mix it with soot from the chimney and paint my shoes. In winter we wore woolen clothes and got 'em at Christmas, too.

"We was woke up in the mornin' by blowing of the conk. It was a big shell. It called us to dinner and if anything happened 'special, the conk allus blew.

Eda Rains

"I seed run-away slaves and marster kep' any he caught in a room, and he chained 'em till he coul' reach their marsters.

"We didn' get larned to read and write but they took care of us iffen we was sick, and we made medicine outta black willow and outta black snake root and boneset. It broke fevers on us, but, Lawsy, it was a dose.

"After freedom they tol' us we could go or stay. I stayed a while but I married Claiborne Rains and lived at Jacksonville. We had ten chillen. The Lawd's been right good to me, even if I'm blind. Nearly all my ole white folks and my chillen has gone to Judgment, but I know the Lawd won't leave me here too long 'fore I 'jines em."

Millie Randall

Millie Randall, was born in Mississippi, but spent most of her slavery days on the Dan McMillan farm, near Big Cane, Louisiana. She is about 80 years old, though her estimate of her actual age is vague. She now lives in Beaumont, Texas.

"I was jes' 'bout six year old when peace was 'clared and I done been born in Mississippi, but us move to Bayou Jacques, tother side of Big Cane, in Louisiana. I mus' be purty old now.

"My name' Millie Randall and my mammy, she call' Rose, but I don't know nothin' 'bout my paw. My old massa name' Dan McMillan and he wife she name' Laura. It were a old wood country where my white folks was and us live way out. Dey raise de corn and de cotton and when dey wasn't workin' in de field, dey diggin' out stumps and movin' logs and clearin' up new ground. Dey have lots of goats and sheep, too, and raises dey own rice.

"Dey give us cullud folks de ration in a sack right reg'lar. It have jes' plain food in it, but plenty for everybody.

"Missy have de big plank house and us have de little log house. Us have jes' old plank beds and no furniture. Us clothes make out good, strong cloth, but dey was plain make.

"All us white folks was mean, I tells you de truf. Yes, Lawd, I seed dem beat and almost kilt on us own place. What dey beat dem for? 'Cause dey couldn't he'p demselves, I guess. De white folks have de niggers like dey want dem and dey treat dem bad. It were de old, bully, mean overseers what was doin' de beatin' up with de niggers and I guess dey would have kilt me, but I's too little to beat much.

"I heered 'bout dem Yankees drivin' dey hosses in de white folks' house and makin' dem let dem eat offen de table. Another time, dey come to de plantation and all de niggers locked in de barn. Dose soldiers go in de house and find de white boss man hidin' in 'tween de mattresses and dey stick swords through de mattress and kilt him.

Millie Randall

"Some de white folks hides dey silver and other things that worth lots of money and hang dem down in de well, so de Yankees not find dem. But dey find dem anyway. Dey breaks open a store what was lock up and told de niggers to git all dey wants. De women ketches up de bottom of dey skirt round de waist and fill dem up with everything dey wants.

"After freedom old massa not 'low my mammy have us chillen. He takes me and my brother, Benny, in de wagon and druv us round and round so dey couldn't find us. My mammy has to git de Jestice of de Peace to go make him turn us a-loose. He brung us to our mammy and was we glad to see her.

"I don't 'member 'xactly when I git marry. It was at Big Cane and when I git marry I jes' git marry, dat's all. Dey was three chillen but dey all dead now and so my husban'."

Laura Redmoun

Laura Redmoun was born about 1855, a slave of the Robertson family, in Jonestown (now absorbed by Memphis) Tennessee. Laura is a quaint, rotund figure of a woman, a living picture of a comic opera mammy. She lives at 3809 Mayo St., Dallas, Texas.

"The funny thing 'bout me is, I's a present to the white folks, right off. They's lookin' for my mammy to have a baby and, Gawd bless, I's borned twins, a boy and a girl. When I's six months old, Miss Gusta, my old missy's daughter, marries Mr. Scruggs, and I's give to her for a weddin' present.

"Miss Gusta am proud of me and I slep' right on the foot of her bed. We lived at 144 Third Exchange Street in Memphis. She didn't have but two slaves, me and Lucy, the cook. Law, I didn't know I was no slave. I thunk I's white and plumb indiff'ent from the niggers. I's right s'prised when I finds out I's nigger, jus' like the other black faces!

"I had good times and jes' played round and got in devilment. Sometimes Mr. Scruggs say, 'I's gwine whip dat brat,' but Miss Gusta allus say, 'No you ain't gwine lay you hands on her and iffen you does I'm gwine quit you.' Miss Gusta was indiff'ent to Mr. Scruggs in quality. He fooled her to marry him, lettin' on he got a lot of things he ain't.

"I seen sojers all toggered up in uniforms and marchin' and wavin'. Plenty times they waves at me, but I didn't know what it's all 'bout.

"Miss Gusta allus took me to church and most times I went to sleep by her feet. But when I's 'bout eight the Lawd gits to workin' right inside me and I perks up and listens. Purty soon the glory of Gawd 'scended right down on me and I didn't know nothin' else. I run away up into the ridges and crosses a creek on a foot log. I stays up 'round them caves in tall cane and grass where panthers and bears is for three days 'fore they finds me. They done hear me praisin' Gawd and shoutin', 'I got Jesus.' When they finds me I done slap the sides out my dress, jes' slappin' my hands down and praisin' the Lawd. That was a good dress, too. I heared tell of some niggers wearin' cotton but not me--I weared percale.

"They done take me home and Miss Gusta say, 'You ain't in no fittin' condition to jine a church right now. You got to calm down 'siderable first.' But when I's nine year old she takes me to the Trevesant St. Baptist church and lets me jine and I's baptised in the Mississippi river right there at Memphis.

"'Bout that time the Fed'rals come into Memphis and scared the daylights out of folks. Miss Gusta calls me and wrops my hair in front and puts her jewelry in under the plaits and pulls them back and pins them down so you couldn't see nothin'. She got silverware and give it to me and I run in the garden and buries it. I hid it plenty good, 'cause we like to never found it after the Fed'rals was gone. They come right up to our house and Mr. Scruggs run out the back door and tried to leap the rail fence in the backyard. He cotched the seat of his pants on the top rail and jes' hung there a-danglin' till the Fed'rals pulls him down. He hurt his leg and it was a bad place for a long time. When I seed him hangin' there I cut a dido and kep' screamin', 'Miss Gusta, he's a-dyin',' and them Fed'rals got plumb tickled at me.

"They went in the smokehouse and got all the sugar and rice and strowed it up and down the streets and not carin' at all that victuals was scarcer than hen's teeth in them parts!

"Then Miss Gusta done tell me I wasn't no slave no more, but, shucks, that don't mean nothin' to me, 'cause I ain't never knowed I was one.

"In them times the Ku Klux got to skullduggerin' round and done take Mr. Scruggs and give him a whippin' but I never heared what it had to do about. He don't like them none, noways, and shets hisself up in the house. He a curious kind of man, it 'pear to me, iffen I's to tell the plain out truth. I don't think he was much but kind of trashy.

"When I's seventeen Miss Gusta sickened and suffered in her bed in terrible fashion. She begs the doctors to tell her if she's a-dyin' so she could clear up business 'fore she passed away. She took three days and fixed things up and told me she didn't want to leave me friendless and lone. She wanted me to git married. I had a man I thunk I'd think well of marryin' and Miss Gusta give me away on her bed at the weddin' in her room. She told my husband not to cuff me none, 'cause I never been 'bused in my life, and to this day I ain't never been hit a lick in my life.

Laura Redmoun

"My first baby was born the year of the big yellow fever in New Orleans. I had six chillen but they all died when they's little from creepin' spasms. I advertises round in the papers and finds my mammy and she come and lived with me. She's in a pitiful shape. 'Fore the ceasin' of war her master done sold her and the man what bought her wasn't so light on his niggers. She said he made her wear breeches and tote big, heavy logs and plow with oxes. One of the men knocked her on back of the head with a club and from that day she allus shook her head from side to side all the time, like she couldn't git her mind straight. She told me my paw fell off a bluff in Memphis and stuck a sharp rock right through his head. They wrapped him in a blanket and buried him. That's all I ever knowed 'bout him.

"My husband was a good man and a good worker. We farmed and I worked for white folks. We took a notion to come to Texas and I been in these parts ever since.

"I don't have no complaint to make. I seen some hard times, but I's able to do a little work and keep goin'. They is so many mean folks in the world and so many good ones, and I'm mighty proud to say my white folks was good ones."

Elsie Reece

Elsie Reece, 90, was born a slave of John Mueldrew, in Grimes County, Texas. Elsie came to Fort Worth in 1926 to live with her only remaining child, Mrs. Luffin Baker, who supports Elsie with the aid of her $7.00 monthly old age pension.

"I's borned in Grimes County, ninety years ago. Dat am long time, child. It am heap of change since den. We couldn't see dem airplanes flyin' in de air and hear folks sing and talk a thousand miles away. When I's de young'un de fartheres' you could hear anybody am 'bout a quarter mile and den dey has to holler like a stuck hawg.

"My massa's name am John Mueldrew and he have a small plantation near Navasota, and 'bout twenty cullud folks, mos' of 'em 'lated to each other. There was seven chillen in mammy's family and I's de baby. Pappy dies when I's a year old, so I don't 'member him.

"Dey larnt me to weave cloth and sew, and my brudder am de shoemaker. My mammy tend de cows and Uncle John am de carpenter. De Lawd bless us with de good massa. Massa John die befo' de war and Missie Mary marries Massa Mike Hendricks, and he good, too. But him die and young Massa Jim Mueldrow take charge, and him jus' as kind as he pappy.

"Nother thing am change a heap. Dat buyin' all us wears and eats. Gosh 'mighty, when I's de gall, it am awful li'l us buys. Us raise nearly all to eat and wear, and has good home-raised meat and all de milk and butter us wants, and fruit and 'lasses and eggs and tea and coffee onct a week. Now I has to live on $7.00 a month and what place am I bes' off? Sho', on de massa's place.

"We'uns has Sundays off and goes to church. Old man Buffington preaches to us after dinner. Dere am allus de party on Saturday night on our place or some other place nearby. We gits de pass and it say what time to be home. It de rule, twelve o'clock. We dances de quadrille and sings and sich. De music am fiddles.

"But de big time and de happy time for all us cullud folks am Christmas. De white folks has de tree in de big house and somethin' for all us. When Missie Mary holler, 'Santa Claus 'bout due,' us all gathers at de door and purty soon Santa 'pears with de red coat and long, white whiskers, in de room all lit with candles. He gives us each de sack of candy and a pair of shoes from de store. Massa never calls for work from Christmas to New Year's, 'cept chores. Dat whole week am for cel'bration. So you sees how good massa am.

"Young Massa Jim and Sam jines de army and I helps make dere army clothes. I's 'bout fourteen den. Lots of young men goes and lots never comes back. Sam gits his right leg shot off and dies after he come home, but Jim lives. Den surrender come and Massa Jim read de long paper. He say, 'I 'splain to yous. It de order from de gov'ment what make it 'gainst de law to keep yous slaves.' You should seed dem cullud folks. Dey jus' plumb shock. Dere faces long as dere arm, and so pester dey don't know what to say or do.

"Massa never say 'nother word and walks away. De cullud folks say, 'Where we'uns gwine live? What we'uns gwine do?' Dey frets all night. Nex' mornin' massa say, 'What you'uns gwine do?' Uncle John say, 'When does we have to go?' Den massa laughs hearty and say dey can stay for wages or work on halves.

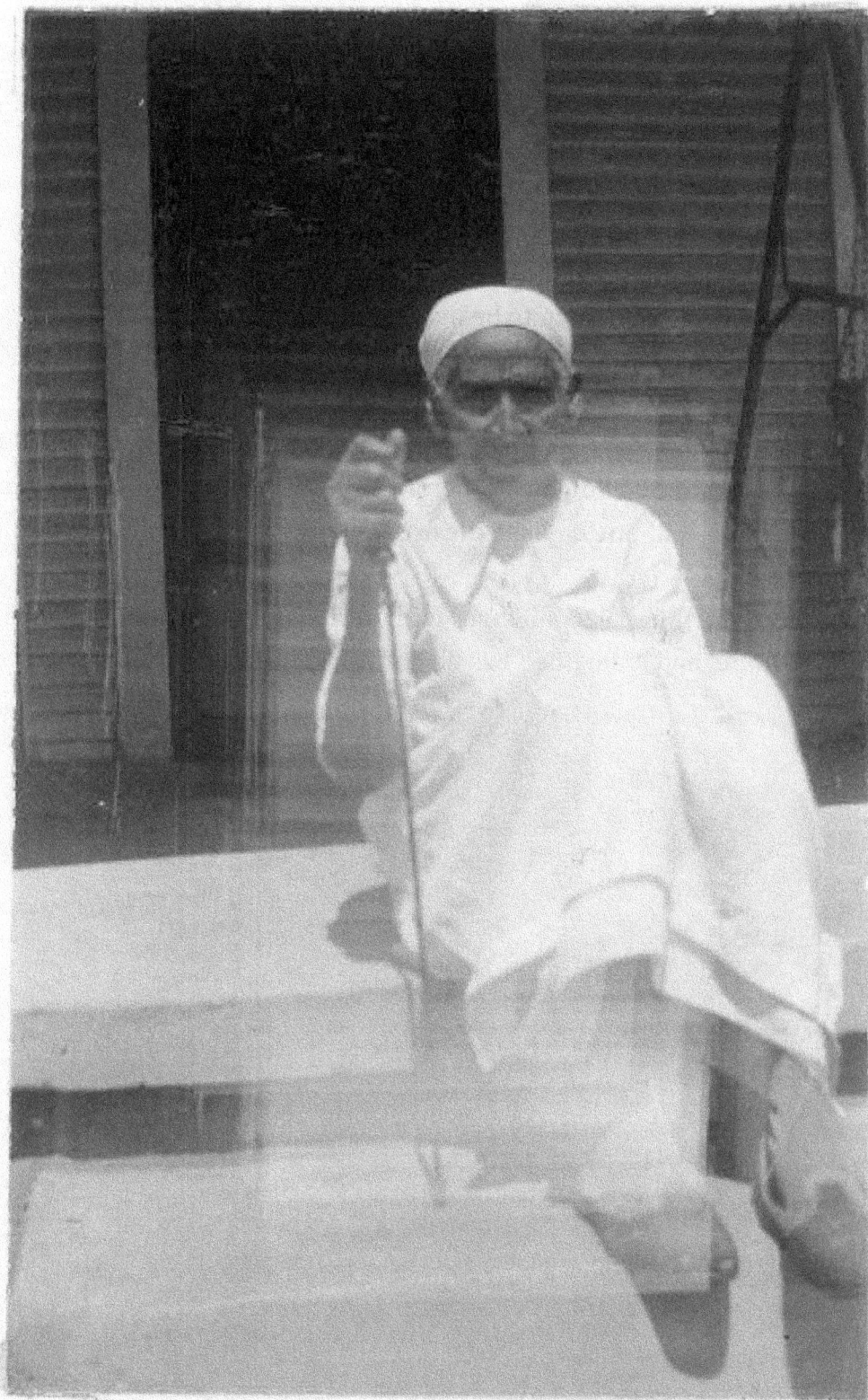

Elsie Reece

"Well, sir, dere a bunch of happy cullud folks after dey larnt dey could stay and work, and my folks stays nearly two years after 'mancipation. Den us all move to Navasota and hires out as cooks. I cooks till I's eighteen and den marries John Love. He am de carpenter and right off builds a house on land he buy from Dr. Terrell, he old massa. I has four chillen, and dey all dead now. He died in 1881, 'way from home. He's on his way to Austin and draps dead from some heart mis'ry. Dat am big sorrow in my life. There I is, with chillen to support, so I goes to cookin' 'gain and we has some purty close times, but I does it and sends dem to school. I don't want dem to be like dey mammy, a unknowledge person.

"After eight years I marries Dave Reece and has two chillen. He am de Baptis' preacher and have a good church till he died, in 1923. Den soon after I gits de letter from old Missie Mary, and she am awful sick. She done write and visit me all dem years since I lef' de old plantation. I draps everything and goes to her and she am awful glad to see me. She begs me not to go back home, and one day she dies sudden-like with a heart mis'ry. She de bes' friend I ever has.

"I comes to Fort Worth in 1926 and lives with my daughter. I's paralyze in de right side and can't work no more, and it am fine I has de good daughter."

Mary Reynolds

Mary Reynolds claims to be more than a hundred years old. She was born in slavery to the Kilpatrick family, in Black River, Louisiana. Mary now lives at the Dallas County Convalescent Home. She has been blind for five years and is very feeble.

"My paw's name was Tom Vaughn and he was from the north, born free man and lived and died free to the end of his days. He wasn't no eddicated man, but he was what he calls himself a piano man. He told me once he lived in New York and Chicago and he built the insides of pianos and knew how to make them play in tune. He said some white folks from the south told he if he'd come with them to the south he'd find a lot of work to do with pianos in them parts, and he come off with them.

"He saw my maw on the Kilpatrick place and her man was dead. He told Dr. Kilpatrick, my massa, he'd buy my maw and her three chillun with all the money he had, iffen he'd sell her. But Dr. Kilpatrick was never one to sell any but the old niggers who was past workin' in the fields and past their breedin' times. So my paw marries my maw and works the fields, same as any other nigger. They had six gals: Martha and Pamela and Josephine and Ellen and Katherine and me.

"I was born same time as Miss Sara Kilpatrick. Dr. Kilpatrick's first wife and my maw come to their time right together. Miss Sara's maw died and they brung Miss Sara to suck with me. It's a thing we ain't never forgot. My maw's name was Sallie and Miss Sara allus looked with kindness on my maw. We sucked till we was a fair size and played together, which wasn't no common thing. None the other li'l niggers played with the white chillun. But Miss Sara loved me so good.

"I was jus' 'bout big 'nough to start playin' with a broom to go 'bout sweepin' up and not even half doin' it when Dr. Kilpatrick sold me. They was a old white man in Trinity and his wife died and he didn't have chick or child or slave or nothin'. Massa sold me cheap, 'cause he didn't want Miss Sara to play with no nigger young'un. That old man bought me a big doll and went off and left me all day, with the door open. I jus' sot on the floor and played with that doll. I used to cry. He'd come home and give me somethin' to eat and then go to bed, and I slep' on the foot of the bed with him. I was scart all the time in the dark. He never did close the door.

"Miss Sara pined and sickened. Massa done what he could, but they wasn't no pertness in her. She got sicker and sicker, and massa brung 'nother doctor. He say, 'You li'l gal is grievin' the life out her body and she sho' gwine die iffen you don't do somethin' 'bout it.' Miss Sara says over and over, 'I wants Mary.' Massa say to the doctor, 'That a li'l nigger young'un I done sold.' The doctor tells him he better git me back iffen he wants to save the life of his child. Dr. Kilpatrick has to give a big plenty more to git me back than what he sold me for, but Miss Sara plumps up right off and grows into fine health.

"Then massa marries a rich lady from Mississippi and they has chillun for company to Miss Sara and seem like for a time she forgits me.

"Massa Kilpatrick wasn't no piddlin' man. He was a man of plenty. He had a big house with no more style to it than a crib, but it could room plenty people. He was a medicine doctor and they was rooms in the second story for sick folks what come to lay in. It would take two days to go all over the land he owned. He had cattle and stock and sheep and more'n a hundred slaves and more besides. He bought the bes' of niggers near every time the spec'lators come that way. He'd make a swap of the old ones and give money for young ones what could work.

"He raised corn and cotton and cane and 'taters and goobers, 'sides the peas and other feedin' for the niggers. I 'member I helt a hoe handle mighty onsteady when they put a old woman to larn me and some other chillun to scrape the fields. That old woman would be in a frantic. She'd show me and then turn 'bout to show some other li'l nigger, and I'd have the young corn cut clean as the grass. She say, 'For the love of Gawd, you better larn it right, or Solomon will beat the breath out you body.' Old man Solomon was the nigger driver.

"Slavery was the worst days was ever seed in the world. They was things past tellin', but I got the scars on my old body to show to this day. I seed worse than what happened to me. I seed them put the men and women in the stock with they hands screwed down through holes in the board and they feets tied together and they naked behinds to the world. Solomon the overseer beat them with a big whip and massa look on. The niggers better not stop in the fields when they hear them yellin'. They cut the flesh most to the bones and some they was when they taken them out of stock and put them on the beds, they never got up again.

"When a nigger died they let his folks come out the fields to see him afore he died. They buried him the same day, take a big plank and bust it with a ax in the middle 'nough to bend it back, and put the dead nigger in betwixt it. They'd cart them down to the graveyard on the place and not bury them deep 'nough that buzzards wouldn't come circlin' round. Niggers mourns now, but in them days they wasn't no time for mournin'.

"The conch shell blowed afore daylight and all hands better git out for roll call or Solomon bust the door down and git them out. It was work hard, git beatin's and half fed. They brung the victuals and water to the fields on a slide pulled by a old mule. Plenty times they was only a half barrel water and it stale and hot, for all us niggers on the hottes' days. Mostly we ate pickled pork and corn bread and peas and beans and 'taters. They never was as much as we needed.

"The times I hated most was pickin' cotton when the frost was on the bolls. My hands git sore and crack open and bleed. We'd have a li'l fire in the fields and iffen the ones with tender hands couldn't stand it no longer, we'd run and warm our hands a li'l bit. When I could steal a 'tater, I used to slip it in the ashes and when I'd run to the fire I'd take it out and eat it on the sly.

"In the cabins it was nice and warm. They was built of pine boardin' and they was one long row of them up the hill back of the big house. Near one side of the cabins was a fireplace. They'd bring in two, three big logs and put on the fire and they'd last near a week. The beds was made out of puncheons fitted in holes bored in the wall, and planks laid 'cross them poles. We had tickin' mattresses filled with corn shucks. Sometimes the men build chairs at night. We didn't know much 'bout havin' nothin', though.

"Sometimes massa let niggers have a li'l patch. They'd raise 'taters or goobers. They liked to have them to help fill out on the victuals. 'Taters roasted in the ashes was the best tastin' eatin' I ever had. I could die better satisfied to have jus' one more 'tater roasted in hot ashes. The niggers had to work the patches at night and dig the 'taters and goobers at night. Then if they wanted to sell any in town they'd have to git a pass to go. They had to go at night, 'cause they couldn't ever spare a hand from the fields.

"Once in a while they'd give us a li'l piece of Sat'day evenin' to wash out clothes in the branch. We hanged them on the ground in the woods to dry. They was a place to wash clothes from the well, but they was so many niggers all couldn't git round to it on Sundays. When they'd git through with the clothes on Sat'day evenin's the niggers which sold they goobers and 'taters brung fiddles and guitars and come out and play. The others clap they hands and stomp they feet and we young'uns cut a step round. I was plenty biggity and liked to cut a step.

"We was scart of Solomon and his whip, though, and he didn't like frolickin'. He didn't like for us niggers to pray, either. We never heared of no church, but us have prayin' in the cabins. We'd set on the floor and pray with our heads down low and sing low, but if Solomon heared he'd come and beat on the wall with the stock of his whip. He'd say, 'I'll come in there and tear the hide off you backs.' But some the old niggers tell us we got to pray to Gawd that he don't think different of the blacks and the whites. I know that Solomon is burnin' in hell today, and it pleasures me to know it.

"Once my maw and paw taken me and Katherine after night to slip to 'nother place to a prayin' and singin'. A nigger man with white beard told us a day am comin' when niggers only be slaves of Gawd. We prays for the end of Trib'lation and the end of beatin's and for shoes that fit our feet. We prayed that us niggers could have all we wanted to eat and special for fresh meat. Some the old ones say we have to bear all, 'cause that all we can do. Some say they was glad to the time they's dead, 'cause they'd rather rot in the ground than have the beatin's. What I hated most was when they'd beat me and I didn't know what they beat me for, and I hated them strippin' me naked as the day I was born.

"When we's comin' back from that prayin', I thunk I heared the nigger dogs and somebody on horseback. I say, 'Maw, its them nigger hounds and they'll eat us up.' You could hear them old hounds and sluts abayin'. Maw listens and say, 'Sho 'nough, them dogs am runnin' and Gawd help us!' Then she and paw talk and they take us to a fence corner and stands us up 'gainst the rails and say don't move and if anyone comes near, don't breathe loud. They went to the woods, so the hounds chase them and not git us. Me and Katherine stand there, holdin' hands, shakin' so we can hardly stand. We hears the hounds come nearer, but we don't move. They goes after paw and maw, but they circles round to the cabins and gits in. Maw say its the power of Gawd.

"In them days I weared shirts, like all the young'uns. They had collars and come below the knees and was split up the sides. That's all we weared in hot weather. The men weared jeans and the women gingham. Shoes was the worstes' trouble. We weared rough russets when it got cold, and it seem powerful strange they'd never git them to fit. Once when I was a young gal, they got me a new pair and all brass studs in the toes. They was too li'l for me, but I had to wear them. The brass trimmin's cut into my ankles and them places got mis'ble bad. I rubs tallow in them sore places and wrops rags round them and my sores got worser and worser. The scars are there to this day.

"I wasn't sick much, though. Some the niggers had chills and fever a lot, but they hadn't discovered so many diseases then as now. Dr. Kilpatrick give sick niggers ipecac and asafoetida and oil and turpentine and black fever pills.

"They was a cabin called the spinnin' house and two looms and two spinnin' wheels goin' all the time, and two nigger women sewing all the time. It took plenty sewin' to make all the things for a place so big. Once massa goes to Baton Rouge and brung back a yaller gal dressed in fine style. She was a seamster nigger. He builds her a house 'way from the quarters and she done fine sewin' for the whites. Us niggers knowed the doctor took a black woman quick as he did a white and took any on his place he wanted, and he took them often. But mostly the chillun born on the place looked like niggers. Aunt Cheyney allus say four of hers was massa's, but he didn't give them no mind. But this yaller gal breeds so fast and gits a mess of white young'uns. She larnt them fine manners and combs out they hair.

"Onct two of them goes down the hill to the doll house where the Kilpatrick chillun am playin'. They wants to go in the doll house and one the Kilpatrick boys say, 'That's for white chillun.' They say, 'We ain't no niggers, 'cause we got the same daddy you has, and he comes to see us near every day and fetches us clothes and things from town.' They is fussin' and Missy Kilpatrick is listenin' out her chamber window. She heard them white niggers say, 'He is our daddy and we call him daddy when he comes to our house to see our mama.'

"When massa come home that evenin' his wife hardly say nothin' to him, and he ask her what the matter and she tells him, 'Since you asks me, I'm studyin' in my mind 'bout them white young'uns of that yaller nigger wench from Baton Rouge.' He say, 'Now, honey, I fotches that gal jus' for you, 'cause she a fine seamster.' She say, 'It look kind of funny they got the same kind of hair and eyes as my chillun and they got a nose looks like yours.' He say, 'Honey, you jus' payin' 'tention to talk of li'l chillun that ain't got no mind to what they say.' She say, 'Over in Mississippi I got a home and plenty with my daddy and I got that in my mind.'

"Well, she didn't never leave and massa bought her a fine, new span of surrey hosses. But she don't never have no more chillun and she ain't so cordial with the massa. Margaret, that yallow gal, has more white young'uns, but they don't never go down the hill no more to the big house.

"Aunt Cheyney was jus' out of bed with a sucklin' baby one time, and she run away. Some say that was 'nother baby of massa's breedin'. She don't come to the house to nurse her baby, so they misses her and old Solomon gits the nigger hounds and takes her trail. They gits near her and she grabs a limb and tries to hist herself in a tree, but them dogs grab her and pull her down. The men hollers them onto her, and the dogs tore her naked and et the breasts plumb off her body. She got well and lived to be a old woman, but 'nother woman has to suck her baby and she ain't got no sign of breasts no more.

"They give all the niggers fresh meat on Christmas and a plug tobacco all round. The highes' cotton picker gits a suit of clothes and all the women what had twins that year gits a outfittin' of clothes for the twins and a double, warm blanket.

"Seems like after I got bigger, I 'member more'n more niggers run away. They's most allus cotched. Massa used to hire out his niggers for wage hands. One time he hired me and a nigger boy, Turner, to work for some ornery white trash name of Kidd. One day Turner goes off and don't come back. Old man Kidd say I knowed 'bout it, and he tied my wrists together and stripped me. He hanged me by the wrists from a limb on a tree and spraddled my legs round the trunk and tied my feet together. Then he beat me. He beat me worser than I ever been beat before and I faints dead away. When I come to I'm in bed. I didn't care so much iffen I died.

"I didn't know 'bout the passin' of time, but Miss Sara come to me. Some white folks done git word to her. Mr. Kidd tries to talk hisself out of it, but Miss Sara fotches me home when I'm well 'nough to move. She took me in a cart and my maw takes care of me. Massa looks me over good and says I'll git well, but I'm ruint for breedin' chillun.

"After while I taken a notion to marry and massa and missy marries us same as all the niggers. They stands inside the house with a broom held crosswise of the door and we stands outside. Missy puts a li'l wreath on my head they kept there and we steps over the broom into the house. Now, that's all they was to the marryin'. After freedom I gits married and has it put in the book by a preacher.

"One day we was workin' in the fields and hears the conch shell blow, so we all goes to the back gate of the big house. Massa am there. He say, 'Call the roll for every nigger big 'nough to walk, and I wants them to go to the river and wait there. They's gwine be a show and I wants you to see it.' They was a big boat down there, done built up on the sides with boards and holes in the boards and a big gun barrel stickin' through every hole. We ain't never seed nothin' like that. Massa goes up the plank onto the boat and comes out on the boat porch. He say, 'This am a Yankee boat.' He goes inside and the water wheels starts movin' and that boat goes movin' up the river and they says it goes to Natches.

"The boat wasn't more'n out of sight when a big drove of sojers comes into town. They say they's Fed'rals. More'n half the niggers goes off with them sojers, but I goes on back home 'cause of my old mammy.

"Next day them Yankees is swarmin' the place. Some the niggers wants to show them somethin'. I follows to the woods. The niggers shows them sojers a big pit in the ground, bigger'n a big house. It is got wooden doors that lifts up, but the top am sodded and grass growin' on it, so you couldn't tell it. In that pit is stock, hosses and cows and mules and money and chinaware and silver and a mess of stuff them sojers takes.

"We jus' sot on the place doin' nothin' till the white folks comes home. Miss Sara come out to the cabin and say she wants to read a letter to my mammy. It come from Louis Carter, which is brother to my mammy, and he done follow the Fed'rals to Galveston. A white man done write the letter for him. It am tored in half and massa done that. The letter say Louis am workin' in Galveston and wants mammy to come with us, and he'll pay our way. Miss Sara say massa swear, 'Damn Louis Carter. I ain't gwine tell Sallie nothin',' and he starts to tear the letter up. But she won't let him, and she reads it to mammy.

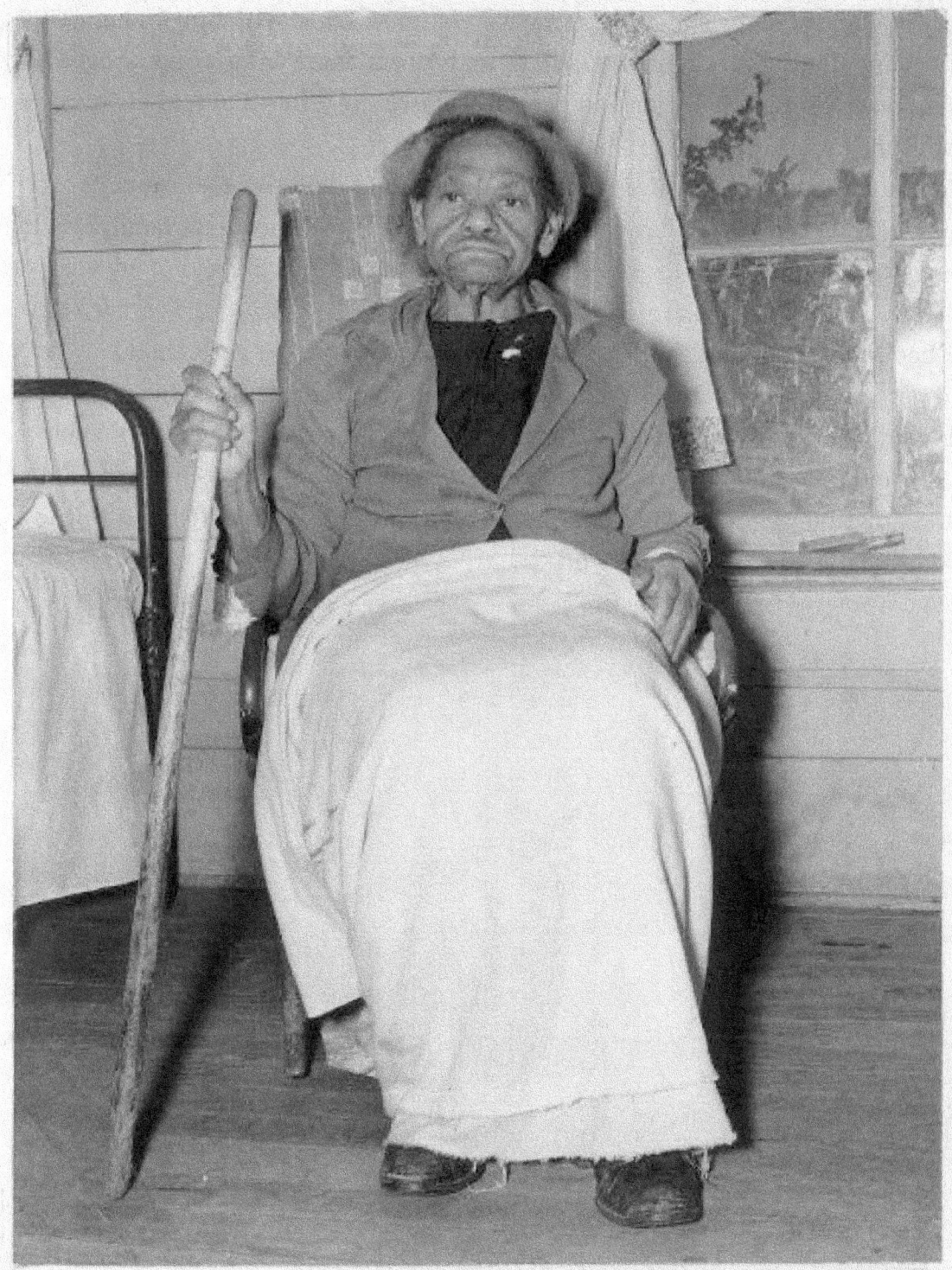

Mary Reynolds

"After a time massa takes all his niggers what wants to Texas with him and mammy gits to Galveston and dies there. I goes with massa to the Tennessee Colony and then to Navasota. Miss Sara marries Mr. T. Coleman and goes to El Paso. She wrote and told me to come to her and I allus meant to go.

"My husband and me farmed round for times, and then I done housework and cookin' for many years. I come to Dallas and cooked seven year for one white family. My husband died years ago. I guess Miss Sara been dead these long years. I allus kep' my years by Miss Sara's years, 'count we is born so close.

"I been blind and mos' helpless for five year. I'm gittin' mighty enfeeblin' and I ain't walked outside the door for a long time back. I sets and 'members the times in the world. I 'members now clear as yesterday things I forgot for a long time. I 'members 'bout the days of slavery and I don't 'lieve they ever gwine have slaves no more on this earth. I think Gawd done took that burden offen his black chillun and I'm aimin' to praise him for it to his face in the days of Glory what ain't so far off."

Walter Rimm

Walter Rimm, 80, was born a slave of Captain Hatch, in San Patricio County, Texas. After Walter was freed, he helped his father farm for several years, then worked as a cook for fifteen years on the King Ranch. He moved to Fort Worth and cooked for Mrs. Arthur Goetz for twenty-five years. He lives at 913 E. Second St., Fort Worth.

"You wants to know 'bout slavery? Well, I's had a deal happen 'sides dat, but I's born on Captain Hatch's plantation, 'cross de bay from Corpus Christi. He had somewheres near fifty slaves, and mammy told me he buyed her in Tennessee and pappy in South Carolina. Massa Hatch buys and sells niggers some dem days, but he ain't a nigger trader.

"Dem sales am one thing what make de 'pression on me. I hears de old folks whisper 'bout gwine have de sale and 'bout noon dere am a crowd of white folks in de front yard and a nigger trader with he slaves. Dey sets up a platform in middle de yard and one white man gits on dat and 'nother white man comes up and has a white woman with him. She 'pears to be 'bout fifteen years old and has long, black hair down her back. Dey puts her on de platform and den I hears a scream, and a woman what look like de gal, cries out, 'I'll cut my throat if my daughter am sold.' De white man goes and talks to her, and fin'ly 'lows her to take de young gal away with her. Dat sho' stirs up some 'motion 'mongst de white folks, but dey say dat gal have jus' a li'l nigger blood and can be sold for a slave, but she look white as anybody I ever seed.

"I pulls weeds and runs errands while I's a child. We has some good eats but has to steal de best things from de white folks. Dey never give us none of them. We has roastin' ears better'n dey cooks dem now. We puts dem, shucks and all, in de hot ashes. Mammy makes good ashcake, with salt and corn meal and bacon grease and flats it out with de hands.

"Massa and missus took dey goodness by spells like. Sometimes dey was hard to git 'long with and sometimes dey was easy to git 'long with. I don't know de cause, but it am so. De mostest trouble am 'bout de work. Dey wants you to work if you can or can't. My pappy have de back mis'ry and many de time I seed him crawl to de grist mill. Him am buyed 'cause him am de good millhand. He tells us his pappy am white, and dat one reason he am de run-awayer. I's scairt all de time, 'cause he run away. I seed him git one whippin' and nothin' I can do 'cept stand dere and cry. Dey gits whippin's every time massa feels cross. One slave name Bob Love, when massa start to whip him he cuts his throat and dives into de river. He am dat scairt of a whippin' dat he kilt himself.

"My pappy wasn't 'fraid of nothin'. He am light cullud from de white blood, and he runs away sev'ral times. Dere am big woods all round and we sees lots of run-awayers. One old fellow name John been a run-awayer for four years and de patterrollers tries all dey tricks, but dey can't cotch him. Dey wants him bad, 'cause it 'spire other slaves to run away if he stays a-loose. Dey sots de trap for him. Dey knows he like good eats, so dey 'ranges for a quiltin' and gives chitlin's and lye hominey. John comes and am inside when de patterrollers rides up to de door. Everybody gits quiet and John stands near de door, and when dey starts to come in he grabs de shovel full of hot ashes and throws dem into de patterrollers' faces. He gits through and runs off, hollerin', 'Bird in de air!'

"One woman name Rhodie runs off for long spell. De hounds won't hunt her. She steals hot light bread when dey puts it in de window to cool, and lives on dat. She told my mammy how to keep de hounds from followin' you is to take black pepper and put it in you socks and run without you shoes. It make de hounds sneeze.

"One day I's in de woods and meets de nigger run-awayer. He comes to de cabin and mammy makes him a bacon and egg sandwich and we never seed him again. Maybe he done got clear to Mexico, where a lot of de slaves runs to.

"De first we knows 'bout war am when some Union ships comes into de Bay and shoots at Corpus Christi. When dat shootin' start, all de folks round us takes to de woods and sev'ral am still gone. Dey am shakin' all over.

"'Bout de third year of de war massa moves up to Clinton, but he moves back, 'cause he can't make no money dere. Den he have all de quarters move up close to de big house, so if we tries to make de run for it in de night he can cotch us. Dat no use, 'cause de ones what am still with him won't run anyway.

"One day I seed massa settin' on de gal'ry and him face all screw up. He says, 'Go git you mammy and everybody.' I goes a-flyin'. My shirt tail don't hit my back till I tells everybody. Massa am cryin' and he reads de paper and says, 'You is free as I is. What you gwine do?' Mammy says, 'We am stayin' right here.' But next mornin' pappy borrows a ox-team to tote our stuff away. We goes 'bout sixty miles and stays 'bout six months, den takes a place where we can make a crop. Den massa tells us we can live on de old place without de rent and have what we can make. So we moves back and stays two years.

"Den we moves sev'ral places and sometimes old missus comes to see us and say, 'Ain't you shame? De Yankees is feedin' you.' But dey wasn't, 'cause we was makin' a crop.

"When I gits up big 'nough to hire out, I works for old man King on some drives, 'fore pappy and mammy dies of de fever. Den I marries Minnie Bennett, a light cullud gal, what am knowed as High Yaller. Her mammy am a white woman. She was kidnapped in Kentucky by some white men and dey dyed her hair and skin and brung her to Texas with some slaves for sale. Massa Means, in Corpus, buyed her. She was so small all she 'membered was her real name was Mary Schlous and her parents am white and she lived in Kentucky. Massa Means comes in de next mornin' and busts out cussin', for dere am black dye all over de pillow and his slave am gettin' blonde, but dem slave traders am gone, so he can't do nothin'.

"He 'cides to keep her and she grows up with de slaves jus' like she am a nigger. She gits used to bein' with dem and marries one. She has one child 'fore freedom, what am Minnie. She has to run away to git freedom, 'cause Massa Means won't let her have freedom. Lots of slaves has to do dat.

"Well, after I marries Minnie, we goes to de famous King Ranch. It was only in two sections den and I hires as cook on de San Gertrudis section, but am sent to de other section, de Fuerta Agua Dulce, and works dere fifteen years.

"Old man King has plenty trouble in dem days. One time some Mexicans comes to Brownsville and takes everything as dey goes. Old man King had two cannons and when dey has battle dey finishes with one cowboy dead and one Mexican dead. No cannons was fired, though. He has more troubles with rustlers and fellows who don't like de way he's gittin' all de land. Dey tries to kill him lots of times, but he fools dem and dies in bed.

Walter Rimm

"I comes to Fort Worth and cooks. Minnie dies 'fore long of de stomach mis'ry. I works for a Missus Goetz and marries Agnes Skelton, what works dere, too. We has five chillen and I works dere for twenty-five years, till I goes blind. I's allus de big, stout fellow, helpin' somebody, and after I's blind I has to 'pend on other people to help me. De white folks sho' been good to me since I been in dis shape, and de state sends me $13.00 a month to pay de bills with. Dat a big help, but I's 'bout three, four weeks 'hind now.

"One old man King's daughters am here and looks me up, and leaves me a couple dollars. I gits 'long some way.

"I sets here and thinks 'bout old times. One song we use to sing was 'Throw de Smokehouse Keys Down de Well.' Dat 'cause dere so many thieves in de country everybody have big locks on de smokehouse if dey 'spects to keep dey meat."

Mariah Robinson

Mariah Robinson, born in Monroe, Georgia, does not know her age, but from certain facts and her appearance, is probably 90 or over. Her master was Judge Hill. He gave Mariah to his son-in-law, Bob Young, who brought her to Texas. She now lives in Meridian, Texas.

"I's borned over in Georgia, in dat place call Monroe, and mammy was Lizzie Hill, 'cause her massa Jedge Hill. I's hones', I don't know de 'zact date I's borned. Missy Joe, my missy, put de record of all ages in de court house for safe keepin', to keep de Indians from burnin' dem up, and dey's burnt up when de court house burns. All I knows is my younges' sister, what live in Georgia, writ me 'bout a year ago and say, 'Last Thursday I's 81 year old.' Dere is five chillen 'twixt my and her age and dere is six chillen younger'n me. Dat de best I can give of my age.

"Jedge Hill's daughter, Miss Josephine, married Dr. Young's son, what lived in Cartersville, in Georgia, but had done moved to Texas. Den my missy give me to Miss Josephine to come to Texas with her to keep her from de lonely hours and bein' sad so far 'way from home. We come by rail from Monroe to Social Circle and dere boards de boat 'Sweet Home'. Dere was jus' two boats on de line, de 'Sweet Home' and de 'Katie Darling.'

"Us sails down de Atlantic Ocean to New Orleans, myself and my aunt Lonnie and uncle Johns, all with Miss Josephine. When us gits to New Orleans us 'rested and put in de trader's office. Us slaves, I mean. Dis de way of dat. Our massa, Massa Bob Young, he a cotton buyer and he done left Georgia without payin' a cotton debt and dey holds us for dat.

"Miss Josephine wires back to Georgia to Dr. Young and he come and git us out. He come walkin' down de street with he goldheaded walkin' cane. Us upstairs in de trader's office. I seed him comin' and cries out, 'O, yonder comes Massa Young.' He looks up and shooked he goldheaded walkin' stick at me and says, 'Never mind, old boss have you out in a few minutes.' Den he gits de hack soon as us out and sends us to de port, for to cotch de boat. Us gits on dat boat and leaves dat evenin'. Comin' down de Mississippi 'cross de Gulf us seed no land for days and days and us go through de Gulf of Mexico and lands at de port, Galveston, and us come to Waco on de stagecoach.

"Us lives four year on Austin St., in Waco, dat four years 'fore de war of 1861. Us boarded with Dr. Tinsley and he and Gen'ral Ross was good friends. I worked in a sewin' room doin' work sich as whippin' on laces and rufflin' and tuckin'. Den us come to Bosque

County right near Meridian, 'cause Massa Bob have de ranch dere and de time of de freedom war us lives dere.

"Us be in de house at night, peepin' out de window or pigeon hole and see Indians comin'. De chief lead in front. Dey wild Comanches. Sometime dere 50 or 60 in a bunch and dey did raidin' at night. But I's purty brave and goes three mile to Walnut Spring every day to git veg'tables. I rid de donkey. Miss Josephine boards all de Bosque County school chillen and us have to git de food. I seed droves of wild turkey and buffaloes and antelopes and deers. I seed wild cats and coons and bunches of wolves and heered de panthers scream like de woman.

"Us lived in a log cabin with two chimneys and a long shed-room and cooked in de kitchen fireplace in de skillet, over it de pot racks. Us made meal on de steel mill and hominy and cheese. I got de prize for spinnin' and weavin'. I knitted de stockin's but Miss Joe had to drap de stitch for me to turn de heels and toes.

"Durin' de freedom war Massa Gen'ral Bob Young git kilt at de last battle. Dat de Bull Run battle and he fit under Gen'ral Lee. Dat left my missy de war widow and she mammy come live with her and she teached in de school. I stays with dem four year after freedom and I's one of de family for de board and de clothes. They's good to me and likes to make me de best lookin' and neatest slave in dat place. I had sich as purty starched dresses and dey holp me fix de hair nice.

"Us used de soft, dim candlelight and I make de candle sticks. Us have gourd dippers and oak buckets to dip water out de well and us make wooden tubs out of stumps and battlin' sticks to clean de clothes.

"I done already met up with Peter Robinson. He's de slave of Massa Ridley Robinson what was gwine to California from Alabama, with all he slaves. Massa Robinson git kilt by de Mexican and a white man name Gibb Smith gits to own Peter. He hires him out to a farmer clost by us ranch and I gits to meet him and us have de courtship and gits married. Dat 'fore freedom. Us marries by Ceasar Berry, de slave of Massa Buck Berry. Ceasar am de cullud preacher. Pete was 'telligent and 'liable and de good man. He played de fiddle all over de country and I rid horseback with him miles and miles to dem dances.

"Peter could write de plain hand and he gits to haul lumber from Waco to make de Bosque County court house. He larns more and gits to be de county's fust cullud trustee and de fust cullud teacher. He gits 'pinted to see after de widows in time of war and in de 'construction days. Fin'ly he is sent to Austin, de capital of Texas, to be rep'sentive.

"Pete and me begot ten chillen. My fust chile am borned two months 'fore freedom. After us slaves is freed us hired out for one year to git means to go free on. Us held by de committee call 'Free Committee Men.' De wages is ten dollars de month to de family. After us ready to go for ourselves, my missy am de poor widow and she have only three cows and three calves, but she give one of each of dem to Pete and me.

"After leavin' Miss Joe us move here and yonder till I gits tired of sich. By den us have sev'ral chillen and I changes from de frivol'ty of life to de sincereness, to shape de dest'ny of de chillins' life. I tells Pete when he comes back from fiddlin' one night, to buy me de home or hitch up and carry me back to Missy Joe. Dat lead him to buy a strip of land in Meridian. He pays ten dollar de acre. We has a team of oxen, call Broad and Buck, and we done our farmin' with dem. Pete builds me a house, hauls de lumber from Waco. Twict us gits burnt out, but builds it 'gain. Us makes de orchard and sells de fruit. Us raises bees and sells de honey and gits cows and chickens and turkeys. Pete works good and I puts on my bonnet and walks behind him and draps de corn.

"He gits in organizin' de fust cullud church in Meridian, de cullud Cumberland Pres'terian Church. Us has ever lived de useful life. I works at cookin' and washin' and ironin'. I helps de doctors with de babies.

"But de dis'bility of age have to come and now I is 'most disabled and feels stunted and pov'ty stricken. I'd like to work now, but I isn't able."

Susan Ross

Susan Ross was born at Magnolia Springs, Texas, about 1862, a slave of Chester Horn. Her features and the color of her skin, together with a secretive manner, would point to Indian blood. She lives with a daughter in the east part of North Quarters, a Negro settlement in Jasper, Texas, and is still active enough to help her daughter in their little cafe.

"Susan Ross my name and I's born at Magnolia Springs durin' de war, sometime befo' freedom come, I guess 'bout 1862. Pappy's name Bob Horn and he come from Georgia, and mammy name Hallie Horn, and she think she part Indian, but she ain't sho'. Chester Horn our massa and he have big plantation at Magnolia Springs, and he kep' one big family connection of slaves. Sometime he sold some of dem and he sold my brother, Jack, and my aunt, too. My other brother name Jim and Sam and Aaron and Bill Horn, and my sisters name Mandy and Sarah and Emily.

"Massa have li'l houses all over de plantation for he slaves. Massa and he folks punish dey slaves awful hard, and he used to tie 'em up and whip 'em, too. Once he told my mammy do somethin' and she didn't and he tie and whip her, and I skeert and cry. Mammy cook and work in de field.

"I jes' 'member I used to see sojers dress in blue uniforms walkin' all over de country watchin' how things goin'. Massa want one my brothers go to war, but he wouldn't, so I seed him buckle my brother down on a log and whip him with whips, den with hand saws, till when he turn him loose you couldn't tell what he look like. My brother lef' but I don't know whether he went to war or not.

"I 'members when de men was goin' to war, somebody allus come git 'em. Lots of 'em didn't want to go, but dey has to.

"Me go to school after us free. When my oldes' brother hear us is free he give a whoop, run and jump a high fence, and told mammy goodbye. Den he grab me up and hug and kiss me and say, 'Brother gone, don't 'spect you ever see me no more.' I don't know where he go, but I never did see him 'gain.

"After freedom, pappy and mammy moves off to deyselfs and farms. I marry when I's fourteen and de Rev. George Hammonds, he perform de ceremony. We marry quiet at home and I wore blue dress and my husband gran' black suit. I have four chillen and five gran'chillen. My husban, he work here and yonder, on de farm and what he kin git.

"I's de widow now and gits $11.00 pension, but have only git it four times. I lives here with my daughter and us make a li'l in dis yere rest'ran'.

"I never did see but one ghost, but I sho' see one. I cookin' at de hotel in town and have to git up and go down de railroad track to my work befo' it git light. One mornin' a great, tall somethin', tall and slender as a porch post, come walkin' 'long. He step to one side, but he didn't have no feets. I reckon he have a head, but I couldn't see it. As I pass him I didn't say nothin' and he didn't either. He didn't have time to, befo' I broke and run for my life. Dat's de onliest ghost I ever see, but I often feel de spirits close by me."

Annie Row

Annie Row, 86, was born a slave to Mr. Charles Finnely, who owned a plantation in Nacogdoches Co., near Rusk, Texas. She has lived at 920 Frank St., Fort Worth, since 1933.

"I was sho' born in slavery and as near as I knows, I mus' be 'bout 86 year old, from what my mammy tells me. I figgers that, 'cause I was old enough to clean de wool when de War starts and dey didn't generally put de chilluns to work 'fore they's ten year old.

"Marster Charley owned my mammy and my four sisters and two brothers but my pappy was owned by Marster John Kluck, and his place was 'bout five mile from Marster Charley's plantation. My pappy was 'lowed a pass every two weeks for to come and see him's family, but him sees us more often than that, 'cause him sneak off every time him have de chance.

"Allus cullud folks lived in de cullud quarters. De cabins was built with logs and dey have no floor. Dey have bunks for to sleep on and de fireplace. In de summer time mos' de cullud folks sleeps outside, and we'uns had to fight mosquitoes in de night and flies in de day. They was flies and then some more flies, with all dere relations, in them cabins.

"De food am mostly cornmeal and 'lasses and meat that am weighed out and has to last you de week. De truth am, lots of time we'uns goes hungry. Everything dat am worn and eat was raised on de place, 'cept salt and pepper and stuff like that. Dey raise de cotton and de wheat, and de corn and de cane, 'sides de fruit and sich, and de chickens and de sheep and de cows and de hawgs.

"De marster has two overseers what tends to de work and 'signs each nigger to do de certain work and keep de order. Shoes was made by a shoemaker what am also de tanner. Cloth for de clothes was made by de spinners and weavers and that what they larned me to do. My first work was teasin' de wool. I bets you don't know what teasin' de wool am. It am pickin' de burrs and trash and sich out of de wool for to git it ready for de cardin'.

"Now for de treatment, does yous want to know 'bout that? Well, 'twarnt good. When dis nigger am five year old, de marster give me to him's son, Marster Billy. That am luck for me, 'cause Marster Billy am real good to me, but Marster Charley am powerful cruel to hims slaves. At de work, him have de overseers drive 'em from daylight 'til dark, and whups 'em for every little thing what goes wrong. When dey whups dey ties de nigger over de barrel and gives so many licks with de rawhide whup. I seed slaves what couldn't git up after de whuppin's. Some near died 'cause of de punishment.

"Dey never give de cullud folks de pass for to go a-visitin', nor 'lows parties on de place. As fer to go to church, shunt that from yous head. Why, we'uns wasn' even 'lowed to pray. Once my mammy slips off to de woods near de house to pray and she prays powerful loud and she am heard, and when she come back, she whupped.

"My mammy and me not have it so hard, 'cause she de cook and I 'longs to Marster Billy. Him won't let 'em whump me iffen he knows 'bout it. But one time, when I's 'bout six year, I stumbles and breaks a plate and de missy whups me for that. Here am de scar on my arm from that whuppin!

"After dey has argument dey never whups me when Marster Billy 'round. Lots of time him say, 'Come here, Bunch,'--dey calls me Bunch, 'cause I's portly--and him have something good for me to eat.

"After that, it wasn't long 'fore de War starts and de marster's two boys, Billy and John, jines de army. I's powerful grieved and cries two days and all de time Marster Billy gone I worries 'bout him gittin' shoot. De soldiers comes and goes in de crib and takes all de corn, and makes my mammy cook a meal. Marster Charley cuss everything and everybody and us watch out and keep out of his way. After two years him gits a letter from Marster Billy and him say him be home soon and that John be kilt. Missy starts cryin' and de Marster jumps up and starts cussin' de War and him picks up de hot poker and say, 'Free de nigger, will dey? I free dem.' And he hit my mammy on de neck and she starts moanin' and cryin' and draps to de floor. Dere 'twas, de Missy a-mournin', my mammy a-mournin' and de marster a-cussin' loud as him can. Him takes de gun offen de rack and starts for de field whar de niggers be a-workin'. My sister and I sees that and we'uns starts runnin' and screamin', 'cause we'uns has brothers and sisters in de field. But de good Lawd took a hand in that mess and de marster ain't gone far in de field when him draps all of a sudden. De death sets on de marster and de niggers comes runnin' to him. Him can't talk or move and dey tote him in de house. De doctor comes and de nex' day de marster dies.

"Den Marster Billy comes home and de break up took place with freedom for de niggers. Mos' of 'em left as soon's dey could.

"De missy gits very con'scending after freedom. De women was in de spinnin' house and we'uns 'spects another whuppin' or scoldin', 'cause that de usual doin's when she comes. She comes in and says, 'Good mornin', womens,' and she never said sich 'fore. She say she pay wages to all what stays and how good she treat 'em. But my pappy comes and takes us over to de Widow Perry's land to work for share.

"After that, de missy found Marster Billy in de shed, dead, with him throat cut and de razor side him. Dere a piece of paper say he not care for to live, 'cause de nigger free and dey's all broke up.

"After five years I marries George Summers and we lives in Rusk. We'uns has seven chilluns. He goes and I marries Rufus Jackson and on Saturday we marries and on Monday we walks down de street and Rufus accident'ly steps on a white man's foot and de white man kills him with a pistol.

"I marries 'gain after two years to Charles Row. Dat nigger, I plum quits after one year, 'cause him was too rough. Him jealous and tote de razor with him all de time and sleep with it under him pillow. Shucks, him says he carry on dat way 'cause him likes me. I don't want any nigger to shew his 'fection for me dat way, so I transports myself from him.

"I makes a livin' workin' for de white folks 'til four year ago and now I lives with my daughter, Minnie Row. Guess I'll live here de balance of my life--'twont be long."

Gill Ruffin

Gill Ruffin, an ex-slave, was born in 1837 on the Hugh Perry plantation, in Harrison County, Texas. He and his mother were sold to Charley Butler, in Houston County, and about a year before the Civil War they were bought by Henry Hargrove, who had purchased Gill's father from Hugh Perry; thus the family was reunited. Gill now lives two miles southwest of Karnack, on State highway No. 42.

"I was bo'n on the Hugh Perry plantation over near Lee. My papa was name Ruben Ruffin and mama's name was Isabella. We was sold several times, but allus kep' the name of Ruffin. I was jus' a nussin' babe when Marster Perry sold mammy to Marster Butler and he carried us to Houston County. Papa was left at the Perry's but Marster Hargrove bought him and then he bought mammy and me. That's the first time I 'member seein' my papa, but my mama had told me 'bout him.

"De first marster I remember, marster Butler, lived in a big, two-story log house with a gallery. The slaves lived a short piece away in little log cabins. Marster Butler owned lots of land and niggers and he sho' believed in makin' 'em work. There wasn' no loafin' roun' dat white man. Missus name was Sarah and she made me a houseboy when I was small. I allus took de co'n to mill and went after things Missus would borrow from de neighbors. She allus made me ride a mule, 'cause de country was full of wild prairie cattle and varmints. Missus had a good saddle pony, and I allus rode behin' her when she went visitin'.

"When I growed up Marster Butler took me outta de house and put me to work in de field. We had an overseer dat sho' made us step. We was used rough durin' slavery time. We lived in log houses with wooden bunks nailed to de walls and home-made plank tables and benches. They give us one garment at a time and that had to be slap wore out 'fore we got another. All us niggers went barefoot. I never sees a nigger with shoes on till after de surrender.

"We didn' have no gardens and all we et come from de white folks. They fed us turnips, greens, and meats and cornbread and plenty of milk. We worked every day 'cept Sunday and didn' know any more 'bout a holiday den climbin' up a tree back'ard. They never give us money, and we hit de field by sun-up and stayed dere till sundown. The niggers was whipped with a ridin' quirt.

"The woods was full of run-aways and I heered them houn's a runnin' 'em like deer many a time, and heered dat whip when they's caught. He'd tie 'em to a tree with a line and nearly kill 'em. On rainy days we was in de crib shuckin' corn, and he never let us have parties. Sometimes we went fishin' or huntin' on Sat'day afternoon, but that wasn' often.

"Marster Butler was shot. He run a store on the place and one day a white boy was pilferin' roun' and he slap him. De boy goes home and tell his pappy and his pappy kill Marster Butler. So me and my mammy was sold to Marster Hargrove, who owned my pappy. That was freedom to me, 'cause Marster Henry didn' cuff his niggers roun'. I worked roun' de house mostly, and fixin' harness and buggies and wagons.

"I never knew but one nigger to run away from Marster Hargrave. He slip off and goes to Shreveport. That was Peter Going. Marster missed him and he goes to fin' him. When he fin's him in Shreveport, he say, 'Come on, Peter, you knowed what you was doin' and you's goin' to pay for it.' Marster tied him behin' de buggy and trots de hosses all way back home. Then he ties Peter to a tree and makes him stay dere all night with nothin' to eat. Peter, nor none of the res' of the niggers didn' ever try to run off after that.

Gill Ruffin

"I don' 'member much 'bout de war. I see the infantry one time over thar close to where Karnack is. I was sittin' on a mule when they pass. All they say is, 'Better git on home, nigger.'

"Marster lef' for de war but didn' stay long. He wouldn' tell us niggers we was free after surrender and we worked on the plantation more'n a year after that.

"After I lef' the Hargroves I lived with my pappy and mammy till I married Lucinda Greer and we raised two boys and two girls to be grown and married. They all dead now, and since my wife died, about 8 years ago, I live here with Will Jones, my grandson."

Martin Ruffin

Martin Ruffin, 83, was born a slave of Josh Perry, near old Port Cadde, on Cadde Lake. He stayed with his master until 1876, then lived with his parents on the farm until 1880. He then moved to Marshall, Texas, where he cooked for hotels and cafes until 1932. Since he has been unable to work, the Red Cross has helped him, and he draws a $12.00 monthly old age pension.

"I's born right here in Harrison County, on Josh Perry's plantation, what was right near Port Cadde, on the lake. I was only eleven year old when the niggers was freed.

"Will Ruffin was my daddy and he come from North Car'lina. Mammy was Cynthia and was born in Texas. I wasn't big enough to tote water to the field when war started, but I driv up the cows and calves and helped tend massa's chillen.

"Massa Perry had more'n a thousand acres in his place and so many niggers it looked like a little town. The niggers lived in rough houses, 'cause they so many he had to make 'em live most anyway.

"The growed slaves et cornbread and bacon and 'lasses and milk, but all the chillen got was milk and bread and a little 'lasses. Massa have fifteen or twenty women carding and weaving and spinning most all the time. Each nigger had his task and the chillen gathered berries in the weeds to make dyes for clothes. Us wore only white lowell clothes, though. They was sho' thick and heavy.

"The overseer was named Charley and there was one driver to see everyone done his task. If he didn't, they fixed him up. Them what fed the stock got up at three and the overseer would tap a bell so many times to make 'em git up. The rest got up at four and worked till good dark. They'd give us a hundred lashes for not doing our task. The overseer put five men on you; one on each hand, one on each foot, and one to hold your head down to the ground. You couldn't do anything but wiggle. The blood would fly 'fore they was through with you.

"When I's a li'l fellow, I seed niggers whipped in the field. Sometimes they'd take 'em behind the big corn crib and fix 'em up.

"Slaves sold for $250 to $1,500. Sometimes they swapped 'em and had to give 'boot.' The 'boot' was allus cash.

"Sam Jones preached to us and read the Bible. He told us how to do and preached Hell-fire and jedgment like the white preachers. Us had service at our church when one of us died and was buried in our own graveyard.

"The niggers sung songs in the field when they was feeling good and wasn't scart of old massa. Sometime they'd slack up on that hoe and old massa holler, 'I's watchin' yous.' The hands say, 'Yas, suh, us sees you, too.' Then they brightened up on that hoe.

"Corn shuckings was a big occasion them days and massa give all the hands a quart whiskey apiece. They'd drink whiskey, get happy and make more noise than a little, but better not git drunk. We'd dance all night when the corn shuckin' was over.

"I heared the cannons rumbling at Mansfield all through the night during the war. It was dark and smoky all round our place from the war. I stood there on Massa Perry's place and seed soldiers carry 'way fodder, and meat and barrels of flour to take to war.

Martin Ruffin

"Massa didn't tell us we was free for three or four days after freedom. Then he said, 'You is free; don't leave, I'll pay you.' The niggers didn't know what he meant at first, then someone say, 'We is free--no more whippings and beatings.' You ought to see 'em jump and clap their hands and pop them heels.

"My daddy and mammy left and went to a farm to work for theyselves, but I stayed till I was near 'bout growed. Then I stayed with daddy and mammy and then came to Marshall. Weeds was mostly here then. I cooked all round town for 'bout fifty years. I didn't marry till I's forty-two. I was working at the Capitol Hotel for $15.00 a week. Rube Witt, a cullud Baptist preacher, married me and Lula Downs and us raises five chillen.

"My wife is dead and I ain't been able to work for five years. The relief and the Red Cross carried me till I got my pension and I's sho' thankful to git that $12.00 a month."

Florence Ruffins

Florence Ruffins was born of ex-slave parents in DeKalb, Texas. She talks of spirits, ghosts and spells, reciting incidents told her by her father and mother, who were supposed to have the "power and the spirit." She lives with a daughter at 1020 W. Weatherford St., Fort Worth, Texas.

"Does I believe in de ghosties? I shos does and I tells yous why I knows dere am ghosties. First, I's hear and see dem and lots of other folks I's talked to has. Den my pappy and my mammy both could see dem, and dey has special powers, but dey was good powers. Dey has no use for de evil spells all all sich.

"In de old days 'fore surrender de cullud folks talks 'bout ghosties and haunts, but since education am for de cullud folks, some of dem larns to say spirit, 'stead of ghost. Now dey has de church dat say de preacher kin bring de ghost--but dey calls it de spirit--to de meetin' and talk with 'em. Dat am de spiritualist-tism church.

"I's tellin' you de things I hears my mammy and pappy tell, and some I's seed for myself. What I seed, I kin be de witness for and what my mammy and pappy says, I kin be de witness for dat, 'cause I's not gwine lie 'bout what de dead people says.

"Dere am only one way to best de ghost and it am call de Lawd and he will banish 'em. Some folks don't know how to best 'em, so dey gits tan'lized bad. Dere a man call' Everson, and he been de slave. De ghost come and tell him to go dig in de graveyard for de pot of gold, and to go by himself. But he am 'fraid of de graveyard and didn't go. So de ghost 'pears 'gain, but dat man don't go till de ghost come de third time. So he goes, but he takes two other men with him.

"Everson digs 'bout five foot, where de ghost tolt him to, and he spade hit de iron box. He prises de cover off and dat box am full of de gold coins, fives and tens and twenties, gold money, a whole bushel in dat box. He hollers to de two men and dey comes runnin', but by de time dey gits dere, de box am sunk and all they can see is de hole where it go down. Dey digs and digs, but it ain't no use. If him hadn't taken de men with him, him be rich, but de ghost didn't want dem other men dere.

"In dat dere same country, dere am a farm what sho' am hanted. Many famlies tries to live in dat house, but am forced to move. It am sposed de niggers what de cruel Massa on dat farm kilt in slave times, comes back to tan'lize. De ghosties comes in de night and walks back and forth 'cross de yard, and dey can see 'em as plain as day. Dere am nobody what will stay on dat farm.

"My pappy am comin' home on de hoss one night and he feel like someone on dat hoss behin' him. He turn and kin see something. He say, 'What for you gits on my hoss?', but dere am no answer. He tries to touch dat thing, but he pass his hand right through it and he knew it a ghost, and pappy hops off dat hoss and am on de ground runnin' quicker dan greased lightning. Pappy sees dat hoss, with de hant on him, gwine through de woods like de deer.

"Right here in dis house, a person die and dey spirit tan'lize at night. It come after we goes to bed and patters on de floor with de bare feet and rattles de paper. Dat sho' git me all a-quiverment. I has to get de Bible and call de Lawd to banish dem. But I seed de shadow of dat ghost often and it am a man ghost and it look sad."

Aaron Russel

Aaron Russel, 82, was born a slave of William Patrick, who owned Aaron's parents, a hundred other slaves, and a large plantation in Ouachita Parish, near Monroe, Louisiana. Aaron remained with the Patrick family until he was 26, then moved to Texas. He farmed all his life, until old age forced him to stop work. He then moved to a suburb of Fort Worth, to be near his children.

"Massa William Patrick give my mammy de statement. It say I's borned in 1855 and dat make me 82 year old. Massa Patrick, he own de big plantation clost to Monroe, over in Louisiana. Dat de big place, with over a hunerd niggers.

"When de war start I's 'bout six year old, but I has de good mem'ry of dem times. Massa have no chillen so nobody goes from dat place, but lots de neighbor boys us knows goes to de army.

"At first everything go good after war start, but de last end am not so good. De trouble am de Yanks come and takes de rations from massa. Dey takes corn and meat and kilt several hawgs and takes two yearlin's. Dey sho' makes massa mad. Him git so mad him cry. If massa hadn't 'spect sich and hide de rations, us sho' suffer, but back of de cotton field massa done have us dig de pit. In de pit us put de hay and lay de rations in dere, sich as corn and smoke' meat and 'taters. De Yanks don't find dat stuff. But what de sojers takes make it nip and tuck to git by.

"All us niggers 'cited when de sojers takes de rations. De older ones wants to fight dem Yanks. Dere'd been trouble iffen massa didn't say to dem to keep 'way. All us like massa, him treat us fine, and us willin' fight for him.

"De sojers come back after dat and use one massa's buildin's for headquarters, for long time. Dat befo' de battle at Vicksburg. At first us young'uns scart of dem, but after while us play with them. After de Vicksburg battle dey goes off and us sorry, 'cause dey treat us with candy and things. But massa glad git shet of dem.

"Us young'uns have de fun with de old niggers. Massa know and sho' have de good laugh. I'll tell you 'bout it:

"'Twas dis-away. De old niggers scart of hants. Us young'uns takes de long rawhide string and makes de tick-tack on de cabin roof where Tom and Mandy 'livin'. I climbs de tree 'bout 50 foot high back de cabin and holds de string. It go thump on de roof, 'bout darktime. Tom and Mandy settin' in dere, talkin' with some folks. Us keep thumpin' de tick-tack. Tom say, 'What dat on de roof?' Dey stops talkin'. I thumps it 'gain. Mandy say, 'Gosh for mighty! What am it?' One nigger say, 'De hants, it de hants,' and dem cullud folks come 'way from dere right now. I hears de massa laugh for to split de sides. And Tom and Mandy, dey wouldn't stay in de cabin dat night, no, sir, dey sleeps in de yard.

"De bell ring 'fore daylight and de work start. When de cullud folks starts out in de mornin' it like de army. Some goes to de fields, some to de spinnin', some to de shoeshop, and so on. De hours am long, but massa am good. No overseer, but de leader for each crew.

"I 'member when Massa call us and say, 'You's free.' Us didn't 'lieve him at first. He say he put each fam'ly on de piece of land and us work it on shares. Him have lots of married couples on he place. I knows most plantations de cullud folks treated like cattle, but massa different. Him have de reg'lations. If dey wants to marry dey asks him and dey has de cer'mony, what am step over de broom laid on de floor.

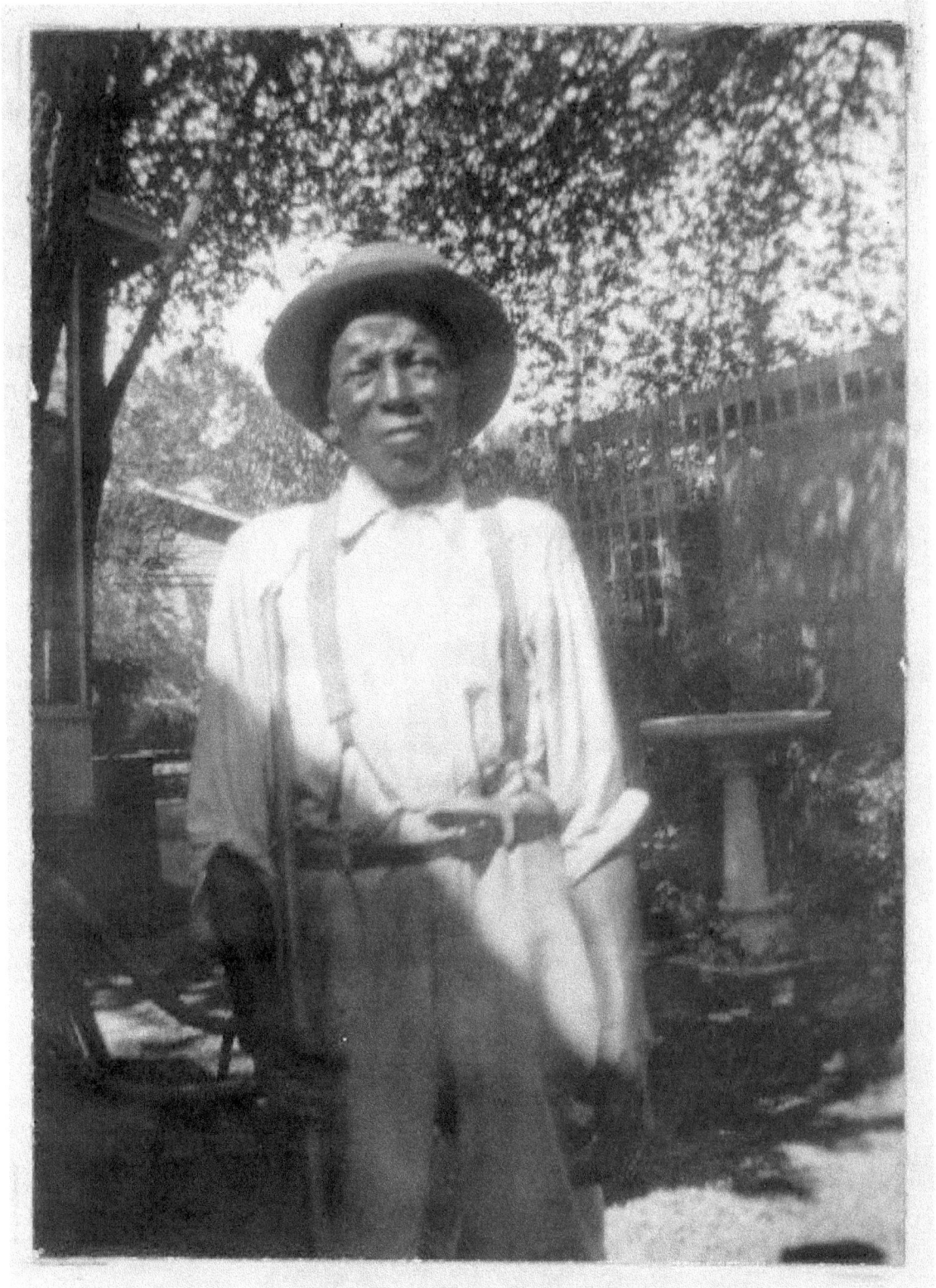

Aaron Russel

"My pappy stay with massa and farm on shares. I stays till I's 26 year old and den gits de piece of land for myself. Us gits 'long good, 'cause us stay on massa's place and he 'structs us what to do. He say to stay out of de mess and keep workin'. For long time us never leave de place, after de war, 'cause of trouble gwine on. Dere am times it wasn't safe for no cullud person to go off de plantation. Some foolish niggers what listen to some foolish white folks gits de wrong 'structions. Dey comes to think dey can run de white folks. Now, when dey starts sich, 'course de white folks don't 'low sich. Some of dem stubborn niggers has to be edumacated by de Ku Klux Klan. Dat am de tough edumacation and some dem niggers never gits over de lesson. Dem dat do never forgit it!

"I never hears dat any cullud folks gits de land offen dere massa. I heared some old cullud folks say dey told it to be sich. Sho', de igno'mus fools think de gov'ment gwine take land from de massas and give it to dem! Massa Patrick tell us all 'bout sich. Like niggers votin'. I's been asked to vote but I knows it wasn't for de good. What does I know 'bout votin'? So I follows massa's 'structions and stays 'way from sich. If de cullud folks can do de readin' and knows what dey do, maybe it all right for dem to vote. De way 'twas after surrender, 'twas foolishment for niggers to try votin' and run de gov'ment. I wants to go some other place iffen dey do. De young'uns now gittin' edumacated and iffen dey larn de right way, den dey have right to vote. I jus' farms and makes de livin' for my family. My first wife dies in 1896 and I marries in 1907 to Elsie Johnson. She here with me.

"My life after freedom ain't so bad, 'cept de last few years. Times lately I's wish I's back with de massa, 'cause I has plenty rations dere. It hard to be hongry and dat I's been many times lately. I's old now and can't work much, so dere 'tis. I has to 'pend on my chillen and dey have de hard time, too. I don't know what wrong, I guess de Lawd punish de folks for somethin'. I jus' have trust till he call me to Jedgment."

Peter Ryas

Peter Ryas, about 77 years old, was born a slave of Volsant Fournet, in St. Martinville Parish, Louisiana. He speaks a French patois more fluently than English. Peter worked at the refineries in Port Arthur for sixteen years but ill health forced him to stop work and he lives on what odd jobs he and his wife can pick up.

"I's borned 'bout 1860, I guess, in a li'l cypress timber house in de quarters section of de Fournet Plantation. Dat in St. Martinville Parish, over in Louisiana. Dem li'l houses good and tight, with two big rooms. Two families live in one house. Dey 'bout ten houses.

"M'sieu Volsant Fournet, he my old massa and he wife name Missus Porine. Dey have eight chillen and de baby boy name Brian. Him and me, us grow up togedder. Us allus play togedder. He been dead three year now and here I is still.

"All dem in my family am field workers. I too li'l to work. My mama name Annie and papa name Alfred. I have oldes' brudder, dat Gabriel, and 'nother brudder name Marice, and two sisters, Harriet and Amy.

"Old massa's house have big six or eight room. Galleries front and back. Us cullud chillen never go in de big house much.

"Old massa he done feed good. Coosh-coosh with 'lasses. Dat my favorite dem day. Dat make with meal and water and salt. Dey stir it in big pot. Sometime dey kill beef. Us have beef head and neck and guts cook with gravy and spread on top coosh-coosh. Dat good food.

"Down on Vermilion Bayou am alligators. Dey fish and snakes, too. Us eat alligator tail steak. Taste like fish. Jes' skin hide off alligator tail. Slice it into steak. Fry it in meal and hawg fat. Dat like gar fish. Sometime git lamper eel. Dey hard to cotch. Perches and catfish and mud-cat easy to cotch. Water bird, too. Duck and crane. Crane like fish. Us take boat, go 'long bayou, find nesties in sedge grass.

"Old massa allus good. He 'low papa and some to have li'l patch round dey door. Dey eat what dey raise. Some sells it. Papa raise pumpkin and watermelon. He have plenty bee-gum with bees. After freedom he make money awhile. He sell de honey from dem bees.

"Dat plantation full cotton and corn. Us chillen sleep in de cotton-house. It be so soft. In de quarters houses chillen didn't have no bed. Dey slept on tow sack on de floor. Dat why dem cotton piles felt so soft.

"Massa have special place in woods where he have meanes' niggers whip. He never whip much, but wartime comin' on. Some de growed ones runs away to dem Yankees. He have to whip some den. He have stocks to put dey neck in when he whip dem. Massa never chain he slaves. I seed talkin' parrots. Massa didn't have one, but other massas did. Dat parrot talk. He tell when de nigger run away or when he not work.

"Us white folks all Catholic. Us not go to church, but all chillen christen. Dat in St. Martinville Catholic Church. All us christen dere. After freedom I start go to church reg'lar. I still does.

"Dey ain't give us pants till us ten year old. In winter or summer us wore long, split tail shirt. Us never even think of shoes. After I's twelve papa buy my first pair shoes. Dey have diamond brass piece on toe. I so 'fraid dey wear out I won't wear dem.

"De war goin' on. Us see sojers all de time. Us hide in bresh and play snipe at dem. All de white folks in town gang up. Dey send dere slaves out on Cypress Island. Dey do dat try keep Yankee sojers from find dem. It ain't no use. Dem Yankee find dat bridge what lead from mainland to island. Dey come 'cross dat bridge. Dey find us all. Dem white folks call deyselves hidin' us but dey ain't do so good. Dey guard dat bridge. But some de niggers dey slip off de Island. Dey jine de Yankees.

"Dey plenty alligators in dat bayou. Sometime I wonder if dem niggers what try go through swamp ever git to Yankees. Dem alligators brutal. I 'member black gal call Ellen, she washin' clothes in bayou. Dey wash clothes with big rocks den. Dey have wooden paddle with hole and beat clothes on rocks. Dis gal down in de draw by herself. She washin' clothes. Big alligator had dug hole in side de bank. He come out and snap her arm off jes' 'bove elbow. She scream. Men folks run down and killed alligator. Us chillen wouldn't watch out for alligator. Us play in li'l flat, bateaux and swing on wild grapevine over water. I done see snakes. Dey look big 'nough swallow two li'l niggers one bite. Dey alligator turtles, too. If dey snap you, you can't git loose less you cut dey neck slap off. I kill lots dem.

"Dey old mens on plantation what they think witch mens. Dey say could put bad mouth on you. You dry up and die 'fore you time. Dey take your strengt'. Make you walk on knees and hands. Some folks carry silver money 'round neck. Keep off dat bad mouth.

"Old massa oldes' son, Gabriel, he Colonel in war. He and old massa both Colonels. Lots sojers pass our place. Dey go to fight. Dem with green caps was white folks. Dem with blue caps was Yankees. Us hear guns from boats and cannons.

"After war over massa come home. Dey no law dem time. Things tore up. Dey put marshal in to make laws. Some folks call him Progo(provost) Marshal. He come 'round. See how us doin'. Make white folks 'low niggers go free. But us stay with massa a year. Dey finish crop so everybody have to eat.

"Den us papa move to Edmond LeBlanc farm. Work on shares. Second move to Cade place, run by Edgar DeBlieu. Jes' railroad station, no town. I shave cane for money.

"In 1867 or 1877 yellow fever strike. People die like dem flies. Dat fever pay no 'tention to skin color. White folks go. Black folks go. Dey die so fast dey pile dem in wagons. Dey pay mens $10.00 to go inside house and carry dem out to wagon. Lots niggers makes $10.00. Dat fever strike quick. Man come see me one mornin! He all right. Dat man dead 'fore dark. It bad sickness. It sev'ral years after dat dey have smallpox sickness. It bad, too.

"All us stay 'round farm till I's 22 year. I never go to school. In 1882 I marry Viney Ballieo. She Baptist. I marry in Baptist church. Cullud preacher. Never white preachers 'round dere. Allus white priests. Viney die and all us four chillen dead now. I marry Edna LeBlanc in 1917.

"I git dissatisfy with farmin' in 1911. I come to Lake Charles. To Port Arthur nex' year. I work at refinery sixteen year. I too old now. Us git what work us can. Jes' from dere to here."

Josephine Ryles

Josephine Ryles, known to the colored people as "Mama Honey", was born a slave of James Sultry, Galveston insurance agent. She does not know her age. She lives in Galveston, Texas.

"Sho, I'm Josephine Ryles, only everyone 'round here calls me 'Mama Honey' and I 'most forgot my name till you says it right den. Honey, I'll be glad to tell you all I 'member 'bout slavery, but it ain't much, for my mind ain't so good no more. Sometimes I can't 'member nothin' a-tall. I'm too old. I don't know how old, but me and dat Gulf got here 'bout de same time, I reckon.

"I'm borned in Galveston and James Sultry owns my mother and she de only slave what he have. He have a kind of big house on Church St and my mother done de housework and cookin' till she sold in de country. I wishes you could've talked to her, she knowed all 'bout slavery, and she come from Nashville to Mobile and den to Texas. Her name Mary Alexander and my daddy's name Matt Williams and Mr. Schwoebel own him.

"Den us sold to Mr. Snow what live in Polk county. Us gits sold right here in Galveston without gwine no place, my mother and me and my li'l brother. My daddy couldn't go with us and I ain't never seed him 'gain. Mr. Snow live out in de country and have a big place and a lot of field hands and us live in cabins.

"My mother was de cook for de white folks and my li'l brother, Charlie Evans, was de water toter in de fields. He brung water in de bucket and give de hands a drink.

"Plenty times de niggers run 'way, 'cause dey have to work awful hard and de sun awful hot. Dey hides in de woods and Mr. Snow keep nigger dogs to hunt 'em with. Dem dogs have big ears and dey so bad I never fools 'round dem. Mr. Snow take off dere chains to git de scent of de nigger and dey kep' on till dey finds him, and sometimes dey hurt him. I knows dey tore de meat off one dem field hands.

"My mother used to send me and my brother out in de woods for de blackberry roots and she make medicine out of dem. You jes' take de few draps at de time. Den she take de cornmeal and brown it and make coffee out of it.

"I didn't pay much 'tention to dat war till Mr. Snow says us free and den us go to Galveston and she git work cookin' and I stays with her.

"I can't tell you much. My mind jes' ain't no more good no more."

TRANSCRIBER'S NOTE

Original spelling has been maintained; e.g. "*stob*—a short straight piece of wood, such as a stake" (American Heritage Dictionary).—The Works Progress Administration was renamed during 1939 as the Work Projects Administration (WPA).

HISTORIC PUBLISHING
©2017 All Rights Reserved

Historic Publishing Slave Narrative Series™

Florida Slave Narratives
ISBN: 978-1-64227-001-3

Texas Slave Narratives & Photographs—Part 3
ISBN:978-1-64227-012-9

Kentucky Slave Narratives: A Folk History of Slavery in the United States From Interviews
with Former Slaves
ISBN:978-1946640758

www.ingramcontent.com/pod-product-compliance
Lightning Source LLC
Chambersburg PA
CBHW080619030426
42336CB00018B/3022